The crucial issue in Africa during the rest of this century is whether it can devise a *new* kind of society. Kenneth Kaunda in Zambia and Julius Nyerere in Tanzania have determined the direction of their two countries, and the fate of their experiments—both of which are capturing the idealism of younger Africans—is of transcendent importance to the development of society there and on other continents as well.

If Africa follows the traditional pattern, it might well become another South America—as the number of coups that have taken place and the rise of a consumption-oriented class might indicate. In this respect, the author points out, even such momentous matters as the struggle in South Africa and the race question must not be allowed to distract attention from the crucial battle between the rural masses and the urban elite.

To meet the challenge, Nyerere has set his hand to proving that a rural society based on cooperation rather than competition is a practical ideal. Kaunda has a more com-

(continued on back flap)

Two African Statesmen

By the same author:

John Hatch

Two African Statesmen

Kaunda of Zambia
and Nyerere of Tanzania

Henry Regnery Company
Chicago

Maps by Elizabeth Hatch
and Cartographic Enterprises

Printed in the United States of America
Library of Congress Catalog Card Number: 76-6268
International Standard Book Number: 0-8092-8405-7 (cloth)
                                    0-8092-7979-7 (paper)

To Maria Nyerere and Betty Kaunda who have borne the heat of the day, the terrors of the night and the loneliness of solitude.

CONTENTS

ACKNOWLEDGEMENTS

A book of this kind clearly owes much to the recollections, perspectives and knowledge of many people other than the author. I have consulted hundreds of friends, colleagues and acquaintenances of the two Presidents whose life stories are told here. I offer my thanks to them all. From amongst them I would especially like to express my gratitude to R. R. Mellor, of the Library Records Department of the British Foreign and Commonwealth Office, for his help in providing me with details of President Nyerere's student days in Britain; to Jill Hollings for allowing me to read and quote from letters received by her from President Kaunda and his wife during his days in detention and prison, and for compiling the index; to the late David Carmichael, who was responsible for finding a place for President Nyerere in Scottish educational institutions and for his student welfare in Scotland; and last, but not least, to Elizabeth for drawing the invaluable maps. Responsibility for everything in the text remains, of course, mine alone.

AFRICA

1976 STATES AND CAPITALS

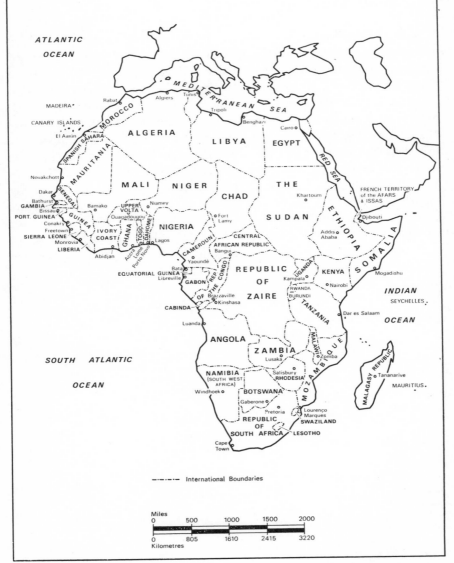

ATLANTIC
OCEAN

MEDITERRANEAN SEA

MADEIRA•

CANARY ISLANDS

Rabat   Algiers   Tunis

Tripoli

Benghazi   Cairo

MOROCCO

El Aaiún

ALGERIA   LIBYA   EGYPT

SPANISH SAHARA

MAURITANIA

RED SEA

Nouakchott   MALI   NIGER   CHAD   THE

Dakar   Khartoum   FRENCH TERRITORY
of the AFARS
& ISSAS

Bathurst   SENEGAL   Bamako   Niamey   SUDAN

GAMBIA   Djibouti

Bissau   UPPER   ETHIOPIA

PORT. GUINEA   GUINEA   VOLTA   Fort   Addis
Ababa

Conakry   Ouagadougou   Lamy

Freetown   IVORY   GHANA   NIGERIA   Addis
Ababa   SOMALIA

SIERRA LEONE   COAST   TOGO   DAHOMEY   CENTRAL   Mogadishu

Monrovia   Lagos   AFRICAN REPUBLIC

LIBERIA   Accra   Lomé   CAMEROUN   Bangui

Abidjan   Porto Novo

Bata   Yaoundé   INDIAN

EQUATORIAL GUINEA   REPUBLIC   UGANDA   KENYA   SEYCHELLES•

Libreville   GABON   OF   Kampala   OCEAN

THE CONGO   Brazzaville   ZAIRE   RWANDA

OF   Kinshasa   BURUNDI   Nairobi

CABINDA   TANZANIA   Dar es Salaam

Luanda   Dar es Salaam

SOUTH   ATLANTIC   ANGOLA   ZAMBIA   MALAWI

OCEAN   Lusaka   Zomba   MALAGASY REPUBLIC

NAMIBIA   Salisbury   Tananarive

(SOUTH WEST   RHODESIA   MAURITIUS•

AFRICA)   MOZAMBIQUE

Windhoek   BOTSWANA

Gaborone   Lourenço
Marques

Pretoria   SWAZILAND

REPUBLIC   LESOTHO

OF

SOUTH AFRICA

Cape
Town

—·—·—· International Boundaries

Miles
0   500   1000   1500   2000

0   805   1610   2415   3220
Kilometres

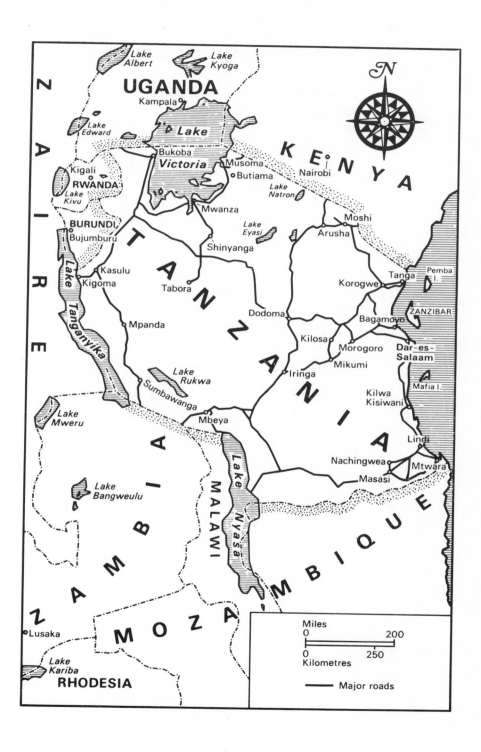

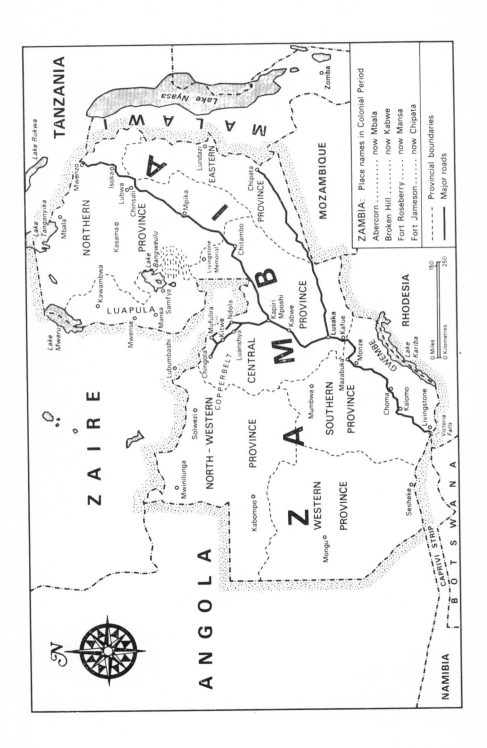

Introduction

Kenneth Kaunda and Julius Nyerere will be measured by historians alongside Gandhi and Nehru, Kenyatta and Nkrumah, Senghor, Houphouet-Boigny, Bourguiba and Touré, Castro, Bustamante, Manley and Williams, Mao and Lee Kuan Yew. They are mid-twentieth-century nationalist leaders who have won their fight against colonial rule and then taken responsibility for pioneering their new states' governments. Their names will rank high in the anti-imperialist honours, each contributing his unique strategy to the battle against colonialism; but Kaunda and Nyerere will be judged more significantly as statesmen offering original policies on the national and international scenes.

Both men come within the category of 'philosopher-king'. Each conceived the objective of defeating colonialism and gaining national independence as a foundation from which to build a new kind of society. Each man started from a single conviction – in both a fundamental belief in the right of all human beings to equal opportunities – and developed a political philosophy from this seed. Their philosophies have been growing throughout their lives and this process has been visible through their speeches, writings and actions. Both have collaborated with close colleagues in the development of their ideas and both have always tried to apply the beliefs they express in the policies for which they and their governments have been responsible. At times their ideas have differed in emphasis if not in principle, as is to be expected when we consider the differences between their two countries and the issues they have had to face. Kaunda terms his philosophy 'Humanism', Nyerere uses the more conventional expression, 'Socialism'. Both, however, have devoted their lives to, first, convincing their people that the principle of equality is moral; and then to devising policies which translate that principle into practice.

To have survived as chief executives of their states for over a decade in the turbulence of modern Africa is a notable feat in itself. Kaunda's Zambia was, first, in the eye of the storm over the Central African Federation; then the chief victim of Ian Smith's declaration of Rhodesian independence and the policy of economic sanctions which was devised to defeat the rebellion. Tanganyika suffered the first of the east African mutinies in 1964, joined herself to revolutionary Zanzibar in the Republic of Tanzania a few weeks later, broke relations with Britain over Rhodesia and then became the chief butt of Amin's aggressive policies. So life has hardly been smooth for either president.

Moreover, both of their countries suffered continually from the economic frustrations experienced by all Third World nations. Tanzania has been basically poor throughout modern times. Neither the Germans nor the British who ruled Tanganyika introduced much genuine development into the land. Zambia has had a different experience. Its copper wealth has sometimes given the appearance of affluence, yet the majority of the people remain poor. Kaunda's greatest task has been to try and equalise living conditions between the comparatively well-paid copper-miners, together with a business–bureaucratic middle class, and the mass of poor peasants or urban workers. In both countries the impact of fluctuating commodity prices, and especially the massive rise in the price of oil from 1973, has hindered economic progress. Yet both men have been entirely wedded to the concept of planned economic development based on an evolution of social justice.

The unique importance of Kaunda and Nyerere to Africa stems from their profound personal belief in the innate and equal worth of the human being. Both are deeply religious men, although their approaches may differ, Nyerere being a Roman Catholic, Kaunda with a more ecumenical approach. This re-inforces the belief. It is from this conviction that arises their passionate devotion to social justice, to a non-racialism which welcomes Europeans and Asians as citizens and has led them to condemn Amin's racialist attitudes, which makes each a man of peace rather than of violence.

Their role in modern Africa has therefore been to set an example of puritanism during a period in which the excesses which followed the end of colonialism have often brought resentment and revolution to other African states. Each has tried to maintain amongst his people the traditional African spirit of community, of discussion rather than dialectic, of co-operation instead of competition. This has led them to institute single-party states, in which full discussion is held within the party, but on a basis of accepted common objectives; to outlaw elitism together with its accompanying race for personal wealth; to create new institutions which protect society from personal or group authoritarianism; to remove tribalism from the political arena.

This example is having a profound effect throughout Africa. Many of the younger generation of Africans are attracted to its Spartan ideals; they increasingly judge their own régimes by comparison with the efforts of Kaunda and Nyerere and their colleagues in Zambia and Tanzania.

It was these two presidents who took the initiative in late 1974 to resolve the delicate issues of southern Africa by the method of discussion in place of the only alternative, bloody guerrilla warfare. Their efforts provoked mixed reactions in other parts of the continent where some, often those who would be least affected by such a war, continued to utter demagogic war-cries against the white supremacists. Nyerere and Kaunda are the last to be accused of hesitation in supporting anti-colonialist or anti-white supremacist movements. Their record in Mozambique, Angola, Rhodesia, Namibia and South Africa, constantly at the expense of risks to the security of their own countries, speaks for itself. Yet they realise the tragedy which will befall many of their own people and their neighbours if the issue of democracy in southern Africa can only be settled by force. They laid the foundations of their policy in 1969 when, in the Lusaka Declaration, they posed the stark alternatives of democratic change through negotiation or force. The initiative of 1974 was made when, for the first time, a leading white politician, Johannes Vorster of South Africa, publicly recognised the validity of this choice. The drama of the struggle for democracy in the southern regions of the continent will continue for many years yet. It affects most parts of the world, for it is based on the universal human dilemma over relations between different ethnic groups. Kaunda and Nyerere have already taken the leading roles; they are likely to be the crucial characters in the denouement.

Both presidents have always insisted on acting through teams of colleagues, in which, although each may be the most influential single figure, decisions are reached collectively. Nevertheless, no one in Tanzania or Zambia, nor in the rest of the continent, doubts that each man has been and remains the seminal influence. Their philosophies, though owing something to the impact of their colleagues, have developed directly from their personal characters. In their turn, their personalities have been moulded by their home life, their education, their subsequent experiences and their own wills. Both are warm, sensitive, humorous human beings, with prejudices alongside principles, conceits beside humility, anger as well as laughter. It is men, fallible, lovable, dedicated, irritating, above all honest about themselves as well as towards others, that this book tries to portray. It so happens that from their characters has arisen a set of actions, attitudes and ideas which is important to Africa and the world; yet the most profound perception offered by a study of their lives is an insight into two human personalities.

Childhood

If they had chosen careers according to personal taste, Julius Nyerere would have become an intellectual and Kenneth Kaunda a farmer. Even after he had been President of Tanzania for several years, Nyerere confided to me that he was looking forward to an opportunity for retirement, to the chance of spending the rest of his life in contemplation, writing and discussion. As early as 1957, when at the heart of the battle for Zambian independence, Kaunda told me that he was seriously considering returning to his beloved Chinsali farm.

These inclinations have been reflected in the attitudes with which the two men have approached the business of government. Nyerere not only found the energy to translate *Julius Caesar* into Swahili – a daring choice for any modern African leader – but wrote Africa's greatest charter, the Arusha Declaration. Kaunda was not content to insist on the principle of 'one man, one vote'; having recognised the value of poultry from his farming days, he coined the slogan 'an egg a day for every Zambian'.

The policy directions of Tanzania and Zambia have been largely determined by the personalities of their respective presidents; the characteristics from which the two men draw their power to influence colleagues and peoples are rooted in childhood experience. Both of them acquired a peace of spirit, a sense of security and a quiet self-confidence from ordered, affectionate family life. Yet the backgrounds of their families differed widely. Whereas Nyerere lived as one of many children sired by a polygamous father, Kaunda's father was an African missionary sent to Northern Rhodesia by the Scottish Church mission from Livingstonia in Nyasaland.

Nyerere's childhood was the more characteristically African. His mother, Mugaya, was the fifth wife of Nyerere Burito. His father was sixty-one years old at the time of the marriage, his mother fifteen. As is customary in polygamous societies, his father took most of his wives in the latter part of his life when he was established as a patriarch, with some little wealth, having achieved status and wisdom. Before his death at over eighty he had twenty-two wives and twenty-six surviving children.

At school, as a young man in Makerere University College, and then at Edinburgh University, Julius Nyerere was to come under the influence of external, alien educational perspectives. As a national political leader, before and after independence, he encountered people and institutions with attitudes vastly different from those of his homeland. These influences have certainly affected his personality. Yet they have been added to the foundations laid by his own society, rather than undermining or changing them. The roots of his nature grew from the seeds planted by the Zanaki community in which he was reared, and by a home life within that community. Later experiences enriched and broadened his perceptions, but from a secure, unshakeable base.

The Zanaki is a small ethnic group, or tribe, of some forty thousand inhabitants living to the south-east of Lake Victoria. They live amongst the hills, whilst to the west stretches the vast Serengeti Plain, a magnificent panorama of bush and sky broken only by outcropping rocks, its multiplicity of animals a joy to the wildlife connoisseur.

The origins of the Zanaki, like those of their neighbours, are still a mystery, for anthropological history made a late start in this area. Certainly their forebears took part in one of the group migrations, caused by scarcity of land, lack of food or the pressure of enemies, which account for the presence of most African peoples in their present habitat. Perhaps of more recent importance was the effect of colonial incursions from Europe. The Germans came first in an attempt to establish an empire over east Africa. Like other European imperialists they sought to maintain their hegemony by employing existing local authorities as their bureacrats. Accepting conventional nineteenth-century European assumptions, they expected all African communities to be governed by a chief. In fact, the Zanaki, like many other African societies, had evolved a vastly different form of government. They did not use the system of chieftainship; so the Germans invented it for them.

The Germans, like all European colonists of the late nineteenth and early twentieth centuries, sought local individuals on whom they could pin responsibility for the conduct of their communities, for collecting taxes and transmitting orders. They divided the Zanaki into eight village groups, appointing a chief over each. In one of them, Butiama, Nyerere Burito, later father of Julius Nyerere, became chief shortly after the German arrival. The name Nyerere can be translated from Ki-Zanaki as 'caterpillar', commemorating a plague of the insects which attacked Zanaki lands in the year of his birth, 1860. Similarly, Kambarage, the original name given to Julius, originates from an ancestral spirit who dwelt in the rain; there was a downpour on the day of his birth in 1922.

The subtleties of Zanaki government did not directly affect his early life, yet they made an impression on him. Government was representative, albeit only of male tribal members. The Zanaki, like most other African communities, sought agreement rather than the dialectic of conflicting views on which Western democracy has been based. Nyerere's father was elected chief (or, more properly, 'omwami') by his clan, which was based on the village of Butiama. He was assisted by the clan elders and by general meetings of the clan, at which every male was expected to attend. The laws and customs of the community were known clearly by every family. Thus the task of government was to interpret customary law when disputes arose or to make decisions on matters of common action, rather than to institute frequent new legislation.

The responsibility of the omwami was to ensure the protection of the community, to maintain order and obedience to the laws, to settle cases of dispute and to give a lead to his people in matters of general welfare. Cases of inheritance and land dispute occupied him most frequently, but he always had the advice of the council of elders, its hearings being open to all members of the community. To allow him to give his attention to these duties the omwami was paid – usually in cattle, meat, grain, sheep, goats, fowl, hoes or beer. If he was considered rapacious or inefficient, the withholding of such dues would usually prove effective; in cases of serious dissatisfaction he could be deposed by a council meeting.

It was not the fact that he was the son of the omwami which most impressed itself on the young Nyerere. He grew up in a system which expressed the African concept of representative government, one that appeared to bring peace and contentment to his community. Although later he was to observe at first hand the various systems of Britain, America, Russia and China, they seemed to him to have evolved in contrasting circumstances to those of his own people. Customary African clan government did not have to be transplanted whole to the national level; but the principles from which it had grown have always seemed to Nyerere to be more compatible with the needs of his nation than those of other societies.

Of more profound influence than the forms of tribal government, though, was the character of family and community life. Nyerere was brought up in the mud hut of his mother, Mugaya. From infancy he was used to doing small jobs around the shamba (or smallholding), tending goats or fowl, and helping in the planting and raising of the standard crops (millet, maize and cassava). When he was eight he was allocated the task of taking his mother's goats to pasture, staying out with them all day and returning as light faded for the family's single daily meal, usually of millet-porridge and maize. Sometimes his father would arrive with a small piece of meat or fish; during the season vegetables and fruit supplemented the diet, whilst the children could find a ripe paw-paw or munch peanuts.

During his boyhood Nyerere was introduced by his mother and other female relatives into the lore of the community and the spirituality of the society in which he lived. This was perhaps his deepest educational experience. Such an African society may tend towards the conservativism characteristic of pastoral life. It is nevertheless profoundly spiritual, offering a sure personal stability. This can form a permanent foundation for those with the initiative to build a richer, wider life.

It is difficult to describe African religion in modern European terminology. Perhaps it might have been better understood by medieval Europeans. It certainly excites a greater empathy in Asia or amongst the indigenous peoples of the Caribbean or Central and South America. For most Africans religions are total, or 'holistic'. They embrace every aspect of life. Thus land, forests, lakes, rivers, mountains, moon, sun, and animals are all parts of the African's religious community. Moreover, those who have died play an equally important role with the living, for all African religions embrace the concept of life after death. Ancestor worship, or the inclusion of ancestors as an essential part of the family and wider community, is therefore almost universal.

Nyerere was brought up in this atmosphere of a totality of life and a continuity from the past through the present to the future. Later he was to join the Roman Catholic church, an act made the easier by its profession of universality, which he accepted in its broadest ecumenical sense. Roman Catholic Christianity seemed but a refinement of the religious concepts in which he had been reared.

He also accepted the humane values professed by Catholics. He has always enjoyed telling of the encounters his father had with Christian missionaries. According to Nyerere, his father would emphasise the principle of rejecting revenge. In particular, he accepted the precept 'Love your brother'. His literal acceptance of the Christian virtues preached by the missionaries must have disconcerted them, for they never returned. Christianity had nothing to teach the old man who had practised throughout his life, under German and British rule, the virtues which they tried to preach to him.

Nyerere's father, certainly one of the major influences on his early life, represented the calm, secure peace of ageless custom, the head of family and clan, centre of a cosmic society in which age was identified with wisdom. He was responsible for guiding the living generations of his community across the span on this earth which bridged past and future. He saw to it that the young learnt and observed the habits and traditions of the tribe, that they showed respect for ancestors and elders, that the traditional sacrifices were made to good and evil ancestral spirits, and to the gods recognised by the tribe. In this way fears of the unknown were assuaged, the welfare of the people was safeguarded, the continuity of community life was preserved.

The fact that Nyerere lived within a chief's family brought him into special contact with those responsible for maintaining tribal custom. His father was a regular visitor to Mugaya's hut, for she was probably his second favourite wife. She was the only one of the wives who could play the Bantu game, bao,* the favoured leisure pastime of candle-lit evenings. Neighbouring omwami – Ihunyo from Busegwe village, Marwa of Butuguri, or Makongoro from Ikuzu – would often visit Nyerere's father in his mother's home. They would talk of tribal matters while playing bao. Ihunyo, the best player, was impressed by the young Nyerere's skill at the game. The impact made by his cleverness when playing with Inhunyo was one of the influences which led to Nyerere eventually being sent to school.

The similarities in one aspect of personality between Nyerere and his father are too striking to be attributed to coincidence. The elder Nyerere was noted for his slow, careful assessment of evidence before taking decisions. He was equally notable for his sense of fairness, for his protection of people's rights. Most of those who knew the father see here the strongest influence on the development of his son's character.

Nyerere's mother must also have had a special influence on her son, although less has been heard about it. At the independence celebrations in 1961 her pride as she regarded her son and her seven grandchildren in the garden of the Prime Minister's house was one of the most touching sights in the week of national rejoicing. It was his mother, as the closest female relative, who was mainly responsible for training Nyerere in tribal manners and custom. Despite all his later international experiences, he has never forgotten those early lessons.

It is difficult for those brought up in monogamous society to appreciate the position of women in a polygamous community. The man is certainly regarded as a patriarch, and tribal custom decrees that the most important events of the day centre on his needs. Amongst the Zanaki, for example, each of the wives would bring the food she had cooked to her husband. It was a terrible disgrace for him to refuse the offerings of any of them, although his preference for that prepared by the best cook was recognised. He would then eat his meal, either alone or with his children and one of the younger wives. The rest of the women would then eat together.

It is often supposed that there must be enormous jealousy amongst the wives of a polygamous community. Of course jealousy exists, as it does in all human groups, yet the jealousy of African polygamous wives arises from other causes than the generally supposed sexual issue. The common factor in all African communities is a love of children, to which must be added a traditional experience of their economic value. Pride is therefore taken in a husband who sires a large family, with resulting approval for his taking of many wives. Where friction appears amongst the wives it is

* 'Bao' is a table game for two played on a board with indentations into which small balls are dropped by the contestants. It is very popular amongst the elders.

from other causes, usually overability in cooking or other personal prejudices.

Nor is precedence or status a common cause of envy. The first, or senior, wife has her accepted prior role. It is equally accepted that a husband may well have a favourite wife. Each of the others has her secure status, recognised by custom. In an African polygamous community tradition and acceptance of human nature usually complement each other.

Another woman who influenced Nyerere as a boy was his sister-in-law, wife of his elder half-brother Edward. She was the daughter of another local chief and showed much affection for her husband's small brother. As a result Julius spent much time in her hut and consequently got to know Edward better than the other boys of the family. As Edward was engaged in tribal matters – he later became chief himself – and as his wife had been brought up in a chief's family, Julius received an additional grounding in tribal custom to that provided by his mother and other female relatives.

This was important to him. He has never lost the influence of tribal learning. It was not just superficial things, like having his teeth filed in the Zanaki shape or treating each of his relatives in the appropriate manner. Tribal influence goes right to the roots of life. As a young man, Julius was to become a Christian, a Roman Catholic. He has never been merely a nominal member of the church. He has always practised his religion and participated in its observances. His Christianity and its formative influence on the way he lives his life is different from that of the average devout European Christian. For Nyerere, a religious faith provides both a broad perspective of life's meaning and a guide to all his actions, trivial or momentous. In this respect his acceptance of Christianity represents simply his choice of one path in a spiritual journey whose frontiers were already established by his childhood learning.

In an African community, religion, or spirituality, embraces the totality, the holism of life for the individual and the group. Every child will absorb a great deal of natural information: how to track animals, to find the way through the bush, and the elements of agriculture and husbandry. By the time he left home for school at the age of twelve Julius had been accustomed to tend goats, cattle and fowl, to accompany the men on hunting expeditions – regarded by British administrators as poaching – to fashion Zanaki bows and the arrows which were dipped in thick black poison, taught the method and timing of sowing, reaping and storing, the care and repairing of huts, and many similar practical attainments. Still more significantly, though, he had been brought up to relate all these tasks and their objects to the rest of his life. The animals, crops, land, trees, sun, moon, sky, mountains and rivers formed part of the same cosmos inhabited by men, women and children. Unknown or magical elements also played a part in this holistic world, their efficacy unquestioned, their healing, protective or menacing attributes accepted. All this was bound together by a profound belief in the continuity of life, after as well as before death. Thus the vague concept of an omnipotent creator controlling all the elements was reinforced by the more personal belief in ancestral spirits with a direct influence on individuals and the community.

This life-image may be described as 'a tribal training', but the phrase offers but a superficial conception of its totality. The fact is that the young Nyerere, like most boys of his age, was already provided with an imaginative framework of the universe within which human meanings, purpose, morality, and relationship were established. His later adoption of Roman Catholicism provided simply an extra perspective of understanding.

Nyerere also took with him from his tribal upbringing into his school-days the concept that a leader's first duty was service to the community; that the interests of the group superseded those of any individual member; that the leader is responsible to the community which has the right to call him to account for his stewardship, to remove him if it so wills; that the welfare of society depends on co-operation not competition. This was the Zanaki legacy which the young Nyerere inherited from his family, clan and tribe, which he took with him when, at the age of twelve, he first left them.

Nyerere's opportunity to go to school arose largely from his close relationship with his elder brother, Edward. Although Ihunyo, the local chief from Busegwe and tribal rainmaker, had urged Nyerere's father to send him to school, his persuasion did not immediately succeed. After all, there were many boys in the family, the two oldest of whom had already been to school. This seemed sufficient, and, in any case, why should there be discrimination in favour of one rather than another? But Edward's intervention persuaded his father. Edward had adopted a boy called Wambura Wanzagi, a son of his wife's sister. He was of the same age as Julius and the two boys became friendly. Wambura could already read and write and was considered clever. The district commissioner was impressed by him and urged Edward to send him to school. At this point Edward suggested to his father that Julius should also be sent as his companion. The two boys left their family homes next day for Musoma, some thirty miles away on the shores of Lake Victoria. There they became boarders at Mwisenge School for the next three years.

It was at this point that a specific European influence entered Nyerere's life. Yet, although the teaching was European in method, the contents were not entirely antithetical to his upbringing nor to his future needs. In addition to English, for instance, he learnt Swahili, an immense boon to his later role as an east African. Moreover, in the grass hut which provided boarding facilities, he learnt with the other boys to prepare and cook their daily meal, a practical addition to the knowledge he had acquired at home.

One European influence which affected Nyerere at Musoma was that of the Christian church. He had made friends with Ihunyo's son, Marwa, who attended the religious instruction class held twice a week. His friend persuaded him to try the class because there was little else to do during class time. He heard the Fathers criticising tribal gods and was convinced by their arguments. He found it good to believe in a single god and a future life. He has retained those beliefs ever since.

Whilst he was away at school Nyerere's father fulfilled tribal custom by paying bride-price to secure him a wife. The practice of the bride-price, or lobola, is often ignorantly described outside Africa as 'buying a wife'. In fact it is an important form of social cement within African communities. The deposit, usually of cattle, generally is used to enable the brothers of an affianced girl to deposit their bride-price, thus facilitating relationships between families and clans. It also serves as an insurance for good behaviour, being returnable in whole or part in cases of neglect, cruelty and divorce. Nevertheless, despite its important social and economic functions, the practice of bride-price provided further evidence of male dominance in African society.

In Nyerere's case it was particularly important. His older brothers were already provided for, but if his father had died he might have been left without resources. For he would then have become the responsibility of a nephew or uncle whose own sons would have taken precedence in claiming the wealth necessary for marriage.

In the event Julius did not marry the girl chosen by his father. When he did become engaged to the girl of his own choice the cattle which had been deposited by his father were returned to him.

At Mwisenge Nyerere had tended to be bored by the lack of challenge, by a scarcity of learning. In 1936, however, having headed the examinations for the whole territory, he was admitted to the government school in Tabora. This was an entirely different institution. It formed a part of Britain's educational policy which was witnessed throughout the Empire. Education was built on a pyramidal structure just as in Britain herself, so in the colonies the first principle of policy was elitism. In Britain the hereditary ruling class was provided with public (actually private) schools to conserve its conformity and preserve its status. In the colonies similar schools were established, like King's School in Lagos or the Alliance in Kenya. There an elite chosen by colonial administrators would be trained in the same mores, destined to provide an indigenous class capable of administering their own country under colonial rule, preserving the British manner of life.

Tabora was one of these schools. It was designed on the lines of British public schools to educate sons of chiefs to become Tanganyika's ruling class, under British control. It incorporated all the traditional British elitist traditions, inculcating the concepts of the sportsman, of fair play, of privilege, and even incorporating the practice of fagging.

By his achievements at Mwisenge the young Nyerere had proved that he possessed outstanding gifts. They assured him a place in Tabora. For six years he studied there, becoming especially proficient in Biology and English. Yet it was less his studies than his social attitudes which distinguished his career there. Already he rebelled against some of the conventions. He resented the privileges accorded prefects and the bullying in which they engaged. Although eventually appointed a prefect himself, he used his persuasive influence to reduce the powers of that office and the special prerogatives prefects claimed. Thus early, before the age of twenty, he was demonstrating his personal interpretation of tribal experience.

It was also at Tabora that the young pupil first began to develop and express his ideas concerning the future of African society. He discussed the organisation of his tribe with boys from other communities and took part in the debating society. It was Nyerere, in fact, who took the initiative in founding the society. One of the debates was held on the issue of brideprice; Nyerere took a critical view of the practice.

In the Tabora school Julius became more interested in Christianity. The White Fathers, who have a fine record of missionary activity and possess the great advantage of being truly international rather than governed from any particular state, had a mission in Tabora. From there they held catechism classes. Nyerere came to be convinced of the Christian approach, accepting the value of a faith in a defined god. Yet he was not baptised until 1943, after the death of his father.

At the end of his school career in 1943 Nyerere, with the support of his brother Edward and his Tabora headmaster, E. S. Williams, gained a bursary and a place in Makerere College. This institution, situated near Kampala in Uganda, was one of Britain's early ventures into providing higher education for Africans in east Africa. It had been founded in 1922 with the main purpose of training clerks to serve the colonial administration. Significantly it was established in Uganda, where the Baganda had been offered privileged opportunities for education and economic advance. But the institution was also designed to provide training for students from Kenya and Tanganyika, though it was often alleged that the poor school system in Tanganyika made it impossible for the territory to fill its quota.

When Nyerere became a Makerere student one of the main functions of the college was to train teachers. It was with the object of becoming a teacher that Julius applied for admission. He secured his qualification to teach, but it was at Makerere that we can begin to discern the development of political ideas which were to dominate his life.

In contrast to the early experience of Nyerere, Kenneth Kaunda was reared from the start in a Christian home. His father, David, was sent from the Scottish church mission of Livingstonia in Blantyre, Nyasaland (now Malawi), to initiate missionary activities in the Chinsali district of Northern Rhodesia (now Zambia). Kenneth was born two years after Nyerere, in 1924, by which time his father had been working in Northern Rhodesia for twenty years. Kenneth was the eighth child born to David and his wife, being given the name Buchizya, or 'unexpected one'.

David Kaunda first was headmaster of the mission school and then an ordained minister of the church. He and a small group of missionaries created a community at Lubwa in the midst of the lovely rolling country around Chinsali. They took their message into the villages of the whole district; but Lubwa remained the centre.

It was here that Kenneth spent his infancy and boyhood. Although at first sight there may appear to be nothing in common between the Zanaki tribal community which gave Nyerere his first impressions and the Christian mission society in which Kaunda was reared, certain aspects of the early life experienced by the two boys held significant similarities. The first was a sense of peace and security. Tribal custom and rural pursuits provided this for Nyerere. No less peaceful was the atmosphere in Lubwa, where David Kaunda and his colleagues had built a community based on the security of conviction in the power of God and the moral surety of belief in Christ's teachings.

Both communities were essentially rural. Lubwa is in the heart of Bemba country. The Bemba language was the first known to the young Kaunda and remains his mother tongue. As son of a missionary Kaunda was naturally not introduced to tribal customs or ritual. Yet the Lubwa mission was essentially a part of the local society. It was a rural community, where in the dry season the men went out into the forest to chop branches from the trees, stacked them in piles on the land and burnt them slowly so as to sterilise the soil, into which seeds were planted for the millet crop which forms the staple diet.

The Kaunda family sustained itself from its own lands. Near Lubwa they cultivated crops for their table. Ten miles away they grew rice in a river bed. After his father's death when he was eight, Kenneth, his brothers and sisters helped their mother to maintain the family life which entailed working in the house and on the lands, carrying water for domestic needs from the nearest well – two miles away – grinding the millet, gathering firewood, washing cooking pots and clothes, building grain bins or chicken huts.

One further common feature of life amongst the Zanaki and Bemba must be mentioned, for it has had a profound influence on the sensibilities of the two men. Just as the tribal life of the Zanaki was based on communal interests, so Lubwa Christianity created a deep sense of community responsibility. Kaunda has recalled that there were always guests to share the family meals. Visitors and travellers from other villages knew that they would always find a welcome in the home commonly known as 'Galilee', whilst those of his father's friends who could not afford school boarding fees would send their sons to stay with the Kaundas.

Both boys, then, knew peace, security, and the necessity for hard work close to the land during their childhood. They were brought up in an atmosphere in which responsibility to one's neighbour or kinsman was natural. Each was given a deep sense of spirituality, whether it be from the animistic holism of the Zanaki or the hymn-singing and prayers of the Christian mission.

Before the end of their childhoods, however, the paths of the two boys diverged. Whilst it needed persuasion to gain Nyerere the opportunity of an education, which he then could only take by leaving his community for boarding school, it was always assumed that Kaunda would attend the local school. He was then expected to go to South Africa, at that time the only country in southern Africa where higher education was available to Africans. But the death of his father put an end to that possibility. Indeed, so poor was his family after his father died that his mother had to borrow the two shillings and sixpence which he had to present as the fee on his first day at school.

The school at Lubwa was held in the open air, as one still finds in many African village schools. The alphabet was taught through copying from a painted cloth hung on a tree. As the children had no books or slates, they would imitate the letters in the sand, drawing each with their fingers as the teacher moved amongst them correcting their shapes.

When the time came that he was promoted to the higher classes, Kenneth had to find thirty shillings a year for his school fees. To obtain this he was employed during the school holidays at ten shillings a month digging drain ditches and doing odd jobs around the school. He was lucky, for the mission naturally felt some responsibility to help the son of its former minister. The vast majority of boys in Kenneth's generation had no opportunity to accumulate such a sum. Kenneth recognised his good fortune, using the influence he gained later to ensure that as many Zambian children as possible were offered free education. The experience also taught him the value of self-reliance, a quality which he put to practical use both when he became a teacher himself and in his political policies.

Throughout his school-days Kenneth trod the conventional path

expected of a mission-bred boy. His social life was planned by teachers
and mission staff; his domestic life by his mother. Education rated second
only to evangelism in the minds of missionaries. There was an endemic
shortage of African teachers. Therefore, any African pupil showing intelligence and ability was expected to become a teacher as soon as the rudi-
ments of knowledge had been acquired.

The schools themselves were usually based on traditional British
precepts. The Lubwa school was run by the Reverend Maxwell Robertson,
who has always been remembered with admiration by Kaunda. He
believed in discipline, efficiency and the virtue of hard work – the traditional values of the Scottish educational system. He founded the Boy
Scout movement in Northern Rhodesia and gave it a prominent role in
his school. Scout concepts of obedience, group loyalty and practical training seemed ideal for fitting African boys into the place in Northern
Rhodesian society they would be expected to hold. They could also be
used to break through tribal affiliations, as they did with social divisions
in Britain.

School games also played an important part in Maxwell Robertson's
curriculum. They too could inculcate the sense of group loyalty so important to the conventional training of boys. It was from his early introduction
to football at school that Kenneth acquired his life-long passion for the
game. The teams were chosen on a village basis and Kenneth played for
his Galilee village against the other villages represented amongst his fellow
pupils.

The other recreational ardour of his life, music, he acquired outside
school. Initially this came about by accident. He was only nine when his
brother bought a stringed instrument from the friend who had taught him
to play it. Kenneth persuaded his brother to teach him also. It soon became
his favourite occupation to play tunes picked up by miners on the Copper
Belt and brought back to the village. He would play in the open at night
whilst the rest danced to his music. Later he was to buy a guitar, his
constant companion through many vicissitudes for over thirty years. As
he had already learned a love of singing from the hymn sessions conducted
by his father at home, vocal and instrumental music has brought Kaunda
a never-failing means of relaxation.

The conventional pattern of progress took Kenneth smoothly towards
the expected goal of teaching. He himself aimed to follow his father's
example and become a minister of the church. He seems to have been led
in this direction by his mother. And as the usual path to the ministry for
an African was through teaching in the mission school, it was first necessary
for him to be trained as a teacher.

Accordingly, having achieved a sufficiently high status as a pupil, he
was admitted into the teachers' training course, also in Lubwa. So for two

more years he continued to live in the mission, attending what was little more than an extension of his school classes.

It was not until he had completed this two-year course in 1941, at the age of seventeen, that Kenneth left home for the first time. He was chosen as one of the thirty students from all over Northern Rhodesia to attend the first African secondary school recently opened at Munali in Lusaka. The first problem was to find transport for the several hundred miles journey from Chinsali to the capital. The commonest means of transport for Africans throughout the continent is by the lorries which normally carry produce, goods and travellers over long distances. This was the only method available for the young Kaunda to travel any distance from his native district.

Accordingly he secured a place for himself and his baggage on a lorry leaving Chinsali for Mpika. At this town on the Great North Road the party found that they had missed the connecting lorry. They had to wait four days for the next one, which took them to Kapiri Mposhi, the junction for the Copper Belt. Here they reached the railway line which runs north and south through the country from Southern Rhodesia and along which most development took place under colonial rule. They were now able to take the train direct to Lusaka.

It had taken Kaunda and his companions eight days to reach the school at Munali. For him it provided his first real adult experience. He had been accustomed to the regular comforts of life in the mission. He had been used to the fastidiousness of a home in which, for instance, it was customary to bathe every day in privacy. It was the absence of such facilities on this long journey, particularly the sense of disgust over the filthy amenities of the communal wash-place and lavatory at Kapiri Mposhi, which left the most lasting impression on his sensibilities.

At Munali Kenneth came into his element. For the first time he made the acquaintance of genuine science teaching, complete with a laboratory, and revelled in the new opportunity. His mathematics improved and, although disappointed to find that history was confined to a South African context, this subject and English literature were always a joy to him. When he found that he could continue his beloved football and add athletics to it, he really felt that Munali offered him a full life.

Munali, like Lubwa, was organised on British lines. Being a secondary school it offered even greater scope, the boys being organised in a house system, prefects being appointed, the usual British ragging and bullying taking place. Kaunda himself gained a reputation as a disciplinarian, the authority he had learnt at Lubwa being used to protect the younger boys from being bullied.

At this stage of his life Kaunda seems to have developed a vague set of values, largely based on conventional British concepts of discipline, hard work, tough games and fair play. To these were added the spiritual sense of his home life, a personal fastidiousness, and a profound dislike of violence in human relations.

At Munali his vision of life was broadened. The agent of this process was Daniel Sonquishe, a master from South Africa who had taken a Fort Hare degree in the only institution of higher education then open to any substantial number of African students in southern Africa. Sonquishe and Kaunda shared a love of guitar music. They took a dancing troupe on a tour of the Copper Belt during one school holiday. But more importantly it was from Sonquishe that Kaunda and his companions heard their first accounts of life in South Africa. It was this master who introduced Kaunda to the meaning of racial segregation and colour discrimination, which seem to have struck an immediate chord of concern. Sonquishe told the young Kaunda that it was probably too late for Africans in South Africa to secure justice; but it was the responsibility of young men like himself to ensure that the South African experience was never repeated in Northern Rhodesia. The exhortation affected him profoundly.

Although he could have continued his education for two more years at Munali, at the end of his second year Kaunda was called home by the Lubwa missionaries. Teachers were in short supply. As he had by now acquired higher qualifications than most of the existing staff, it was felt that he should put them to the service of the mission school. So, at the age of nineteen, he was appointed boarding master at his old school. The days of his formal education were over. He had become one of the few privileged, educated African young men. He now had to take his place in adult society.

2

Preparations for Politics: Nyerere

After spending six years in Tabora Nyerere proceeded to Makerere College near Kampala in Uganda. In the interim, between gaining his School Leaving Certificate at Tabora and entering Makerere, the young student returned home. At nearby Musoma he was baptised with a group of fellow young men in the Nyegina mission. There seems to have been some idea within the church that he might succeed his father as chief, which, if he had followed the custom of polygamy, would have prevented him from becoming a member of the church. However, as his father had died in 1942 and been succeeded by his brother Edward, this impediment was removed. He was named Julius at the baptism ceremony, an enforced change of name which irritated him. But thereafter he wished to be known by his new Christian name.

Makerere College played a similar role during the inter-war years in east Africa to that of Fourah Bay in west Africa. As the only institution of higher education available to Africans, it provided an opportunity for the tiny elite to obtain qualifications enabling it to gain a toe-hold in the professions and in the administration of the colonies. After the second world war it attained the status, first of a university college attached to London University, then of a constituent college of the University of East Africa, and finally of the separate University of Uganda.

Tanganyikans frequently complained that under colonial rule the lack of secondary schools prevented their country from filling its quota of students. As late as 1949 no more than thirty-two of the 222 students came from Tanganyika; no women from the country were admitted until 1952. But Nyerere found little difficulty in securing acceptance. Both the headmaster at Tabora and his brother, the new chief, were anxious that he should continue his education. He was granted a bursary and began his studies at Makerere at the beginning of 1943.

Nyerere's two years at Makerere coincided with the latter half of the second world war, the defeat of Nazi Germany and the great international debates about Fascism, Communism and Democracy. These were not, however, the issues which principally concerned colonial students of the time. Many of their compatriots joined the armed forces of the imperial powers. Julius' own elder brother, Burito, of whom he was very fond, served in the British army and was killed, though no one knows where.

To most colonial subjects, though, and certainly to almost all students from colonial countries, the war was being fought between two groups of imperial states. They disliked the obvious racialist philosophy of Hitler and his Nazis. They were especially incensed with Mussolini's conquest and occupation of Ethiopia, welcoming the restoration of the Emperor to Addis Ababa in 1941. But they were not impressed by British, French or Belgian claims to be fighting against racial imperialism when they saw their own countries remaining under the colonial rule of these same states, or experienced the continued practice of racial discrimination in the colonies where they lived. The Atlantic Charter of 1943 caused some little stir, but they were not surprised when Winston Churchill declared that its high-minded principles did not apply to the British Empire. Franklin Roosevelt acquired some prestige in colonial circles for his opposition to Churchill's imperialist assertions. In Africa the Brazzaville Conference of 1944, where Charles De Gaulle promised that Africans should participate in drafting the new French constitution after the war as a reward for their support against Vichy, made a more direct impression.

Although this was the background context in which Nyerere spent his student life at Makerere, these were not the issues which mainly occupied his mind there. As most Makerere students had spent two more years at school than he, he found that he had to work extra hard at his studies. He had been well prepared in Biology and found little trouble with the English classes. In other subjects required for a teacher's training, though, he had some leeway to make up.

Already, however, Nyerere's main interest had begun to centre on ideas and concepts, rather than on the specific subjects of a curriculum. He was attracted by what philosophy of life, its meaning and its organisation had been propounded. At this stage he was enormously impressed by the essays of John Stuart Mill. Already he had acquired such a fluency of style and originality of perception that he twice won first prize in the east African literary competition. It is significant that his second prize was gained by an essay on the subjection of women in tribal society, in which he applied Mill's analysis to the issue in the society he knew personally.

It was his exploration for concepts which also guided Nyerere's social life as a student. He was not interested in games or dancing, nor in the usual activities organised by the Students' Union. But he and his friend, Andrew Tibandebage, founded a society known as Catholic Action, which arranged annual retreats, pilgrimages to honour Christian martyrs, and a choir.

After his experience in Tabora it was natural that Julius should partici-pate in the Makerere Debating Society. His performances there left a lively impression on his fellow-students. He probed much deeper into human affairs than the usual dilettante student and thus stimulated his companions into a more serious attitude towards political issues. It followed naturally that in his second year Nyerere branched out from religious to political activity. He and another close friend, Hamza Mwapachu, created a new political organisation which they called the Tanganyika African Welfare Association. Tibandebage became chairman with Nyerere as secretary. Yet when they canvassed for membership they were told that an organisation already existed which should be able to satisfy their needs. This was the Tanganyika African Association.

The TAA had been formed in 1929, largely under the guidance of Sir Donald Cameron, the governor of the time. It was one of those loose, ambiguous organisations commonly established by progressive British governors during the inter-war years. It was neither simply social nor purely political. It served as a meeting ground for the tiny elite, and consequently held social functions. But as it was expected, at least by progressive British administrators, that adult men were interested in other topics than gossip, it also provided the opportunity for political discussion. The subject of national policy, considered as the sole prerogative of the British government, might be frowned upon; but it was never necessary to ban it formally.

By the time that Nyerere and his friends were at Makerere, however, the TAA had subsided into an organisation which was largely confined to social activities. Nevertheless, as the world war drew to its close, the young Africans who had begun to consider the political future of their country saw it as the one body which might provide a channel for their efforts. Already in Mwanza and the Lake Province ideas had begun to develop. Within a few years this was to become the main core of political activity in Tanganyika.

Makerere was also a college attended by many more Ugandans and Kenyans than by students from Tanganyika. It was situated in the heart of Buganda, where the Baganda had a long history of political activity. Moreover, political discussion and action were even more lively in Kenya. Towards the end of the war both Asians and Africans increased the volume and insistence of their political demands in that country. In 1944 Eliud Mathu became the first African appointed to the Legislative Council in Nairobi. These were events which inevitably influenced the intellectual climate of Makerere. The Tanganyikan students might be less experienced in political activities and have had fewer opportunities to see their elders engaged in political organisation, but they were affected by the east African climate of new political aspiration and were stimulated into applying the lessons learnt from others to their own country.

Thus Nyerere and a few other Tanganyikan students decided to organise a branch of the TAA in the college. They did not have a very clear idea of the existing structure of the Association, for communications in Tanganyika were still very rudimentary. But one of their number, Vedast Kyaruzi, knew of the branch in Bukoba, his home town. So the idea of a new political organisation was abandoned in favour of joining the TAA. Their efforts to form a Makerere branch appear to have received little encouragement from the Dar es Salaam headquarters. Communication was never certain, whilst politically active officials, usually civil servants, tended to find themselves transferred to other posts. Nevertheless, the branch was formed, providing Nyerere with his first experience of direct political organisation.

The formation of the Makerere branch of the TAA coincided with the first stirrings of a national concept of politics in Tanganyika. Early in the following year a branch of the Association was formed in Mwanza. Under the leadership of Joseph Chombo, a civil servant who had joined the organisation in 1938, it was to become one of the principal agents of political consciousness in the post-war decade. It contrasted with the tribal or religious unions which had so far held the stage in African organisation not only in being unrestricted by tribal, religious or occupational qualifications, but in its distinctive political interests. The Mwanza branch always considered the welfare and rights of both rural and urban Africans to be its responsibility. As branches spread throughout the Lake Province over the next two years, the concept of African advancement superseded tribal, religious or status considerations, laying the foundations for a genuinely national perspective.

Although this was the political environment in which Nyerere and his friends exchanged their ideas in Makerere, and although several of his companions were soon to transfer their activities to Dar es Salaam, Nyerere himself was not one of the most active politicians amongst the students. He was a learner rather than a preacher, collating his own philosophy from his reading and listening. He felt the need to probe deeper than the often superficial analysis of most politically conscious students. His main contribution to student politics was to turn minds to the wider issues involved in serious political change.

Nyerere's father had died in 1942. During the time that he was studying at Makerere Nyerere's mother had to stay with one of his uncles. So, as soon as he had obtained his Diploma in Education, in 1945, he returned to the Zanaki district and spent the summer in building a house for her. He had also to consider now where he was going to teach.

The choices offered him held some little significance. It was expected that he would join the staff of Tabora. He had been a pupil there, it was a government school and consequently was able to pay maximum salaries. The Tabora headmaster offered him a post; but so did Father Walsh, director of St Mary's College, a new Catholic secondary school, also in Tabora. St Mary's could only offer him £6 5s a month, whereas the government school would pay more than twice as much. The government pointed this out to him by letter, adding that any time he taught teaching in a mission school would not count towards his pension.

Yet Andrew Tibandebage, his college friend, was now on the St Mary's staff and urged Nyerere to join him. Moreover, the government's pressure annoyed Nyerere, who believed that mission teachers were serving the country just as well as those in government schools. He decided to accept Father Walsh's offer and took up the post of History and Biology teacher at St Mary's.

During his time at St Mary's Nyerere continued the process of self-discovery which was developing in Makerere. His reputation for being shy and reserved remained; indeed, it has been a characteristic throughout his life. Yet he was able to establish good terms with his pupils and is remembered by them for the understanding he could communicate to them. As at Makerere, he gained renown for his debating skill, both at St Mary's and at the Tabora government school where inter-school debates were held. Already his value judgements were becoming apparent. In one of these debates in the government school he persuasively argued that education produces more happiness than does wealth.

Yet, although perhaps the most formative hours were those spent in endless discussion with Tibandebage, with whom he shared a house, Nyerere now began to make his first tentative flights into action in addition to developing his theory. He learnt some of the practical difficulties of economic life by helping to operate a co-operative shop designed to undermine the Asian commercial monopoly in Tabora. He was made a price inspector by the government but resigned when he found that the government took no action on his reports. During the evenings he held classes in English for the local inhabitants.

But it was again within the TAA that Nyerere gained his most important experience of practical affairs. He became secretary of the local branch. As the Association had just begun to expand its appeal across the country, his position brought him into contact with a wider spectrum of people than all his previous experience. It was as Tabora's delegate that he made his first visit to Dar es Salaam in April 1946 when he attended the national conference of the TAA. The main issue concerned the whole country. For it was at this time that the British Colonial Office had begun to experiment with forms of association between the three east African territories under its rule.

This issue gave Nyerere his first taste of national and international politics. For some years the governors of Tanganyika, Kenya and Uganda had periodically met together on an informal basis to discuss and decide common problems. During the war the relationship had become closer so as to organise the war effort on a joint east African basis. Immediately after the war the British government proposed to establish a constitutional link between the three territories. It was designed to provide for common services and control over them, but stopped short of a federation.

Tanganyika and, to a lesser extent, Uganda, had always felt suspicious towards any form of closer association with Kenya. From before the war and until the end of the 1950s, Kenya's white settlers held a place in the African racial spectrum subsequently occupied by the white community of Rhodesia. It was widely believed that their ambition was to establish their own independent state on a similar basis to the Union of South Africa. Its strength would be augmented if they could include within it the neighbouring territories of Uganda and Tanganyika. At one point they also held secret negotiations with representatives of the white communities from the Rhodesias.

Thus the Kenyan 'white settler' issue formed the central emotive topic of race relations in Africa during the immediate post-war period. In the light of subsequent events it is curious to remember that African leadership in the three east African territories believed at this time that the preservation of Colonial Office authority offered them the best protection against white ambitions. This tactic became apparent in the 1953 Uganda crisis when Africans revolted against the suspicion that the Colonial Office was planning to hand over authority to a white-dominated east African Federation. Later the Africans of Northern Rhodesia and Nyasaland were to adopt the same strategy.

There were also many Europeans resident in Tanganyika and Uganda who feared that any close association of these countries with Kenya would ruin their race relations and precipitate racial hostilities. Usually, however, when the issue was officially discussed, the majority of those whites in politics accepted the assurances of colonial administrators that the best interests of the territory were being promoted. The argument that economic development would be better advanced in some form of inter-territorial association than as separate territories was particularly popular in colonial circles at this time.

When, immediately after the war, the British Labour government issued its proposals for closer co-operation between the three territories, inevitably argument flared with still greater heat. The first British proposals, however, provoked confusion as well as passion. Far from being welcomed by the white community, their provisions raised a storm of protest. For this plan, contained in Colonial Paper No. 191 of 1945, was based on equal representation of Africans, Asians and Europeans in each of the three territories. It is true that when the official members were added to the representatives of the three resident communities, Europeans in the proposed Central Legislative Assembly would far outnumber Asians and Africans. But to the white settlers this was not the point. They were fighting to secure a majority of their number both against the non-Europeans and against Colonial Office officials. That way alone lay the political authority they sought. They angrily repudiated the notion of mere equality with non-Europeans combined with continued subordination to colonial administrators.

Africans and Asians in the three territories saw the prospect differently. The Asians in Kenya had fought a long battle against white ambitions during the years between the wars. Because they had support from their home-lands, stronger organisation and more wealth than the Africans, they entered the political lists earlier. Indeed, the main struggle for political power in the 1920s and 1930s took place between them and the European settlers.

On the other hand, Africans in each of the territories were only just beginning to emerge as a political force. The Kikuyu in Kenya and the Baganda in Uganda had some experience of fighting against both the colonial government and white ambitions; but they represented only fragments of the African population. Now, with the experience of war service and the democratic ideas preached during that conflict before them, Africans began to recognise that their whole future was at stake.

The response of both Africans and Asians was that they were not prepared to accept the large superiority of European members in the new Assembly, even though most of them were to be colonial officials. Already they had begun to identify colonial administrators with local white settlers. They held that any democratic form of representation would reflect the vastly larger populations of non-Europeans over Europeans of any type. They feared that the colonial administrators were in league with the white settlers in planning a South African kind of future for east Africa.

In Tanganyika there was the special resistance to association with Kenya to add to the unfair proportions of representation. The fact that the Kenya white settlers were not satisfied with equal representation but indignantly denounced the proposals only confirmed suspicions. Few in east Africa doubted that the Kenyan whites intended to gain political control over their country, for they scarcely tried to conceal their ambition. To bring Tanganyika and Uganda into close association with them seemed a sure way to presenting them with dominion over the whole of east Africa. Tanganyika might be governed undemocratically, the inevitable consequence of any colonial relationship; but she had too few white inhabitants to make any serious bid for white domination. She had also been a Mandated Territory, with the League of Nations as final authority. Now she had become a Trust Territory, which brought in the United Nations as final arbiter of British policy. As her race relations had been comparatively harmonious, certainly in comparison with those of Kenya, she had further cause to regard the British proposals with apprehension.

This was the climate of opinion in which Nyerere took part in his first serious political conference. These were the arguments which he heard at the TAA national conference in Dar es Salaam. For himself, his growing sense of the significance of fairness, which we have already noted at school and in college, was affronted. He began to recognise that his conception of justice could only be established by political action on national and on east African scales.

Later in 1946 the new British Colonial Secretary, Arthur Creech Jones, who had a progressive, Fabian reputation for anti-colonialism, toured the east African territories. Surprisingly he seems to have been impressed by the Kenyan white settler lobby. For, to the consternation of political Africans, he amended Paper No. 191, substituting for it Colonial Paper No. 210. The new paper made provision for each territorial legislature to elect one additional member to the Assembly. As Europeans held majorities in all three legislatures, it seemed certain that whites would thereby secure three additional members.

To Nyerere and other politically conscious Africans this appeared as a gross betrayal of the democratic principles for which Britain had professed to fight the war and which had been used as the main recruiting appeal amongst Africans. Their disillusion was aggravated when they discovered that the less racialist 191 paper had been prepared by a Conservative Colonial Secretary before the break-up of the wartime coalition, whereas the 210 proposals which favoured the white settlers were the work of Creech Jones and the Labour government. Nyerere was to experience fluctuating relations with the Labour Party throughout his political life; his initial encounter taught him the gap between profession and practice.

Later Nyerere was to recall his reactions to the British government's retreat from the principle of equal racial representation in an essay. He wrote: 'To our horror and dismay HM Government had indeed dropped the principle of equal racial representation! The Europeans had triumphed and they rejoiced everywhere. The British Socialists can hardly realise how much that event lowered the prestige of the Labour government in the eyes of the Africans and Indians of east Africa. The great faith which they had in the Socialist government was shattered to pieces by that single event and will never be the same again.'

This issue also introduced doubts and suspicions into relations between the new African political thinkers and those who had assumed political leadership. In 1945 the first Africans were appointed to the Legislative Council. The Governor chose two African aristocrats from comparatively wealthy tribes. It was obviously expected in that patronising age that the African members would accept the advice of the colonial government which would train them in the niceties of British parliamentary procedures.

Kidaha Makwaia was a young Sukuma chief who had been to Tabora and Makerere and was later to go to Oxford. Abdiel Shangali was a Chagga, a wealthy coffee planter, with little formal education. He was chairman of the 1946 TAA conference, strongly criticising the Paper 191 proposals debated there.

It was expected that when the Legislative Council came to debate the Paper 210 both African members, together with the Asians, would speak and vote against it. Nyerere and Tibandebage had mobilised opinion in the Tabora district against the proposals, using the TAA to hold several protest meetings. Then they heard that Makwaia was to pass through Tabora on his way to the Legislative Council Meeting.

Nyerere, accompanied by a local chief, went to Tabora railway station to talk with Makwaia whilst his train stopped there. They impressed the young chief with the unprincipled injustice which the proposals represented and urged him to take the opportunity of unreservedly attacking them in his speech. After the TAA conference of the previous year they also counted on Shangali demonstrating still more forceful opposition to Paper 210 than he had showed to Paper 191.

When it was reported in the press that both African members had abstained from voting, weakly asking for more time to consider the proposals, that the Government spokesman had publicly interpreted this abstention as African approval, and that only the Asian members had spoken and voted against the motion, the young African nationalists were furious. To them the two African members had justified all the suspicions that they were nothing more than Government 'stooges'. This event, the first major political experience of Nyerere, soured relations between him and Makwaia for many years. Thus early he learnt that skin colour or racial origins do not determine the degree of integrity.

Almost as soon as he left Makerere, Nyerere felt the urge to continue his studies. There was much more that he wanted to discover, more thinking, reading, listening to do. He had felt political sensations, resented the dominant role of foreigners in his country, recognised that his people needed political education to understand the roots of their grievances. He believed that he had a valuable contribution to make to his country; but he had still to unroll for himself his own political philosophy.

The only way in which he could pursue his studies further and find the opportunity to develop his self-knowledge was to gain a place in some institution of higher education overseas. But there were many obstacles. He felt responsible for maintaining his mother and ensuring that his younger brothers were also given opportunities for education. He was very occupied with his teaching at St Mary's, his debating, reading and political activities with the TAA. With all these responsibilities it took him until 1948 to pass the London Matriculation examination.

There were still difficulties. Father Walsh offered his help in obtaining a scholarship for study abroad, but the colonial government had been warned that Nyerere was politically motivated. At this time it was common in the colonial service to remark that the consequences of higher education amongst 'natives' could be seen in the independence of India!

Moreover, at Christmas 1948 Nyerere became engaged. The couple could hardly have been more compatible if chosen by computer. Maria Gabriel was the daughter of an elder from the North Mara district on Lake Victoria, a little north of Nyerere's own birthplace in Butiama. Her father was one of the first amongst his community to become a Christian. Maria was sent to the White Sisters' School for girls near Mwanza where she gained a teacher's certificate.

Maria and Julius met in Musoma, also on the lakeside. They corresponded whilst he was teaching in Tabora. When he discovered that it was possible that his scholarship to study abroad could include an allowance for his mother and his fiancée he went to her home during the school holidays and proposed to her. It was then that the forethought shown by his father nearly twenty years earlier proved itself. The lobola of six cattle handed over to the father of his prospective child-bride was returned to him by her intended husband. Julius was able to observe tribal custom by passing them on to Maria's parents.

One further, perhaps deeper, obstacle still remained. Nyerere was profoundly conscious of the expense incurred in education. The year after he left Makerere he expressed this concern for the first time in print. During his tour of east Africa, Creech Jones, at that time Under-Secretary of State for the Colonies, had visited the college. Copies of his speech there were distributed to old students. Nyerere commented on his remarks in the first issue of the college magazine, published in November 1946. He wrote, inter alia:

The Secretary of State told the students that they are enjoying a precious gift which masses of the people outside would like to share. I feel that this is a true statement of a plain fact. But I must confess that although while I was at Makerere I had some idea that I was somehow more fortunate than the great masses of my people, yet that statement would have meant nothing or very little to me while I was still at the College; far less, in fact, than it does today.

While I was at Makerere I understood that my government was spending annually something in the neighbourhood of £80 on my behalf. But that did not mean very much to me: after all, £80 is only a minute fraction of the total amount which is collected every year from the African tax-payers. But today that £80 has grown to mean a very great deal to me. It is not only a precious gift but a debt that I can never repay.

I wonder whether it has ever occurred to many of us that while that £80 was being spent on me (or for that matter on any other of the past or present students of Makerere) some village dispensary was not being built in my village or some other village. People may actually have died through lack of medicine merely because eighty pounds which could have been spent on a fine village dispensary were spent on me, a mere individual, instead. Because of my presence at the College (and I never did anything to deserve Makerere) many Aggreys and Booker Washingtons remained illiterate for lack of a school to which they could go because the money which could have gone towards building schools was spent on Nyerere, a rather foolish and irresponsible student at Makerere . . .

But why did the community spend all that money, run all those risks and miss all those chances of schooling? Was it for the sake of building a magnificent but useless apex of a stagnant pyramid? Surely not. The community spends all that money upon us because it wants us as lifting levers, and as such we must remain below and bear the whole weight of the masses to be lifted, and we must facilitate that task of lifting . . .

. . . that reminds me of a short but remarkable speech which was given to the boys and staff of the Government School, Tabora, by Dr Lamont. He likened education to a pair of spectacles: it enables those who have it to see things more clearly than they would have done without it. And he likened the educated person to the eyes: the eyes are not important in themselves, but merely in what they can do for the body. The educated man is not important in himself; his importance lies in what he can do for the community of which he is a member. That analogy will always be with me, and will always make me realise my unworthiness to the community.

We old students envy the present generation at Makerere both for having heard Mr Creech Jones and also for having Dr Lamont as their Principal. May I end by quoting the former once again?

'I hope that this message has gone home to you – do share in the work of your people and don't regard toil as a thing to be done for you. You cannot go forward unless prepared for hard work yourselves . . .'

The analogies and the philosophy represented by these words have always remained with Nyerere. They were to become the central motivating force of his public and private life, to be put into practice as well as to be theoretically believed. It may be that this was the first time that they had actually formulated in his mind, for, as he makes clear in the quoted letter, he did not think like this whilst at Makerere. As his letter was written only about a year after leaving the college, it is reasonable to suppose that the thoughts of Creech Jones and of Dr Lamont subsumed the ideas that had begun to crystallise in his first few months as a teacher.

It was shortly after this time that Dr Lamont was virtually forced out of the principalship of Makerere. He returned to Glasgow University where I was then lecturing. It was from Dr Lamont that I first heard of Nyerere. Within his profound love of east Africa and his great hopes for its future he felt that Julius Nyerere would come to play a unique role.

Nyerere arrived in Scotland almost simultaneously with Lamont. He was originally awarded a three-year scholarship under the Colonial Development and Welfare Scheme in April 1948. This was to allow him to read for a general arts degree in Britain, but was made subject to his eligibility for entrance to a university. It was then found, however, that his qualifications did not meet the requirements of the university entrance boards to read for an arts degree.

In the following year, 1949, his application was re-submitted. He was re-awarded a scholarship, this time for four years, the extra year to enable him to gain the qualifications required for university entrance. But as he was teaching science at St Mary's, the scholarship was allocated for a science degree.

Nyerere arrived in Britain on 12 April 1949. He went to the Colonial Office to discuss the use of his scholarship with officials. He liked the Biology he had been teaching his boys at St. Mary's and it had been his strongest subject in the examinations he had taken. But he had not come to Britain to expand his scientific knowledge. His object was to develop his own philosophy, to read extensively, to listen and exchange ideas with students and staff, to seek the answers to the many queries which increasingly perplexed him. Above all, he was searching to understand why his country was ruled by foreigners, why he and his people had to obey orders given by aliens with little comprehension of African values, traditions or ambitions.

For this purpose it seemed to Nyerere that an arts course would be far more suitable than further study in science. At this point he found an ally in David Carmichael, then responsible for colonial students in the north of England, Scotland and Northern Ireland. Carmichael suggested that the young Tanganyikan could obtain special coaching in Edinburgh where he himself had an office. Nyerere concurred and travelled north to Scotland. It was still expected that he would become a science student at the Robert Gordon Technical College in Aberdeen. However, on applying for a change in his course of studies, he was granted permission from the Colonial Office to take an arts degree provided that he secured the necessary qualifications that year. After spending the next three months in being coached in English, he passed the Higher English examination of the Scottish Universities Preliminary Examination in August 1949. This removed the last impediment to his acceptance for an arts degree. He enrolled at Edinburgh University in October and prepared to spend the next three years in reading for a general arts degree.

It may be wondered why a brilliant student, such as Nyerere had already proved himself, should be content with an ordinary degree instead of taking an honours course. His own answer to this query throws further light on his state of mind at the time. In a letter to George Shepperson, at that time a history lecturer in Edinburgh, published in the *Gazette of Edinburgh University* in October 1960, Nyerere wrote, 'I had never intended to pursue a strenuous course of studies and the subjects I chose enabled me to get a fairly broad one without bothering too much about the details of a specialist. Had I the inclination to take an honours degree, I should have liked to take one in philosophy.'

The ordinary degree course allowed Nyerere to stagger his studies and to take his examinations at the end of each of the three years. In his first year he studied English, Political Economy and Social Anthropology; in the second, British History and Economic History; and in the third, Constitutional Law and Moral Philosophy. At the end of this third academic year, in July 1952, he was awarded his MA degree.

The study involved in this variety of subjects involved a great deal of reading, much of it related to the topics which increasingly dominated his thoughts. Yet Nyerere was never content to confine himself to the prescribed university subjects. He has often said since that he perceived life at the university as the best opportunity he would ever be offered to evolve his own philosophy. He read widely, particularly seeking for clues to the human situation in Africa. He thought and studied deeply on every aspect of race and politics, especially seeking answers to the situation within which his people lived under alien rule in east Africa.

Yet I doubt if it was in reading that Nyerere found his greatest stimulation as a student. This was an unusual period in British academic institutions. Not only had British post-war scholarship schemes brought an expanded flow of colonial students to universities and colleges; many of the students were ex-servicemen, more mature than the normal undergraduate. Scotland, with her long educational reputation and special connections with the colonies, attracted large numbers. Moreover, the excitement of colonial nationalism was at its height. From the Manchester Pan-African Conference of 1945, the independence of the Indian subcontinent and the submission of new colonial constitutions, Africans, Asians and West Indians visualised new horizons. Every political group in the universities where colonial and radical British students mingled found colonial nationalism at the heart of discussion.

Nyerere lived in the British Council residence in Edinburgh. Other colonial students also lived there. Discussions, formal and informal, were constant. On one occasion, I remember, Kojo Botsio, then Minister of Education in the Gold Coast, was a visiting speaker. Only the previous year, in 1951, the Gold Coast had held its first genuine elections, the first African ministers had been appointed. This event naturally added to the excitement of African students.

Another centre of anti-colonial debate was the society known as 'Cosmos', run by colonial students with the help of David Carmichael and a clergyman in whose house it usually met. Once a year Cosmos joined with the International Club in Glasgow to hold an international conference of students in various Scottish conference centres. Nyerere never attended any of these conferences, but he was an occasional visitor to Cosmos, recognised by other colonial students as a quietly passionate anti-colonialist.

The arrival in Edinburgh in 1951 of Dr Kenneth Little, the distinguished social anthropologist, increased the profundity of discussions on colonialism. He quickly organised a seminar especially for colonial students, where the roots of colonial rule were explored. I remember Nyerere as the shrewdest questioner amongst the participants on the occasion on which I led the seminar.

This atmosphere of political excitement and emotional debate centred on the imperial condition undoubtedly had a profound influence on the student Nyerere. Yet it did not affect him in the stereotyped manner. He never became dogmatic, strident or demagogic, as did many colonial students. Those who were fellow-members of this vibrant Scottish student society remember him as 'intense'. He is well remembered by them, especially by those from the West Indies, and almost unanimously they choose this word in their recollections.

The intensity reflected his efforts at profound self-analysis, together with his attempts to find the roots of the peculiar factors which dominated the society into which he had been born. Yet his concentration on these tasks never diminished his good humour nor his humility, both characteristics which impressed his student friends and tutors alike. He continued to prefer indoor to outdoor recreations, working out the *Scotsman* crossword, or playing Lexicon or canasta with Mrs Wilson and her son, a family with whom he became particularly friendly.

Yet out of the maelstrom of colonial issues which surrounded him during his years in Edinburgh, one did focus his attention to the extent that he felt that he had to leave his books for a time and take a personal part in the action. In June 1951 the British government published an official report favouring federation between the two Rhodesias and Nyasaland. Although Attlee's government made it clear that the report was only published for consideration, it was known that white politicians in central Africa were determined to bring the two Rhodesias together, and that they carried considerable weight in Whitehall.

It was also clear from the report that although there were about six million Africans and less than 200,000 whites in the countries concerned, under the proposed federation power would rest squarely in white hands. This was just such a practical issue of colour discrimination as Nyerere had been examining theoretically. It also complemented what he had seen happening in east Africa.

Opposition to the proposed federation, particularly to its imposition without the full consent of the Africans involved, was organised in Britain as well as in Africa. Church groups with African interests joined various political sections in protesting against what was seen as an attempt to foist on central Africa a modified form of South African apartheid. After the Labour Party was defeated in the elections of September 1951, the Conservative Party committed the British government firmly to the policy of federation, whilst many members of the Labour Party joined the movements of protest.

At this time Nyerere was a member of the executive of the World Church Group in Edinburgh. With the deep involvement of the Church of Scotland in central Africa, protest against federation was considerably stronger in that country than in England. It was supported by both main national newspapers, the *Scotsman* and the *Glasgow Herald*. This national criticism of federation was reflected in a mass meeting organised by the World Church Group in the Church of Scotland Assembly Hall in Edinburgh. The meeting was chaired by Sir Gordon Lethem, an ex-colonial governor, who was flanked by the Bishop of Edinburgh, academics and leaders of the Scottish churches. The three speakers were Dr Hastings Banda, now President of Malawi and then practising in London, the Revd Kenneth Mackenzie, a church missionary who had worked in Northern Rhodesia and Nyasaland, and myself, who had just returned from a tour of central Africa. The meeting unanimously passed a resolution condemning closer association between the three African territories 'without the free consent of the African peoples'.

Nyerere attended this meeting. He was provoked into angry denunciation of the scheme which he saw as another example of white domination over African peoples. The inaugural meeting of the campaign was pursued by further meetings on the subject organised in different centres under the auspices of an *ad hoc* body, the Scottish Council for African Questions, set up to combat racialism and colonialism in Africa. Nyerere agreed to speak at some of these meetings, thereby taking his first step into British politics concerned with African affairs.

Yet, with this notable exception, Nyerere did not spend his time as a student in active politics. He had other objectives in preparing himself for what he foresaw to be the future role of service to his country. Whilst in Edinburgh he perceived with ever-growing clarity that his duty lay in that direction, although he was unsure what exact role he ought to play. He spent most of his time in preparation, by clarifying his mind as to his own political philosophy. By the end of the three years he had completed this task, satisfying himself that he had fully prepared himself for whatever role he should feel called to on his return home.

Fortunately, Nyerere recorded at the time the main concepts which he enunciated for himself during these student years. In a University of Edinburgh notebook he wrote an extended essay on the subject, 'The Race Problem in East Africa'. According to his own testimony he expressed in it the precepts he was later to try and put into practice. (This essay was later published in the book *Freedom and Unity*, published by Oxford University Press.)

Already Nyerere was displaying the impatience with double-thought which was to characterise his later impatience with those who refused to express what they really thought. He wrote :

We cannot reach the goal by hypocrisy or wishful thinking. We can only do it by honest thinking, honest talking and honest living. Yet there is too much hypocrisy in east Africa today. The European official and the European settler rule and maintain their prestige mainly by hypocrisy, their inner motives would hardly stand examination; the Indian trader makes his living by downright dishonesty or at best by sheer cunning which is hypocrisy; the African clerk or labourer often disregards fulfilling his part of a contract and even a very educated African will pretend to love the European whereas his heart is nearly bursting with envy and hatred.

Having tilted his lance at sophistry and humbug, Nyerere warned against the assumption that racial animosity was confined, as often supposed, to Kenya. He pointed out that it was in Tanganyika that a British minister (John Dugdale) had walked out of a public gathering on hearing a European state that he would rather dine with swine than with an African. Nor did Nyerere confine his exposure of racial antagonism to Europeans. It was always the attitude, not the race of the individual, which concerned him. He related how an African friend of his had referred to Europeans as Mbwa Hawa, 'These Dogs'. He then declared that he welcomed these outbursts for they revealed the seriousness of the disease. It was the disease itself which he regretted.

Various schemes had been suggested to solve the racial problem in

Africa. But before any policy could succeed, one first principle had to be recognised:

As long as one community has a monopoly of political power and uses that power not only to prevent the other communities from having any share in political power, but also to keep those other communities in a state of social and economic inferiority, any talk of social and economic advancement of the other communities as a solution of racial conflict is hypocritical and stupid. The solution of the problem of racial conflict must depend upon the acceptance by all the communities concerned of the principle of social, economic, and above all, political equality.

Thus early did the young Nyerere reject the theory that economic development of African societies in the colonies would destroy social discrimination and eventually lead to political harmony. As this was the received doctrine of many British politicians, Labour as well as Conservative, it is significant to note how early Nyerere saw through its sophistry. It formed the main argument for those in both parties who supported the Central African Federation, was used to excuse the retention of South Africa in the Commonwealth, was held to justify postponement of independence for the colonies and eventually provided a pretext for continued economic relations with the South Africans. Nyerere saw the absence of political equality as a main reason for continued economic and social discrimination. He was to advance this argument as each of the issues listed above was joined.

Later in the essay Nyerere dealt with the specific racial situation of east Africa in words which can now be seen as prophetic of the policies which he was to employ in political life:

Our problem in east and South Africa is a problem of a White minority which sincerely believes that democracy's cardinal foundation is the will of the people, but which refuses to let the term 'the people' include non-Europeans. Our whole quarrel boils down to the simple question, 'Who are the people of east Africa?' . . .

For a small white minority to come to our country and tell us that they are the people of the country and we are not is one of those many insults which I think we have swallowed for too long. The sooner we tell them that we will no longer tolerate such monstrous impudence the better for all of us. It is even more to their interest than ours that we should refuse to tolerate such insult now when we can still so refuse peacefully, rather than let them grow so chronically insulting that any peaceful means of reparation will seem inadequate . . .

Our east African White neighbours are saying today, 'The people, we are the people.' I shudder too, when I consider what such a doctrine may lead to. The African's capacity for bearing insult is not really limitless . . . They cannot bear insult for ever, and it is well to remember that a day may come when someone may want to incite them; how easy it is to inflame an insulted people ! . . . Such a doctrine may have to be uprooted with all the vulgarity of a bloody revolution . . . A day comes when the people will prefer death to insult and woe to the people who will see that day ! Woe to them who will make that day inevitable ! I hope and pray that such a day will never come. But the European holds the answer. He has only to will that such a day shall never come and it will never come.

This was a sombre warning, the articulation by an African who had the opportunity to think about the condition of his people of sentiments which were soon to sweep the whole continent. Yet Nyerere was entirely sincere when he expressed the hope that bloodshed would never become necessary. He was no bloodthirsty revolutionary. He believed in peaceful change, so long as the absence of violence were not made an excuse for inaction or delay. So he completed his essay by holding out a vision of hope:

The Africans and all the Non-Africans who have chosen to make east Africa their home are the people of east Africa and frankly we do not want to see the Non-Africans treated differently either to our advantage or disadvantage . . . We must build up a society in which we shall belong to east Africa and not to our racial groups. And I appeal to my fellow Africans to take the initiative in this building up of a really harmonious society . . .

We appeal to all thinking Europeans and Indians to regard themselves as ordinary citizens of Tanganyika . . . We are all Tanganyikans and we are all east Africans. The race quarrel is a stupid quarrel, it can be a very tragic quarrel. If we all make up our minds to live like 'ordinary sorts of fellows' and not to think that we were specially designed by the Creator to be masters and others specially designed to be hewers of wood and drawers of water we will make east Africa a very happy country for everybody.

It will be noted that in this essay Nyerere was not only expressing the case for his people's equality; he was also preaching a non-racial doctrine. At that time this was uncommon amongst African politicians and political thinkers. It was more customary to dwell on the injustices suffered by Africans at the hands of Europeans, whether colonial rulers or settlers. There was also considerable animosity felt towards the Asians who had settled in east and South Africa, who were considered to have forged a privileged position, below the Europeans but above the Africans. To Nyerere, though, those who dwelt in Africa were Africans, whatever their racial or national origins. So long as they accepted themselves as no more than equal citizens of the land of their adoption, they were equally entitled to remain there, participating in a fully democratic system. It was to be many years before Nyerere could persuade his fellow-Africans to accept this philosophy.

After receiving his degree Nyerere originally intended to return home by sea in August. However, the British Council arranged for him to take a week's course in July and two further courses subsequently. The idea was for him to study educational institutions in England. For this purpose he was awarded a British Council Visitorship. He contemplated staying longer in Britain to take another degree, but decided that he had achieved his main objective in thinking out his own purpose in life and the principles which would guide him. Consequently he concluded that the time had come to return home. As his August sailing had been cancelled to allow him to accept the British Council invitations, he decided to travel by air, which had the advantage of enabling him to reach Tanganyika as early as the August boat. On 7 October 1952, at the age of thirty, equipped with the product of three and a half years' reading, listening and contemplation, Nyerere flew home to test his theories in practice.

3

Preparations for Politics: Kaunda

During adolescence and youth Nyerere's life evolved out of a traditional environment into that of conventional British educational institutions. Kaunda, two years younger, was reared under greater European influences in the Lubwa mission, but spent his formative years in activities closer to the usual experience of African young men. Since the introduction of money economies by Europeans into African countries during the later years of the nineteenth century, many African men have been pushed and pulled into spells in urban life. Taxes and declining agriculture forced many of them to seek paid employment in mines, factories, petty trading or domestic service. The lure of excitement and desire for consumer goods added momentum to the trek. Long before the end of colonial rule it became almost obligatory in many areas for young men to spend some time in the towns. This was the modern initiation experience, in which a young man gained sophistication and a little capital with which to start married life.

In Kaunda's case the search was less for excitement than for independence. On returning to Lubwa at the behest of the missionaries he was appointed as a boarding master at the mission school. He was only nineteen, self-conscious that all his fellow-teachers were much older. His higher educational qualifications hardly compensated for his youth in African eyes. He soon came to feel that his life was being dominated by the decisions of the missionaries and the desires of his mother. Throughout the first twenty years of his life Kaunda had lived under constant authority. His father had been a strict disciplinarian; after his death his mother played double maternal and paternal roles; the atmosphere of the mission imposed an assumption of duty on the boy; he was expected to be educated in the mission school, to train as a teacher, eventually to become a missionary like his father; it was the missionaries who decided that he should go to Munali and they who decreed that he should return to the Lubwa school. Soon afterwards his mother took a decision which, although he welcomed it, may have added to his sense of having his life determined by others.

Among the visitors to Lubwa were John and Milika Kaweche who at that time were living in Chinsali. Sometimes they would take their daughter, Mutinkhe, to receive medical treatment at the mission dispensary. The Kaweche family later moved to Mpika where they sent Mutinkhe to school. Unusually, her father believed that girls should be given equal educational opportunities with boys. Consequently, instead of leaving school after a rudimentary education, like most of her fellow-pupils, Mutinkhe went through all the standards in Mpika and then proceeded to a boarding school at Mbereshi. The only other girl who had survived to this stage and who had also been offered a place in Mbereshi was unable to accompany her as her parents insisted that she get married.

At Mbereshi Mutinkhe took the Elementary Teachers' Course, receiving her certificate in 1946. She then returned home to Mpika to teach at the local school. It was hoped that her example and her presence on the school staff would attract more girls to attend the school and proceed to become teachers.

However, Mutinkhe never took up her appointment in the Mpika school. Kaunda's mother had, without his knowledge, been considering who would make him a suitable wife. She visited the Kaweches in Mpika, consulted another friend, a neighbour of theirs, and saw Mutinkhe for the first time since she was a small girl. Satisfied with the reports and her own observations, Mrs Kaunda wrote to her son who was attending a Scout camp in Mufilira with his two closest friends, Simon Kapwepwe and John Sokoni. She suggested that on his journey back home he call in Mpika to see the Kaweches' daughter. At the same time she arranged for the neighbours to speak to Mutinkhe's parents about her suggestion that her son would be a suitable match for their daughter.

Mutinkhe, or Betty as she now was more usually called, this being her Christian name, has recalled her curiosity to see the young man whom she had heard might become her husband. She had been told that he and his two friends were staying in Mpika and went to the hut where they were resting. But only two men were there. She had to return the same evening before she saw Kenneth:

The two other men left the room, apparently to give their friend a chance for speaking to me. I was now in no doubt he was the one. He introduced himself and went straight to the point. I became speechless. He asked me several questions to which, as is the custom, I did not reply. As you know, I was born and brought up among the Bemba people. Silence meant consent. Kenneth too, was born and brought up in the same way. He understood. After a few minutes I went home. On the following morning he called on Chitulika the headman of the village and sent him to deliver five shillings to my parents as a token of betrothal. My parents informed me of the engagement token and asked whether I was willing to be engaged to him. I agreed. According to the custom, if the parents accept the present, it means they consent. My parents accepted the five shillings and five shillings was a lot of money, for among the Bemba a sixpence or one shilling used to be enough for this purpose.*

The wedding took place two months later, in August 1946. According to Bemba custom it was celebrated first in Mpika, the bride's home, then in Lubwa, the village of the bridegroom. Kenneth and Betty travelled the 120 miles from Mpika to Lubwa sitting on their luggage on the back of a lorry. At the Lubwa reception all Kenneth's schoolchildren attended and dancing continued all night. The people attending donated pennies to the couple, £3 being collected during the festivities. A few days later Kenneth resumed his duties at the school and Betty, eighteen years old, took over the responsibilities of housekeeping for him.

Kenneth was the product of a dual community, in which tribal custom and Christian beliefs intermingled. He never accepted either uncritically. His individuality began to dominate his personality, insisting that he make personal choices, rather than accept an expected role either within the Bemba community or as a member of the mission. So he remained as a teacher for only four years. Probably because he was little older than his pupils and much younger than the rest of the staff, he had the reputation for imposing strict discipline, which, in any case, was the tradition in which he had been brought up himself whilst at the mission school. The influence of his own schooldays was also shown in his interest in a form of boy scouting. He could not call his pack 'cubs', for that term was reserved for European boys. So he named them 'trekkers', but taught his boys much the same type of conventional values and skills as he had been taught by his own schoolmaster in the African variant of the Boy Scout movement. He also continued his football and guitar-playing enthusiasms, which gave him considerable popularity amongst his boys. One further interest which was to last throughout his life and which also brought emulation from the boys, was his interest in clothes. As he was able to supply most of his food from the garden, he had money to spare to have his suits and shorts styled by a Chinsali tailor. Thus early in life did the young Kaunda set sartorial fashions; he still does so – his tropical suitings have even been imitated in 1970s' Jamaica.

Yet Kaunda had already become far too individualistic to remain content with the conventions he had been taught. As a schoolmaster he joined the Chinsali African Welfare Association whose members consisted largely of teachers and government clerks. It is true that at first he was

* From *Betty Kaunda*, a biography by Stephen A. Mpashi, Longmans of Zambia, 1969.

mainly interested in the social side of the Association, organising dances and football matches. But in joining he became a member of one of the major pre-nationalist streams. Before long he was participating in discussions on issues affecting the welfare of Africans throughout the area, associating with resolutions sent to the District Commissioners or to the mission.

Welfare associations played a crucial role in the preparation of African nationalist movements. The more enlightened colonial officers regarded them as a means of consulting educated African opinion. More often the majority of officials treated them with suspicion, regarding their members, in Lugard's phase, as 'trousered blacks', as semi-educated 'native' agitators, unrepresentative of the ordinary African who was assumed to count the blessings of undisturbed colonial rule.

Thus, from the 1930s onwards, the welfare associations became an issue of political argument inside and outside government circles. The official bodies representing African opinion were formed by the Urban Advisory Councils. But, as these consisted of nominees appointed by District Commissioners, they were usually filled by those prepared to carry out government policies without query. The welfare associations, on the other hand, were composed of members who had joined voluntarily. They therefore attracted those Africans with independent minds and initiative in each locality. It was for this reason that the government continually tried to prevent them from involving themselves in political issues. Inevitably many of them disobeyed such government instructions. They became increasingly concerned with matters of politics as they found that the welfare of their communities was subject to political decision. Consequently, it was frequently the welfare association which provided the early training ground for those Africans who were later to engage in nationalist politics, whilst the associations themselves often supplied the foundation of organisation on which political parties could be constructed.

Before he had been a teacher for four years the young Kaunda began to feel restless. His brother had joined the army and he himself was attracted to break away from the restrictions of mission and home to try his luck in the Army Education Corps. His mother and the missionaries persuaded him that it was his duty to remain at home.

Yet his urge persisted. Eventually it overcame the ties of a happy married life, his mother's home and his promising school career. He and his closest friends decided that they must break out of the Lubwa missionary – domestic syndrome. They decided to seek other experiences, to test themselves in different societies.

Only a year after his marriage Kaunda left Lubwa to search for a new career. At this time he had two special friends. He had first met Simon Kapwepwe as a boy when both had been attending the mission hospital during a period in which Kaunda suffered from sores and frequent bouts of malaria. They were to remain close friends and political colleagues until 1971. The third of the friends was John Sokoni, another Lubwa teacher. The three of them decided to seek wider pastures outside Lubwa.

Sokoni and Kapwepwe initiated the break. They secured teaching appointments in Tanganyika and left for Mbeya. On arrival they became unduly optimistic over the prospects and sent for Kaunda to join them. Seeing this as an opportunity to break the ties which bound him to Lubwa, Kaunda took his wife, now pregnant, to stay with his sister in Chinsali and caught a lorry for Mbeya. There he discovered that his friends' optimism had been misplaced. The poor conditions of service offered by the Tanganyikan Government ended the young men's dreams. They decided to return home immediately.

For the rest of the year the three friends stayed on the family farm near Lubwa. Betty, Kaunda's wife, stayed with them at first, but in November it was decided that she should be with her mother during her confinement. So Kenneth took her to Mpika, where their first child, named Panji Tushuke, was born at the beginning of December.

Yet the expansion of his family responsibilities did not quench Kaunda's yearning to seek wider opportunities. Moreover, he now aspired to become a serious farmer. For this he would need capital. He spent Christmas with his wife and baby boy, entertaining his relatives and their friends on his guitar. Kapwepwe and Sokoni had already gone ahead to Lusaka. In the New Year of 1948 he left his family in Mpika and joined them.

The period of frustrated hopes which had started in Tanganyika continued. Kaunda and Kapwepwe were accepted as Army Education Instructors, only to be discharged within twenty-four hours without being given any reasons. Then Kaunda travelled for five days to a Salvation Army school near Salisbury in Southern Rhodesia, only to find that the post had already been filled. So he re-boarded the bus with his rucksack, box of books, and suitcase of clothes, carrying his blankets on his head and guitar over his shoulder. The bus took him another eighty-five miles beyond Salisbury to another school where a post was vacant.

Already as a youth Kaunda had acquired a fastidiousness which was to stay with him throughout his life and to bring him frequent occasions of acute nausea. One of them had been on his first journey from his home on his way to school at Munali. A second occurred during this journey in Southern Rhodesia. He had been accustomed at his mission home to regular cleanliness of body and clothes. Facilities to maintain this standard had been available when he was in school. Now he felt affronted that he had had no opportunity to bathe or change his clothes for five days. When he found that the only place he could wash was in a cattle pond and that the school meal he was offered was almost inedible, he immediately decided to return home. His homesickness was only aggravated by the plight in which he found himself in a strange and hostile country.

Having secured a little money to pay for his fare from selling some of his clothes, he now found that in Southern Rhodesia he was expected to carry a pass. This was his first practical experience of the politico-social distinction between the life of an African in a British Protectorate and in a self-governing colony. As a British subject in Northern Rhodesia he had never had to apply for a pass, nor were any issued. In Southern Rhodesia, however, he was ordered to show one before he could be sold a railway ticket. Fortunately for him the ticket clerk mistook a church certificate for his pass and sold him a ticket back to Northern Rhodesia. After a hungry and thirsty four-day rail journey he thankfully arrived back in his own country. Characteristically, his first luxury was to be taken by some of his former pupils for a bath!

These experiences abroad in Tanganyika and Southern Rhodesia had given Kaunda a broader view of societies outside the parochial life of Lubwa which was to sharpen his consciousness of African difficulties and opportunities; but they had exhausted his resources. He had been seeking capital to provide the opportunity to start farming. So he now turned to that area of his own country where most young Africans seeking their fortune were accustomed to migrate; the Copper Belt. Here were opportunities not only for jobs in the mines, but in all the services which supplied the mining communities. The mines themselves still preserved a *de facto* discrimination between white and black miners. Nor were there any genuine opportunities for Africans to gain the training necessary for skilled mining employment. Yet, compared with conditions in the rural areas where most Africans were born and brought up, the Copper Belt offered chances to secure much more money.

It was just at this time that trade unionism had begun to develop amongst the African mineworkers' community. Ernest Bevin, Foreign Secretary in Attlee's post-war Labour government, showed scant interest in the political rights of British imperial subjects. But Bevin was first and foremost a trade unionist. During the war Arthur Creech Jones had worked with him in the Ministry of Labour and was strongly influenced by Bevin's ideas. When Creech Jones became Colonial Secretary under Attlee he reflected this influence in his policies.

One consequence of this was the pressure exerted by the Colonial Office for the first time for the encouragement of trade unions in certain colonies. Northern Rhodesia, with its large mining community was one example. Not only was the Labour Officer instructed to assist in the formation of African unions, but a special trade union adviser was appointed. The two men, Richard Luyt, later to be Chief Secretary of Northern Rhodesia and then Governor of British Guiana, and Bill Comrie, from a branch of

Bevin's own union on the Clydeside, were largely responsible for getting the African Mineworkers' Union launched. Together with a remarkable African, Lawrence Katilungu, they steered it through its infancy to become probably the strongest African trade union in the continent.

Kaunda was almost caught up in this new trade union enthusiasm. Certain white miners, seeing the danger to their interests that might be presented by a separate African union, decided to try and attract the Africans into their union. This policy was encouraged by the World Federation of Trade Unions, which was largely under Communist influence. One of its representatives was delegated to recruit African miners and advertised for an organising secretary. Kaunda applied for the job, but before any appointment was made, the scheme was abandoned. Although those who supported it in the white union argued that division would weaken miners in their negotiations with the companies, the Africans realised the danger of being dominated by experienced white trade unionists. They also relevantly asked why the white miners had made no such overtures until an African union was projected. So they rejected the proposal and proceeded to form their own union.

Kaunda decided to return to teaching and applied for a post on the Copper Belt. In the meantime he secured a job as an assistant Welfare Officer in the Nchanga Mine, at £4 a month. This entitled him to a two-roomed hut in the Chingola Compound. He wrote to his wife in Mpika, arranged to meet her at Kapiri Mposhi so that she would not have to negotiate the large Copper Belt towns on her own, and took her and their child by train to Chingola. Such were the conditions of travelling for Africans at that time that there was nowhere for the family to stay in Kapiri Mposhi. They had no option but to spend the cold night in the open.

Betty Kaunda found life in Chingola much easier than she had been used to at Mpika. Instead of having to go into the forest to collect firewood she was able to use charcoal for cooking. There was a communal water tap in the compound, so she did not have to fetch her water from a distance either. The women did their washing together on the cement wash place, so an air of community life was established. Betty began to enjoy the amenities of town life.

It was not to last for long. Although his wife quickly became attached to Chingola, Kenneth was dissatisfied. He found that his job entailed little more than opening the library, most of whose books he had already read. He was bored, finding his active mind starved, with little opportunity for intellectual or physical stimulus.

Thus he was delighted when the Reverend Fergus McPherson, previously at Lubwa, offered him a post as boarding master in Mufilira. Betty was disappointed at having to leave Chingola, but avoided letting her husband see her chagrin. The couple agreed that their first objective was to improve their standard of life.

Accordingly, whilst Kenneth taught the older boys and supervised the boarders, Betty took a post teaching in the primary department. Kenneth was paid £5 13s 6d, and Betty £3 2s 6d a month. As John Sokoni also taught at the school, whilst Simon Kapwepwe was not far away in Kitwe, the trio continued their friendship. They also shared a joint determination to accumulate the money necessary to return to their farming.

Little could be saved from the £2 a week which the Kaundas were earning as teachers. So Kenneth used his ingenuity to supplement their funds. Just across the Congo border, at a town called Mokambo, second-hand American clothes were on sale. People were allowed to cross the border to buy them, but were only permitted to return with one jacket and a dress or shirt. Kenneth organised his schoolboys to cross with him, returning with as many clothes as they could wear. These were then sold locally for a small profit, which, together with anything which could be spared from their salaries, the Kaundas saved for their future plans.

It was at Mufilira also that Kenneth began to practise on a small scale the self-help principle he was later to urge on his people nationally. As many of the African boys found difficulty in securing their school fees, he organised them to grow vegetables in the school gardens. He then bought the vegetables for school use, paying the boys so that they could save for the fees demanded by the school authorities.

The Kaunda family only stayed in Mufilira for one year. Yet it was a year in which Kenneth's experiences began to draw him unerringly into public life. He was first chosen to be the teachers' representative on the Urban Advisory Council, whose members were nominated by the District Commissioner after consultation with the various interest groups of the area. As the Council was purely advisory, with its influence depending entirely on the personality of the particular Commissioner, membership was not a very rewarding or stimulating experience. Nevertheless, it gave Kaunda his first practical experience of the functions of a public committee. He was also elected to attend the Provincial Council, but found his short experience on it scarcely more satisfying.

Of much greater significance was the experience of the Northern Rhodesian colour bar which he encountered for the first time in Mufilira. As described above, he had been surprised and affronted by discovering the attitude taken towards Africans by the authorities in Southern Rhodesia with their pass laws. In the rural community in which he had been brought up as a student and teacher, colour discrimination in his homeland had never intruded itself. It was different in the tough mining townships of the Copper Belt.

As a British Protectorate, Northern Rhodesia was not supposed to practise any form of racial discrimination in its institutions. In fact, although other apologies were offered as explanations, 'Europeans' and 'Natives' were treated separately and differently by government, in education, representation and administration.

Yet, at this stage, before political organisation amongst Africans had advanced beyond the infant stage, it was social discrimination which impressed itself most directly on the African. It was the practice in the towns for Africans to be served in shops only through a side hatch. They were never allowed to enter through the shop door or to examine goods within the shops themselves. Nor was there any social mixing in hotels or public houses.

Naturally, this form of social discrimination, imposed by an alien settler community rather than by law, irked educated Africans more specifically than those who had been accustomed to accepting that they were lesser beings than the Europeans. As education slowly spread amongst the younger African generation, resentment increased. Yet most of the Europeans, many of whom were minimally educated themselves, tended to strengthen rather than diminish their discrimination, indignant that blacks should be acquiring equal and sometimes superior knowledge. Both Africans and Europeans began to recognise that the superior skills which whites had been accustomed to quote as reason for their greater power stemmed from education and training, neither of which bore any relation to skin colour.

A few Europeans recognised that social habits must change as the number of educated Africans grew. They tried to ensure that the educated African was not insulted by those whites who resented the new social situation or saw no reason to modify their traditional attitude of superiority. It is significant that, from his first experience of colour discrimination, Kaunda never accepted the supposition that his education entitled him to receive different treatment from those of his fellow-Africans who had never had his opportunities.

It was a sign that the young Kaunda had begun to be moved by a practical social conscience when he decided personally to challenge discrimination in the shops. He entered a chemist's shop which also stocked books. On being peremptorily told to leave he tried to speak reasonably to the proprietor, only to be forcibly ejected by two white customers. His schoolboys were awaiting the outcome in the street. A shouting match ensued between the whites and the boys, from which the two Europeans hastily withdrew.

On reporting this incident to the District Officer, Kaunda was told that anytime he wanted to buy anything he only had to ask for a note. It was then that Kaunda declared that he did not want any privileges for himself, but that all his people should be treated as dignified human beings. When later, the District Officer himself accompanied Kaunda to the shop and remonstrated with the chemist, the latter apologised. Again Kaunda was assured that if the proprietor had known who he was he would not have been ordered out of the shop; and again he had to explain that he was not seeking personal privileges but the right of all his people to courteous treatment.

This was an isolated incident in Kaunda's life. He did not pursue the issue again for nearly ten years, when he was in the midst of an active political life, in a life-and-death struggle with the Federation. Nor is there any record of the situation in Mufilira having been changed by his gesture. Nevertheless, it was an incident which Kaunda remembered all his life, which taught him in practice the effects of colour discrimination on the sensibilities of his fellow-Africans. It was a seed from which blossomed an intense hatred of racialism in all its aspects.

By 1949 the Kaundas considered that they could afford to risk the return to farming. Kapwepwe and Sokoni shared the resolve. The three of them had already bought bicycles to enable them to attend meetings more freely and watches to get them there punctually. The Kaundas had also purchased a sewing machine to repair the second-hand clothes they bought and sold.

In June 1949, the Kaundas and Sokoni travelled by train to Kapiri Mposhi. There was only enough money to pay Betty's bus fare to her parents' home in Mpika. The two young men were to cycle. Eventually, with the good offices of a friendly lorry-driver, they all arrived back in Chinsali.

The two years from leaving Lubwa to his return in 1949 provided Kaunda with his initial education in politics. He had seen something of Tanganyika, Southern Rhodesia and the Congo, so knew that societies outside his own country had many variations. He had faced the practical difficulties of supporting a family as an African with the privilege of an education, and had seen the much greater difficulties encountered by the majority of his countrymen. He had personally experienced the practice of the colour bar and had witnessed the hostile relations between white and black in the rough mining townships of the Copper Belt.

Kaunda's mission and home background remained an important influence in his personality. He had always been sensitive and highly strung. The impact of his schoolmasters and missionaries made him somewhat pious. Not only did he embrace the Boy Scouts and church choirs; the book he was refused in the chemist's shop was, characteristically, Arthur Mee's *Talks for Boys*, laced with the moralistic tones of the 1920s.

It can therefore be imagined that to subject himself to the indignities of being thrown out of a shop or of risking his liberty in Southern Rhodesia demanded a will inspired by a sense of duty and capable of overcoming instinct. It was this same duty-inspired willpower which compelled him to enter the political arena in defiance of colonial authority.

4

Tanganyika and Northern Rhodesia

Julius Nyerere and Kenneth Kaunda began their political lives within a year or two of each other, around the divide between the 1940s and 1950s. They had prepared themselves in different ways. Both had secured a basic education, but whereas Nyerere had proceeded to the contemplation invited in academic society, Kaunda had wandered around his own and neighbouring countries, mixing teaching with a variety of employment.

The contrast in their environments as they approached public life was, however, even sharper than their youthful experiences. For Tanganyika and Northern Rhodesia, although neighbours, were vastly different countries. At the beginning of the 1950s their differences were much more marked than later, certainly more than when they attained independence and became Tanzania and Zambia respectively.

The first obvious contrast is that whereas Northern Rhodesia was land-locked, Tanganyika had a long sea coast with three valuable harbours. The significance of this difference was not only geographic or economic; it had fundamentally influenced the characters of the two societies. Throughout the European Middle Ages, the east African coast had formed an integral part of the Indian Ocean emporium. Goods and people had been exchanged between east Africa and Arabia, India and the East Indies. Cultural mixing had brought into being a new society on the east African coast, a blend of Arab and African Bantu, speaking its own language and developing its own culture. This was Swahili society, extending in varying concentrations from Somalia through Mozambique. It formed a vital part of Tanganyikan society.

It is true that the wide belt of arid lands which lie behind the coast effectively separated the other peoples of Tanganyika from littoral communities. These inland societies more closely resembled the peoples of Northern Rhodesia. Yet separation was never complete. Trading caravans formed cultural bridges, evidenced especially in the diffusion of the Swahili language.

Nor, indeed, was central Africa unaffected by the activities of the east coast. It was from this region, including both Rhodesias, the Congo and Nyasaland, that materials and manpower provided the coastal city ports with most of their wealth. It was here that the gold, copper and iron were mined to find their way by caravan across the vast areas to the coast. Later it was largely from central Africa and from the east African hinterland that men, women and children were seized in their villages to supply the nefarious slave trade, mainly conducted by Arabs, angrily denounced by Livingstone and others.

Trade is inevitably accompanied by cultural contact. Thus there was never complete separation between the coastal peoples and those of the interior. Nevertheless, a gulf was fixed between their experiences, which, although always connected by fragile bridges, produced important differences in the societies they created.

The first was the impact made by foreigners. The coastline of Tanganyika had seen visitors from Arabia, India, Portugal, Germany and Britain, each bringing their special economic interests with them, often accompanied by political ambitions. Its communities had frequently been interrupted in their evolution, powerfully influenced by alien cultures. The Germans and the British had ruled Tanganyika, taking from her peoples their powers of decision over their own lives. This had aroused resentment, at times amounting to violent rejection. The Maji Maji revolt against the Germans had provided Tanganyikans with that sense of historical martyrdom which is a valuable aid to national consciousness. Resentment against the British rule which replaced that of the Germans after the first world war had never risen to such heights. British authority was, in any case, slightly modified by the League of Nations' mandate, and superseded by a United Nations' trust agreement.

There were constructive as well as destructive elements in this foreign influence. Participation in Indian Ocean trade had brought a knowledge of commercial practices, although many of them were largely forgotten by the twentieth century, most of those remaining being concentrated in Arab or Indian hands. The Germans had built useful railways and roads, also introducing the important sisal cultivation. The British had fostered a certain amount of education, although it was confined to a small minority; had begun some economic development, mainly concentrated on the country's infrastructure; and had maintained an administrative framework more benign than that of the Germans, usually in conjunction with local leaders.

But the most important effect of alien influence was the amalgam of Arab and African cultures out of which Swahili society developed. The major contribution which this society had made to Tanganyika is its language. Although originally a Bantu tongue spoken on the coast, Kiswahili has adopted words from the languages of those who visited or settled along the coast, the Arabs, Indians, Portuguese and British. Because of the trading contacts inland, the language came to be known and used in the hinterland, even as far as parts of central Africa. This gave Tanganyikans an enormous advantage as their political movement developed. It was the only colonial territory in Africa which had its own lingua franca, apart from the languages of imperial rulers. Kiswahili could be understood in virtually all communities of Tanganyika, offering a sense of national unity unknown in other colonial territories, eventually providing it with its own official tongue after independence.

Nor did this valuable asset submerge local tribal or community languages. Most Tanganyikans became bi- or tri-lingual, using both the mother tongues of their own communities and Kiswahili, and in the towns adding English. This again gave the nationalist movement a subconscious advantage. Local loyalties were seen not to be competitive with but complementary to the higher loyalty towards the nation.

This language factor was certainly one influence which allowed the Tanganyikan nationalist movement to develop without that inter-tribal rivalry which handicapped its counterparts in neighbouring Kenya and Uganda. Yet there were other causes.

It has often been asserted that the difference which marked off the tribalism of the nationalist movements in Kenya and Uganda from the absence of tribal schism in Tanganyika was a contrast in tribal size. The argument has been that the lack of large tribes in Tanganyika compared with the Kikuyu of Kenya or the Baganda of Uganda prevented any one tribe in Tanganyika from entertaining ambitions of political domination.

This explanation does not match the facts. For the Sukuma of Tanganyika were almost as numerous as the Kikuyu or the Baganda. Why, then, the contrast in the experience of the three neighbouring countries? Explanations can only be tentative, but they illustrate some of the main features of the country to which Nyerere returned in 1952.

The population of Tanganyika has long been settled in various pockets of the country, due to the necessity of finding fertile land, fisheries or other means of seeking a livelihood. Much of the territory is virtually uninhabitable. The capital was sited at Dar es Salaam, where most of the administrative and commercial headquarters were situated. Yet Dar es Salaam was hundreds of miles away from the home of any large tribe. So no community comparable with the Kikuyu or Baganda lived beside the seat of political power.

Moreover, Dar es Salaam never became the economic Mecca represented by the capitals of Kenya and Uganda. This was partly due to the fact that Tanganyika was basically a poor and agricultural country, the little wealth that could be gained lying in country districts, like the cotton of Sukumaland or the coffee of the Kilimanjaro area. Thus the main economic activities were concentrated on rural areas. When complaints and resentments came to be voiced, they were usually raised in these rural districts over agrarian issues. Anti-colonial activity therefore tended to be diffused, take place far from the political capital and involve local leadership.

This trend was accentuated by the absence of a large settler community. Immediately after the Second World War there were only just over 10,000 Europeans in Tanganyika, compared with about five times that number in Kenya. Many of them were farmers of varying nationalities with little influence in Dar es Salaam. This contrasts sharply with the situation in Kenya, where most of the large settler community came from Britain, many congregated in Nairobi and all considered that the British government had a primary duty to further their interests.

It was not surprising, therefore, that whereas the major anti-colonial movements had been dominated by Kikuyu in Kenya and by Baganda in Uganda, in Tanganyika a faint thread of trans-tribal national consciousness had been established in the years before the war. When taking over the administration from the Germans the British employed a handful of educated Africans from various parts of the country whose outlook was territorial rather than tribal. Through their organisations they laid a slender foundation of national consciousness. From 1929 onwards the African Association fostered this national sense in the branches it opened in various centres. They may have fluctuated in their activity, but some continuity prevailed and their outlook was always territorial, non-tribal. Even some tribal organisations, like the Bukoba Bahaya Union, transformed themselves into branches of the Association. Not only was its object to unite educated Africans on the mainland; it had a lively branch in Zanzibar. It was this branch which inspired the first territorial conference in 1939. At the second, in the following year, the Association was claiming that Africans should represent their own country: 'We are now claiming a voice in the Government. That is, the African now be given a chance to speak on behalf of his country.' By the third conference, held in 1945, it was being resolved 'that efforts be made to enrol all Africans, women and men, in the African Association'. The skein of territorial unity may have been thin, but it was there among the educated and influential; and it surmised a loyalty higher than but yet embracing that to the tribe. In this respect Tanganyika was unique in Africa.

The experience of Kaunda's Northern Rhodesians varied considerably from that of the Tanganyikans. Discoveries of shells and beads in the Southern Province prove that as early as the first millennium trading contacts took place between the inhabitants of this area and the east coast. But this was vastly different from the constant contact with foreigners experienced by the Swahili. It could, perhaps, be compared with the history of Tanganyika's inland communities, in occasional contact with, but never decisively influenced by, those engaged in overseas trade.

The history of all Africa's peoples is one of migration. So the communities which comprised the Northern Rhodesian population came originally from outside that country. In the south of the country the Tonga, Ila, and communities related to them moved into the territory some 800 years ago. They came from the north-east, probably from what became Tanganyika. From the Lunda–Luba medieval empire in the Congo came the Lozi into the upper reaches of the Zambesi, and the Bemba across the Luapula and eventually into the northern plateau. The last major migration was that of the Ngoni, a branch of the Zulu. As a result of Shaka's wars in the south these peoples migrated all over central–east Africa, bringing with them the military prowess learnt from their parent society. In the 1830s they entered Northern Rhodesia and, after a period of military expeditions, settled in the east of the country.

There are many other small or sub-communities, for modern Zambia contains over seventy recognised tribes. These four are the main conglomerates, however, playing a major role in the composition of the nation.

Although Tanganyika was composed of many more ethnic communities than Northern Rhodesia, well over 100, they were not as distinct from each other nor as self-conscious of their separate communal structure. Nor did the Northern Rhodesians possess the inestimable advantage of a lingua franca. Bemba was spoken by many people who did not actually belong to the Bemba tribe, and this diffusion of the language increased as the Copper Belt developed. Yet this affected only a minority of Northern Rhodesians, confined to one area, and certainly did not provide the country with a common language.

Neither did the history of the country encourage even the degree of national consciousness which had appeared in Tanganyika by the end of the war. Much of the experience of inter-tribal contact in the country had been one of conflict, often of warfare and expulsions. They had also suffered from the tragic dislocations of the slave trade, both of domestic slavery amongst their own people and the depredations of the Portuguese and Arabs. In this respect, at least, they shared a common experience with their neighbours in Tanganyika.

The effects of contact with foreigners, however, made a sharp contrast. In the years after Livingstone's death in 1873 missionaries of various denominations settled in Zambia. But throughout the lands north of the Zambesi greater effects on the lives of the inhabitants were wrought by the contests between the British, the Portuguese and the Belgians, with Arab slave traders still operating their own commerce.

It was as a result of deceptions practised by Cecil Rhodes' British South Africa Company that the inhabitants of what later came to be known as Northern Rhodesia lost self-government. In conjunction with members of the British government Rhodes' agents took control of Barotseland from

Lewanika and extended their power outside the Barotse kingdom. This was not accomplished without resistance, which included a battle between British troops from Nyasaland and the Ngoni, from which the BSA made a handsome profit through seizure of Ngoni cattle.

From 1891 the territory was administered by the Chartered Company, with the authority of the British Crown and government behind it. Contact between the new white rulers and the African inhabitants varied. In many areas customary life was hardly disturbed; in others, especially where white settlers appeared or administrative posts were established, tribal life was seriously weakened. The imposition of a hut tax and recruiting for labour in the south certainly undermined traditional communities, whilst the effects of the white man's rule also reduced the authority of the chiefs.

White settlement was slow, at first confined to farmers, many of them Afrikaners from South Africa. As the railway was extended from Bulawayo, first to Livingstone and then to Broken Hill, however, it gradually increased. Those African communities living near the line of rail, therefore, felt the effects of the alien incursion most severely.

In 1924 the administration was transferred from the Company to the Colonial Office. Virtually no improvements had been effected under Company rule, the territory having being allowed to stagnate. By this time, however, demands from industrial countries for minerals had begun to transform its significance. Copper had been mined and smelted for centuries. The first European companies followed earlier African excavations.

The development of copper during the 1920s, mainly by the Selection Trust and Anglo-American, transformed the northern part of the country. In 1924 there were only 1,300 Africans employed on the Copper Belt; six years later there were 30,000. During the years immediately following, the world slump hit the industry shrewdly, but it was not long before the impact of rearmament and then war stimulated further expansion. This mining industry attracted many more Europeans into the country. The figure jumped from 4,000 in 1924 to 13,800 in 1931, declined during the slump, and was not restored to this level until the war years. From the start, European miners were attracted by wages even higher than those paid in South Africa. Semi-skilled white miners could earn £30 a month; African labourers were paid about 15s. a month for underground work.

By the end of the war, therefore, Northern Rhodesia possessed a treble socio-economic structure. The mass of Africans still lived in their traditional, largely subsistence communities, although increasing numbers of their young men left for the copper towns. About 10,000 of them had also served abroad in the British army. Secondly, there were a number of large farms owned by white farmers. Thirdly, there was the Copper Belt, with its well-paid white miners and the commercial enterprises which served them, together with its thousands of black mining labourers and those who provided them and their families with urban services. There were other towns, like Lusaka, the capital, Livingstone and Broken Hill, with an urban life resembling a pale reflection of the copper towns.

Northern Rhodesia had been comparatively remote from the centres of political activity up to this time. Communications with the outside world and inside the country were rudimentary, even the best roads being made from gravel. Yet a number of factors appeared between the wars which presaged argument and conflict in the following years.

The change from Company to Colonial Office control in 1924 was marked by the introduction of 'indirect rule', a concept associated with Lord Lugard, who had attempted to put it into practice as Governor of Nigeria. According to the theory, this allowed colonial administrators to use the services of local indigenous authorities to apply colonial policies. To some extent, therefore, after 1924 African chiefs were used as government agents and given some legal authority.

This policy was resented by most white settlers, who feared that it might lead to Africans securing dangerous powers. The whites were determined that as power was transferred from the Colonial Office it should be handed to them. They therefore continually criticised the colonial servants and their policies, seeking to supersede their authority. One central tactic in this strategy was to seek closer association with the white community of Southern Rhodesia and, more remotely, with South Africans. For it should be remembered that on the farms and in the mines many whites in Northern Rhodesia were South Africans themselves.

Yet the policy of indirect rule had one blind spot in relation to Africans themselves. The administration, like that of Lord Lugard in Nigeria, never came to grips with the fact that many Africans were becoming detribalised, no longer subject to chiefs' authority. As mining was extended the African population of the Copper Belt grew. Many African families became permanent town dwellers. They might still retain a family stake in their village, but they were now settled in the towns where the chiefs' fiat did not run.

Moreover, despite the poor communications within Northern Rhodesia itself, which made movement inside the country very difficult, ever since the imposition of the hut tax many young Africans had been accustomed to seek employment abroad. Many went to Southern Rhodesia, some as far as South Africa, seeking the money wages to enable their families to pay the tax and accumulate a few possessions. Their experiences gave them knowledge of how other countries were run. They were offended by the pass laws customary in the south; but they saw Africans organising themselves. Racial discrimination might be worse in the countries they visited, but they were also provoked into questioning why they were not allowed to walk on the pavements or enter the shops of their own country.

Moreover, the paucity of educational opportunities offered in Northern Rhodesia made it necessary to recruit many clerks from Nyasaland, where mission education was much more widespread. As political consciousness was also more advanced in Nyasaland, their presence stimulated increased discussion of conditions in Northern Rhodesia. The Nyasaland African Congress was founded in 1944. Nyasas working on the Copper Belt started their own branches – with government consent – an example which was soon to be followed by Northern Rhodesians themselves.

As in Tanzania, however, specific political organisation had its predecessors in the welfare movement. As early as 1923 the first welfare association was formed in Mwenzo on the Tanganyikan border. During the 1930s a number of these associations were formed, mostly along the line of rail, usually stimulated by Nyasas or those Lozi who had greater educational opportunities than Africans elsewhere in the country. Although the associations were formed for only quasi-political objects, the Livingstone organisation was complaining about the loss of Tonga land to white farmers in 1930 and against racial discrimination shortly afterwards. The fact that the Livingstone association had members from various northern areas as well as some Nyasas demonstrates that ideas had begun to be diffused through the country. By 1933 an attempt was being made to organise a joint body of all associations in the country, but it seems to have been abortive.

The other focus of African activity came in the growth of African religious organisations. The Watch Tower movement, which gained adherents throughout the continent, attracted many members. It represented resistance to the administration in a religious guise, but its anarchistic outlook did little to prepare its members for future political activity. The most that can be said of it is that, like the welfare associations, it gave Africans some sense of community spirit in the face of an alien administration and taught them something about the intricacies of organisation.

One overt sign that Africans were beginning to stand on their own feet in social affairs was seen with tragic force in 1935. In that year a strike was called in the mines. The fact that most of the clerks in the compound offices were Nyasas may have had some significance. Disturbances ensued in which six Africans were shot dead and many others injured. Although the commission of enquiry made the mistake of ignoring the social conditions and growing consciousness of the Africans and blaming the incident mainly on the Watch Tower movement, some officials had their eyes opened. The Chief Secretary, Charles Dundas, recognised that the compound system, imported from South Africa and aimed at preserving tribal links, would have to be replaced by a stabilised urban African labour-force. The implication of this recognition was that the policy of indirect rule was insufficiently comprehensive for Northern Rhodesian conditions. It would have to be accepted that those African workers who came to work and live in the towns were detribalised, at least so far as authority within their communities was concerned.

It may have been that this revelation of the inadequacies of stereotyped government policy was one of the factors which led to the creation of new bodies to represent African opinion. Just before the start of the Second World War the government established a number of councils designed to provide liaison between the administration and urban Africans. The councils were to be only advisory and their members were to be nominated, not elected. Later provincial councils were created, comprising members of both urban and rural councils, eventually culminating in a national African Representative Council. When in Mufilira Kenneth Kaunda was nominated to membership of both the urban and the Western provincial councils and only just missed being chosen as a member of the Representative Council.

All these councils were without power, but they were able to ventilate African opinion on discrimination, the lack of education and housing and similar social issues. Their significance, however, extended further than the subjects of their debates.

In its curiously stumbling, unfocused manner, British colonial policy was providing Africans with growing political opportunities. The rationale of British policy was that by gradually extending democratic institutions, vaguely modelled on British practice, colonial subjects would slowly gain experience of political procedures, eventually culminating in self-government. Many members of the British governments which put this colonial principle into practice and many more of their administrators would have denied that this was a practical possibility in the foreseeable future. Some would even have repudiated the ultimate objective. Nevertheless, by the creation of the institutions demanded by the policy, self-government was made inevitable, only its timing becoming an issue between the colonial government and subject peoples.

This pattern contrasted sharply with that projected by other European imperial governments. Perhaps the Belgian policy may have ultimately predicted the same outcome, but if so it remained entirely theoretical, no practical steps being taken to initiate the process. In the case of both France and Portugal, however, the objective of self-government never became even theoretical. In both cases, when colonial principles were considered, the only ultimate objective conceived was some form of integrated extension of the metropolitan state to embrace the colonial peoples. As a result, colonial administration as well as principle was carried out in a very different manner from that of the British colonies.

Whether the British administrators in Northern Rhodesia recognised it or approved it, the fact was that the creation of these councils certainly advanced African political consciousness and gave them new opportunities to express it. In particular, the provincial councils served a specially significant purpose. For they brought together the new urban elite and the rural chiefs. Such was the naïvety of some administrators that they expected the chiefs to lead the members from the urban councils. Instead, of course, it was the urban members whose sophistication and greater knowledge of political issues dominated proceedings in the councils.

Up to this point in the description of Northern Rhodesia's evolution the only major difference with the experience of Tanganyika was the presence of the Copper Belt and its social consequences. Arising partly out of the existence of the Copper Belt, however, one crucial dissimilarity did exist. It was to be focal to the divergence of experience between the two countries, and therefore to the careers of Kaunda and Nyerere.

We have already mentioned that the whites who settled in Northern Rhodesia were critical of Colonial Office policy. They considered that it was giving dangerous influence to the Africans, whereas they believed that power should be transferred to themselves, as it had been in South Africa.

From the 1930s arguments about white strategy revolved around the hub of relations with the white community of Southern Rhodesia. In 1936 politicians from the two communities met in conference at Victoria Falls. They issued a declaration that early amalgamation of the two Rhodesias under a self-governing constitution would serve the interests of all inhabitants. Two years later the British government sent out the Bledisloe Commission to advise on the issue of amalgamation of both Rhodesias and Nyasaland. Its report was indeterminate and, in any case, the war quickly overrode the question.

Soon after the war ended, however, white politicians returned to their proposition. There was not always unanimity amongst the Northern Rhodesian whites. Some feared that amalgamation would deprive them of their African labour and copper wealth through the greater attractions and economic strength of the South. Others saw a union as the only alternative to a Colonial Office policy which was allowing Africans to usurp the natural right of white authority.

It should be realised that at this time white settlers in Africa, whether in Kenya, the Rhodesias or South Africa, considered that their community was the only one to count in the countries where they lived. All discussion amongst them on national or colonial policies was confined to what they saw as the interests of white society, which they identified as 'the country'. They simply did not recognise Africans as the same kind of human being, nor as members of national society. The future to which they looked, therefore, was one in which white people would have the most comfortable and secure society in which to live.

Even the colonial government, in the curious dichotomy of its policies, reflected a similar attitude. Despite its declarations that indigenous interests must take precedence over all others – as in the Devonshire and Passfield statements – it was the white settlers who were accorded representation in the quasi-legislatures of those dependencies where white communities had chosen to live. In Northern Rhodesia the whites were allowed to elect eight members of the Legislative Council. At the end of the war five further unofficial members, all white, were nominated, so that for the first time the unofficial members held a majority over the officials. They were also given a minority number of seats in the Executive. It was not until 1938 that a European was first nominated to represent 'African interests', nor until ten years later that the first two Africans were allowed to become members of the Legislative Council. Yet, at the end of the war, the European population of the country still remained under 25,000, whereas the Africans were estimated to total about 1,600,000.

The issue of some form of union between the two Rhodesias, which became focal to the politics of central Africa, was thus seen by the whites in both countries as of concern to themselves alone. In 1941 Roy Welensky, the acknowledged spokesman of white miners and railway workers in the northern territory, formed a Labour Party. It represented only white workers and quickly took the lead in demanding more power for unofficial members of the Legislative Council at the expense of colonial officials. As soon as the war was over Welensky and his party increased their pressure for amalgamation with Southern Rhodesia, a pressure which was complemented by Godfrey Huggins in Salisbury.

Yet the Africans of Northern Rhodesia had already shown to the Bledisloe Commission before the war, in the evidence they were allowed to give, that they were totally opposed to the amalgamation of the two territories. They had displayed complete hostility towards any risk of being placed under the pass laws and more extreme forms of discrimination practised in the south. In this they had found allies amongst the civil servants of the north, who feared that their policy of indirect rule would be sabotaged by association with the south.

In the years immediately following the end of the war the battle lines between the two policies became increasingly clearly defined. The Europeans, led by Welensky and Huggins, having realised that they would find little sympathy at the Colonial Office for their amalgamation ambitions, modified their objective to one of federating their two territories. In 1948 Welensky and the Governor, Sir Gilbert Rennie, had talks about federation in London. They took with them two African civil servants, despite protests from the African welfare associations that they did not represent

African views. With the modification of the white claim from amalgamation to federation surprising encouragement was forthcoming from the British government. The only stipulation made by the Colonial Secretary, Arthur Creech Jones, before discussions were held was that Nyasaland should also be included. The British government did not wish to subsidise the Protectorate for ever.

This was the age of the received theory that economic growth in the colonies would bring political democracy in its train; that the most important progress the Africans could make was to develop their own middle class, along with a trade union movement. Then, as British history proved inevitable, representation would slowly 'broaden down from precedent to precedent'. The prescription for economic growth was the attraction of foreign capital and the preservation of sound European management. Attlee's Labour government faithfully accepted the conventional doctrine of the times, without wasting too much time on any socialist or empirical analysis of conditions in these faraway places inhabited by strange people.

Little recognition was shown in Britain that federation represented simply a modification of the policy adopted with disastrous results in South Africa in 1910. The white communities of the Rhodesias were too small to move directly to independence, as had their fellow whites in the south. But they knew their constitutional history. They realised that once the process of transferring power from the imperial parliament to a colonial society had begun, nothing short of a cataclysm could halt it. And if they were the recipients of the first instalments of that power, neither Whitehall nor Westminster would be able to force them to surrender it, especially as they had many friends in London's corridors of power. Their object, therefore, was to persuade the British government to establish federal institutions which the white community would control, before Africans had gained advances from the Colonial Office in Northern Rhodesia or Nyasaland sufficient to allow them a base from which to challenge. Then the whites would be in an impregnable position to determine the pace of representational advance, whilst confident that they could gain independence from Britain before any threat to white supremacy could be mounted by the Africans.

Some civil servants in both Northern Rhodesia and Nyasaland were unhappy over this prospect of colonial policy being reversed. The Africans were virtually unanimously hostile to it.

From the early days of the war there had been a revival of the welfare association movement. The Mwenzo association had been reformed and others had been established in various parts of the country, including that at Chinsali with which Kaunda was associated. At this time Lieutenant-Colonel Stewart Gore-Browne was the nominated member for African interests in the Legislative Council. The welfare associations tended to look to him for sympathetic advice. He attracted large meetings, although in 1948 he was to lose African trust temporarily when he proposed responsible government and a partition of the territory.

By 1946 the welfare associations decided that the time had come to form a territory-wide organisation. In Lusaka they created the Northern Rhodesian Federation of Welfare Societies under the inspiration of Dauti Yamba, George Kaluwa and Godwin Lewanika, the latter a senior mining clerk who had tried to institute a united association in 1933.

For some time there had been talk about the formation of an African political party. Those who had been to South Africa talked of the need for a 'Congress', and this talk was increased by the formation of the Nyasaland Congress in 1944. The issue of closer association with Southern Rhodesia, which had now become the foremost political issue in the country, brought a new urgency to the idea.

In September 1948 the annual conference of the Federation of Welfare Societies, held in Kaunda's old school at Munali in Lusaka, resolved to reject any form of association with Southern Rhodesia and to demand that the government receive a delegation. It then decided to rename the Federation the Northern Rhodesia African Congress, with Lewanika as first president. One of the delegates to this portentous conference was Simon Kapwepwe, Kaunda's close friend.

The Tanganyika to which Nyerere returned in the early fifties and the Northern Rhodesia where Kaunda began his political work a little earlier, thus showed both similarities and sharp differences. In both countries rural life was stagnant, consisting of little more than subsistence living for the vast majority of Africans, leaving them to suffer from all the diseases associated with malnutrition, in addition to those endemic to the tropics – malaria, bilharzia, and leprosy. Both countries had main railway lines, but the miserable condition of their roads inhibited their use for widespread development. In each the incidence of tsetse fly rendered large tracts uninhabitable for man or beast; two-thirds of Tanganyika and one-third of Northern Rhodesia were plagued by this pest.

Within each agricultural scene were pockets of European farms, the sisal and coffee plantations of Tanganyika, the tobacco and coffee farms of Northern Rhodesia. Colonial governments tended to concentrate their agrarian assistance on European farming, assuming that it alone held any export potential with which to furnish funds for the administration.

Social conditions in the towns were also similar. In the suburbs comparatively wealthy European civil servants, businessmen and, in Northern Rhodesia, miners, lived in comfort often rising to luxury. In Tanganyika there was also an Indian community whose conditions varied from European-style life to the poverty of the African worker. But the mass of the population, the Africans, usually had to make do with squalid tin or thatch shanties, raised from any materials they could find lying waste, built haphazardly wherever open ground could be found, and often without sanitation, drinking-water, cooking or washing facilities.

The big difference in these urban conditions was that so many more Africans in Northern Rhodesia had to endure them because of the existence of the Copper Belt. Tanganyika had no comparable industrial concentration. This left her without the economic potential of Northern Rhodesia, but also without the degree of social tension, conflict, or crises. Dar es Salaam, Tanga, Dodoma, Mwanza, Tabora, Mbeya, certainly presented massive social challenges before they could offer decent living conditions for their inhabitants; but they could not compare in scale with those of Lusaka, Livingstone, Broken Hill, Ndola, Kitwe or Mufilira.

Another major contrast between the two countries was the fact that whereas Tanganyika had a long Indian Ocean coastline, which had provided her people with their maritime history, their international contacts and constant trade, Northern Rhodesia was entirely landlocked. Not only had this isolated her inhabitants from the overseas contacts familiar to their neighbours; it raised barriers to the full exploitation of the mineral wealth for the development of the country. Above all, it left Northern Rhodesia dangerously dependent on communications controlled by others, the Southern Rhodesians, South Africans, Portuguese and Belgians.

Yet the sharpest contrast was to be seen in the political situation of the two countries. Nyerere and the Tanganyika nationalists faced a comparatively straightforward task of devising the tactics to exert pressure on the British government in order to persuade it to transfer power to Tanganyikans. In this they had valuable allies in the United Nations as a result of their status as a Trust Territory. The Europeans in their country were so few, so diffused and so feeble in political pretensions that decolonisation could only replace imperial by African rule.

In Northern Rhodesia, however, the situation was much more complex. The Africans there faced a bitterly prejudiced local white community, with the well-organised miners at the core. This Northern Rhodesian white community had now allied itself with the even stronger whites of Southern Rhodesia, who already held control of their own government and all its servants. This white alliance was implacably opposed to any thought of African government in either territory. It was in the process of building a federation which would allow it to block African progress for the foreseeable future. Behind the federation stood South Africa, the strongest and most profoundly prejudiced state in Africa. In London a majority of politicians, ministers, civil servants, financiers and businessmen was firmly determined that the federation should be given the power it needed to succeed, even if this necessitated a modification of colonial policy in Northern Rhodesia and Nyasaland to prevent African progress endangering the white supremacy on which its success was seen to depend.

Even if, by some miracle, this combination of forces could be defeated, Northern Rhodesia's Africans would then simply reach the same starting point as their Tanganyikan neighbours. For then they would still have to persuade the British government to surrender its imperial power and transfer it to an African régime. In view of the wealth which was being produced by the country's copper and the complex economy produced by it, in addition to the large European community resident in Northern Rhodesia, only an extreme optimist could anticipate this happening.

It should be remembered that when Kaunda and Nyerere began to think seriously about politics and their own role in the future of their countries, European decolonisation had only just begun. It is true that the independence which the Indians, Pakistanis, Burmese and Ceylonese had won from Britain drastically reduced the size of the British Empire, whilst lighting a beacon for other colonial subjects. But that battle had been won after more than half a century of massive struggle by peoples who had been participating in the various fields of government for most of that time. Africans were only just beginning to conceive of the same objectives, had only just opened their era of mass struggle. These were the days before Ghana's first representative elections, with Farouk still on the Egyptian throne, when Winston Churchill was still convinced that he would retain the British Empire. Any prospect of Africans governing their own independent states, especially in east or central Africa, could only arise within vivid imaginations. Nyerere and Kaunda were both imaginative men.

5

Kaunda's Nationalist Politics

At the time that he returned home in 1949 Kaunda was being affected by two contrary influences. He felt the pull of the land, which had led him to save his resources, resign his teaching post and gamble on becoming a successful farmer. Simultaneously, his experiences over the past two years had profoundly stirred his emotions. His hatred of oppression and inequality had been awakened by indignities suffered by himself and even more by what he had seen done to his fellow-Africans. He had realised that he lived in a society where the alien ruled and the colour of one's skin determined the human category to which one was allocated. Under this system, apparently, human rights were accorded to categories, the African, in the lowest, being able to claim only minimal dues.

Kaunda was one of a small number of Africans in Northern Rhodesia whose feelings were provoked by this situation at this time. Dauti Yamba, the Luanshya school teacher, who later became a prominent politician, represented this sense of affront when he told the Western Province Regional Council that 'members of the ruling race should show Africans a little honour, to recognise that they were human beings and, in fact, equal in creation'. The initial resentment was against the insult to men's dignity. This preceded concern over representation or constitutional details. It may have been felt first by those few evolué Africans whose sensibilities were sharpened by the knowledge of other societies gained through education or personal experience; but the expression they gave to it found a ready response by less sophisticated fellow-Africans. It was as though the sense of affront had been lying dormant until suddenly awakened by the protests of those who, in Dr Lamont's phrase, had acquired 'a pair of spectacles'. The various councils which were established soon after the end of the war rang with complaints against the indignities which Africans were forced to suffer in their own homeland.

Although it was this sense of human indignity which dominated the feelings of African spokesmen at this time, it was not long before they realised that political action alone could remove it. So long as aliens ruled the country, recognising their fellow-whites settled there as a privileged category, social protests could result in no more than palliatives at best;

in the vast majority of instances the protests were ignored as nothing more than evidence that educated Africans soon became either upstarts or agitators against the natural order of colonial society. The whites had shown an example of how political organisation forced concessions. Africans began to learn the same lesson. The advent of propaganda and publicity over the issue of closer association with Southern Rhodesia proved a catalyst. It immediately gave urgency to the necessity for political activity.

Kaunda was caught up in this precipitation of African consciousness. He felt the indignities to himself and to his fellow men very deeply. When he sought action to protest against them he found himself in conflict with authority. He began to realise that only through combined activity was there any chance of future relief. By the time he returned to Lubwa he and his friends were already committed to participate in politics. He had to discover whether he could reconcile a political role with his love of farming.

By 1949 association between the two Rhodesias formed the dominant political issue of central Africa; Congress offered the Africans of Northern Rhodesia their only serious opportunity for political activity. Yet the question of amalgamation or federation between the Rhodesias complicated African political strategy. In sharp contrast to the situation in Tanganyika, the path towards African emancipation did not lead directly through the removal of Colonial Office rule. For the white settlers of Rhodesia, in the north and in the south, were themselves fighting to remove British authority. They saw the Colonial Office as the protector of African interests. They believed that they would have to follow the example of the South Africans in ridding themselves of Whitehall and Westminster supervision if they were to gain complete control over the countries where they had settled. This was a central purpose of the schemes first for the amalgamation of the Rhodesias and then, as an alternative, for their federation.

To some extent the African view of the situation coincided with that of the Europeans. Although they disliked the nature of colonial rule, and particularly the way in which it discriminated in favour of white privilege, they preferred its continuation to the alternative of complete domination by European settlers. They knew enough of South African conditions to recognise that once the whites secured control of the government and removed the restraints exercised by the Colonial Office, Africans would become defenceless. They still believed that British rule eventually presumed a transference of power to majorities – i.e., to Africans – even if that horizon was not yet in sight. Thus the political battle in Northern Rhodesia had to be two-pronged. It had to oppose association with Southern Rhodesia at all costs, for this would entrench white supremacy;

it had to demand the retention of Colonial Office authority in order to prevent local white domination, whilst at the same time insisting that colonial powers be progressively transferred to Africans, who formed the vast majority of the inhabitants. This presented an infinitely more complex prospect than that in neighbouring Tanganyika.

Organised African politics in Northern Rhodesia were initiated in an era of revolution within the imperial world. India, Pakistan, Ceylon and Burma achieved their independence from Britain in 1947–8. The emancipation of 500 million colonial subjects and their creation of new, sovereign nation-states had a shattering impact on the colonial scene. The following year another 100 million subjects of European imperialism gained their freedom when Indonesia became independent from Holland. The Vietnamese were fighting the French to rid themselves of alien rule; guerrilla warfare continued in Malaya; there were serious disturbances in the Gold Coast and Nigeria; agitation for self-government mounted in the West Indies. The era of European domination over the poorer peoples of the world had entered its death throes; the mystique of white superiority was fading.

Yet in north, east, central and South Africa white societies refused to observe the trend of history. South Africans turned from the vacillations of General Smuts to the intransigent white supremacy of Dr Malan. The Kenya settlers pressed the Colonial Office to chart a South African future for them before the west African model could overtake them. Europeans in Algeria, Morocco and Tunisia insisted that the French government remain as their protectors. In the Rhodesias first amalgamation and then federation was employed as the strategy to preserve white domination.

Thus, whilst Nyerere's Tanganyika remained on the fringe of the European's laager reaction to events elsewhere in the world, albeit uncomfortably close to it, Kaunda found himself at the very heart of the conflict. It might seem in 1950 that the future of European power in Africa would be determined in Nairobi; in the longer term it was seen to depend on events in Lusaka and Salisbury.

This was the political situation into which Kaunda was plunged in 1949. First, though, he had to find a means of livelihood for his family through the exercise of his farming instincts. He founded a co-operative farm outside Lubwa with some of his friends. Kenneth was appointed as manager and set out to study all he could find on agriculture. He built a four-roomed house, was joined by his elder sister, frequently visited by his brother and other sister, and had his mother near by. For a period, therefore, Kenneth knew the closeness of family life. The combination of growing food and warm family relations gave him a new happiness, the memory of which has never faded. He experienced deep pleasure from planting, watching the germination and harvesting. He grew citrus, vegetables, maize, cassava, beans and corn, and found special pleasure in rearing poultry. The near-by Lubwa mission provided a ready market for his produce. It was hard work, usually taking from sunrise to sunset, but gave him profound satisfaction.

In addition to his farming, Kaunda continued to supplement his income by selling second-hand clothes. He and his companions now had 300 miles to cycle to get to the Congo where the clothes could be bought. They then loaded them on to lorries and cycled home, hoping to arrive there before the lorries in time to check their delivery.

For a time, too, the missionaries at Lubwa persuaded Kenneth to return to teaching on a part-time basis. The shortage of teachers was so acute that he began to teach in the mornings, returning to his farm work in the afternoons. This busy life was only made possible by the assistance of his sister on the farm and his wife in the second-hand clothes' shop.

The contentment which Kaunda experienced from family and farm was enjoyed, however, for only a brief period. He had returned to Lubwa in mid-1949; by the end of the year he became convinced that the district should have its own branch of Congress. He, Sokoni and another old schoolteacher friend, Robert Makasa, approached the Chinsali African Welfare Association. The idea was cautiously accepted, although at this time it was believed that all Congress officials would be sent to prison. Perhaps because of this rumour, the originators of the idea were chosen as the first officers. Makasa became chairman and Kaunda secretary.

It was an overwhelming sense of duty which compelled Kaunda to take this initiative. His work on the farm, in gathering and selling clothes, in his teaching, filled all the hours of his day. Yet he chose to sacrifice some of these satisfying activities to tour the area recruiting for Congress. The feeling of social obligation seems to have stemmed from his profound Christian beliefs. He has told how he and Makasa or Sokoni would cycle up to sixty miles on Friday evenings to meetings in the Chinsali area. They would accompany their cycling with singing hymns in Bemba which had been translated from Church of Scotland hymn books, relying on the God in which they had faith to protect them from the man-eating lions which roamed that district.

The message which Kaunda and his friends took to the people of Chinsali was simple and basically Christian. They tried to persuade them that they were the same kind of human beings as any other. They were not concerned at this stage with the intricacies of constitutions, representation or legislation. They had first to imbue their people with the concept of universal human dignity. As some of their audiences had been in the British army during the war, had seen other societies and had been called on to risk their lives in the defence of the British Empire, this simple message received a ready hearing. It was but a short step to the socially political query of why, on returning home, such ex-soldiers should find themselves excluded from common amenities, like being served in shops or allowed to have meals in cafés. Then would come the crucial political issue: 'Where is this partnership in Northern Rhodesia which Welensky talks about for his federation?' Congress stood for changing these conditions in which Africans were treated as inferior in their own land, for the right of all to be treated as equal human beings. It was from this simple humanistic appeal that Kaunda and his colleagues recruited Congress members and aroused public discussion throughout the Chinsali district.

Yet, simple though the message might seem, Kaunda's political activities were by no means universally understood nor approved. He was one of the pioneers, before it had become customary for Africans to participate in political activities. It was still widely assumed in African society that politics were the prerogative of the European, that it was in the natural order that Europeans made the rules and Africans obeyed them. To many of his fellows, therefore, Kaunda's actions and those of his friends were presumptuous. This viewpoint was strengthened by the youth of those who broke the European monopoly of political activity; in traditional African society young men and women were expected to accept the authority of their elders. To many, the European, whatever his age, was accepted in the role of elder.

This critical reaction to the political preoccupation of these young African pioneers was reinforced by the necessity for them to sacrifice the interests of their families to spend time in organising their Congress. The good African in traditional eyes founded a family, worked the land to sustain it and contributed to the development of his local community. To neglect one's own family for the sake of some vague, generalised ideal was to breach custom. Some conception of the pressures under which Kaunda and his friends laboured may be gained from the words of Betty Kaunda, his wife:

It did affect me as well as his mother, for he began to travel from village to village and from place to place. He stopped teaching, and spent most of his time travelling and very little time on the farm. His mother and I got worried and often said to ourselves, 'What is this Congress business which is taking up all his time? He now can't spare the time to work on the farm.' One day I gathered up the courage to ask him to explain to me what these Congress activities were and their ultimate aim. He told me that he and his friends wanted ultimately to take over the government of the country from the hands of the European colonialists. I, his wife, could not then understand this. I felt pity for him, for I thought he and his friends were aiming for the impossible. White men are very clever and powerful, I thought, how on earth could

Kenneth and Makasa and Sokoni, even if helped by the villagers, take control of the country? Daydreams and pipedreams, at least so they seemed to me then. His mother and I began to get anxious about him.

Betty Kaunda, of course, later understood more thoroughly that Kenneth's efforts were practical as well as idealistic, something more profound than mere dreams; that other Africans in her own country and in other parts of the continent shared her husband's vision and were prepared to sacrifice their own comfort and safety to make it into a reality. She became one of the stalwarts of the Congress, of immense support to her husband. Yet, if she so doubted the sanity of his early efforts, how much more doubtful must strangers have felt?

At the time that Kaunda began to organise Congress in the Chinsali district the momentum of politics in central Africa was already leading towards confrontation between European and African. In October 1948, at an African conference in London, Welensky and Huggins had amended their demand for amalgamation to one for federation. In February 1949 they held a conference of white delegates from the two Rhodesias and Nyasaland; they unanimously resolved that the three countries should be unified under a federal constitution. In November the Northern Rhodesian Legislative Council, under Welensky's leadership, passed a motion asking the British government to establish a federal government for central Africa. The following year Huggins threatened that if greater powers were not transferred from London to the Central African Council, which co-ordinated certain common services between the three territories, his government would withdraw from it.

Gradually the Establishment in London was being persuaded that federation should be supported. Creech Jones, who had toured central Africa after the Victoria Falls conference to sound opinion, had promised the Africans that they would be consulted and that Britain would not abrogate her responsibilities to them. But the copper companies and the British South Africa Company now openly supported federation. Some Colonial Office officials had begun to argue that federation alone could save central Africa from a northward spread of the apartheid doctrine. Industrialists and financiers eager to see the area open up investment opportunities were joined by the military who supported federation on strategic grounds.

It was not wholly surprising, therefore, that early in 1951 the British government passed over the issue to a committee of British and central African civil servants to investigate. What was surprising was the naïveté of a Labour government and of its chief adviser, the liberal-minded Andrew Cohen, in believing that the findings of such a committee could be isolated from political implications. Inevitably the committee found cogent reasons for federation. Equally inevitably they were used to accelerate the momentum of those in central Africa who saw federation as furthering the white settler interest. And although Labour ministers promised that African opinion would be consulted, it was too late. The centre of gravity had been decisively moved towards Welensky and Huggins, who could now quote 'impartial' British officials as having approved their scheme. The fact that the Labour government was defeated before a decision was taken on the committee's report certainly hastened the implementation of federation; for the Conservative government which succeeded it was firmly pledged to the concept. But if it had remained in office Labour would have been faced by imperative demands from Huggins, Welensky and their friends to put its own officials' proposals into practice – and some influential Labour members would have supported the demands.

If Labour ministers, Andrew Cohen and other officials had been more perceptive they would have realised that African opinion was so strongly opposed to any form of closer association that any federal scheme was bound to become a battleground, rather than the 'racial partnership' of their fond hopes. The only form of partnership the Africans had ever experienced was that aptly described in one of Godfrey Huggins' less wary moments as between rider and horse. Africans saw every reason to suppose that the purpose of federation was to perpetuate the role of rider, freed from the restraints the Colonial Office had imposed on his ill use of his horse.

As soon as Welensky returned from amending his amalgamation policy to one of federation in 1948 the Northern Rhodesian Congress prepared a confidential memorandum. It included advice to their members to remain cool and non-violent, but declared that federation and amalgamation were identical, that 'he wants to enslave Africans by bringing in Federation'.

Immediately after the white Victoria Falls conference early in 1949 a group of central Africans in London, led by Dr Hastings Banda of Nyasaland and Harry Nkumbula of Northern Rhodesia, drafted a memorandum which they sent to the Colonial Office. It answered each point of the federal argument, declaring that federation would be dominated by Southern Rhodesian whites, that the policy of segregation and discrimination practised in Southern Rhodesia would be extended to the northern territories, whereas the Colonial Office's 'cardinal principle in administration is guidance or guardianship'.

In Northern Rhodesia, Congress, the African Representative Council and various provincial councils declared their opposition to federation. Mbikusita Lewanika, the Congress president, presented Creech Jones with a petition outlining these objections when he toured the country. The

Colonial Secretary found that opposition in Nyasaland was even more vehemently hostile.

It was this explosive situation which Kaunda entered when he began his efforts to found and develop the Chinsali branch of Congress. The issue of federation itself stimulated the pace of African politics and of Congress in particular. It certainly precipitated Kaunda into the heart of the nationalist maelstrom much more suddenly than would otherwise have occurred.

During the year 1950 he served his political apprenticeship by voluntarily organising the Chinsali branch in the spare time left from farming and collecting clothes from the Congo. But early in 1951 he had to attend the annual conference of Congress in Lusaka. This proved to be a germinal gathering. It concluded with the election of a new president.

The new president was Harry Nkumbula, replacing Mbikusita Lewanika. At this time Lewanika maintained the accepted anti-federal line, although before long he was to join a pro-federal party and sit in the Federal parliament. But he was considered by some Congress activists, including Kaunda, as ineffectual and suspect. Their instinct was to be proved correct. The fact that he came from Barotseland, which had a special relationship with the British Crown and would not be as completely affected by federation as other parts of Northern Rhodesia, may have played some part in arousing suspicion. It was also discovered later that he had reported a prominent white supporter of Congress, Simon ber Zukas, to the police. Zukas was deported in 1952. Lewanika's reputation as a government 'stooge' was consequently justified.

So in Lusaka, Kaunda, Justin Chimba, Reuben Kamanga, Edward Liso and other young militants lobbied to secure the replacement of Lewanika by Nkumbula as president. He was elected by an overwhelming majority. A year later Kaunda was appointed a full-time organiser at £10 a month, although his allowance often arrived late and might only amount to half this sum.

Thus began the crucial association between Kaunda and Nkumbula. The two had first met casually in 1944 when Nkumbula impressed the younger Kaunda by his self-confidence in dealing with an arrogant lorry driver who was intending to leave a sick passenger behind. At that time Nkumbula was a teacher on the Copper Belt and a member of the Western Province Regional Council. He then spent two years at Makerere, one at the Institute of Education and another at the London School of Economics. It was during his period in London that he associated with Hastings Banda in drawing up the memorandum answering the case for federation. Soon after this the government withdrew his scholarship on the grounds that he had failed to pass the preliminary examinations. On his return home he was unable to obtain employment in any professional capacity and had to make a living by selling cowrie shells to members of his Ila community.

Harry Nkumbula was a complex character. A bon viveur, in all senses of the phrase, at times a playboy, he nevertheless can lay claim to being the original father of African nationalism in Northern Rhodesia. When he assumed the presidency Congress was no more than a feeble, disjointed collection of groups. It had thirteen branches and eleven affiliated organisations, but there was no central planning and little co-ordination of activities or policies.

Nkumbula, with advice from Zukas, gave Congress a clear direction and resounding leadership. His predecessor, Lewanika, had spoken many bold words and, indeed, made intelligent proposals. Not only had he condemned federation as self-government for the senior partners alone and called for universal suffrage, probably coining the slogan 'one man, one vote', so far as Northern Rhodesia was concerned; but he suggested a federation of Northern Rhodesia with the east African territories. If this concept had been entertained by the Colonial Office at this time the whole future of Africa would have been drastically different.

Nkumbula, however, was made into a leader by the heightened tensions caused by the urgency of the federal issue. He had nailed his colours on federation to the public mast with Hastings Banda in London. He had absorbed there the spirit and the language of anti-colonialism amongst such organisations as the West African Students' Union and the Fabian Colonial Bureau. Now he not only condemned the federal project but began to teach his people to think of their own self-government, free not only from federal control but from that of Britain and its Colonial Office. As he saw British governments conniving with the schemes of Huggins and Welensky to perpetuate white domination, he declared that 'There existed a cold war between the British government and the indigenous peoples of Africa', and that 'we must have our own parliament, in which Europeans and Indians will have reserved seats'. This was certainly a great leap forward in political vision. He was countered by the Secretary for Native Affairs – a colonial servant – who stated that Northern Rhodesia would never attain African self-government because the European settlers predominated.

Again, in June 1952, Nkumbula returned to the new theme in even more trenchant language. '. . . it is high time that we tell the white people in this country that their support of this plan is not only dangerous to us but to their well being and happiness in this country. This is our country . . . the best government for the black people is a government fully manned and run by the black people of Africa. That is also true of any race.' He was answered again, this time by Welensky. 'We do not want to dominate,' he told a meeting in Ndola, 'but if there is going to be domination, it is going to be my own race that will dominate.'

The federal band-wagon still rolled, more speedily after the Conservatives were returned to power in Westminster late in 1951. Oliver Lyttelton, the new Colonial Secretary, stated categorically that the new government was unequivocally in favour of federation. Conference followed conference, until it was clear that only details remained to be settled. The British government and the leading white politicians in central Africa, with the wholehearted support of international business and finance, closed their eyes to African opposition and to the conflict which it was pledged to wage against the scheme.

There can be no doubt now, when we review this situation with hindsight, that the Colonial Office and its officials were guilty of wishful-thinking in their astigmatism towards African sensibilities. A few reported the turmoil into which the issue of federation had thrown their local people. Most contented themselves with the judgement that only assurances that African land or customs would not be disturbed were needed to appease African fears; that federation was such a remote concept for most Africans that they would take the advice of colonial officials that it was in their interests. For the fact is that most colonial officers and most civil servants, members of parliament and ministers in London, had been accustomed to regard Africans as children, to be told what was best for them and to accept it from their betters.

Some of us tried to warn members of the government at the time. I was in Nyasaland and both Rhodesias in August–September 1951 when Jim Griffiths and Patrick Gordon Walker, then Colonial Secretary and Commonwealth Secretary respectively, were touring the area to sound out opinion. I met the Congresses and could not fail to recognise their bitter and reasoned hostility to federation. I was prevented by a local colonial officer from meeting Griffiths. When I did so, back in Britain a month later, it was too late. The election had taken place, the Labour government had been defeated and Griffiths was no longer Colonial Secretary. Yet even at this time there were many Labour members, and even the left-wing periodical, *Tribune*, that were supporting federation, ignorant of its implications.

It was not that a vast majority of Africans in Northern Rhodesia and Nyasaland at that time knew the details of the federal scheme or were preparing to rise up against them. Rather was it that anyone who understood people and their political potential, instead of thinking in terms of racial categories, could see how federation, by assaulting the whole concept of African dignity, would force a resentment which could only result in conflict. For, when a people's sensibilities are affronted to such a degree, society always throws up that necessary handful of leaders able to articulate the discontent and to organise resistance.

The various agents of colonial rule and the white settlers of central Africa had been so accustomed to ordering society as though it were entirely composed of Europeans, ignoring the African, assuming that he would automatically obey any injunctions declared by them, that they never seriously listened to the rumblings of revolt. If their vision had been broader, they might have stopped to consider what was happening in west Africa, or in Kenya, or even in South Africa, where Africans were revolting against the prospect of permanent white domination, making their own claims to control their own societies. But whenever these comparisons were pointed out, Rhodesian whites, colonial officials and British members of parliament always offered the same alibi, as though by reflex action – Africans in central Africa were 'more backward'.

The year 1952 saw the temperature of what had now become largely a black–white conflict rising sharply. Huggins and Welensky were now in complete alliance with the British government. Their main efforts were directed to emasculating as severely as possible the safeguards for Africans which had been included in the proposals of the civil servants. In Lusaka Nkumbula warned Europeans that their lives would be made intolerable if federation were introduced. Congress raised its militancy by threatening the use of 'mass protest', popularised by Nkrumah in the Gold Coast, if federation were imposed.

It was at this time that Congress set up a Supreme Action Council to direct the battle against federation. Kaunda was one of its original members. The Attorney-General immediately reacted by issuing this statement: 'I am warning you that the Government will not hesitate to use its powers to deal with disorders caused, including general strike planned by your meetings.' Congress responded by deciding to send a delegation, led by Nkumbula, to London to intensify its protests. When it reported back it was received by a specially convened conference, composed of both chiefs and Congress members. This was significant, because the government had been trying to use its influence with the chiefs in order to isolate Congress. By their attendance at this conference, and by the support they displayed for its efforts in opposing federation, the chiefs deliberately warded off the danger that the government might divide African society in order to minimise opposition to its policy.

It had now become obvious that, if it were to exert any permanent influence, Congress would have to become a mass party. The efforts of its few pioneers had failed to impress the local situation or that in Britain. If it were to have any chance of affecting the future of Northern Rhodesia, it would have to prove that it had the support of the mass of the people. This entailed organisation in the rural areas, otherwise the government and settlers would continue to argue that it represented only the tiny minority of urban discontents.

It was at this point that Kaunda was appointed as organising secretary for the Northern Province. This was a huge area to cover. It stretched from Mpika to the Tanganyika border in the north, from the frontier with Nyasaland to the Congo in the west. His sole means of transport in attending meetings or recruiting in the vast province was a bicycle. But in accepting this new employment Kaunda left the narrow field of amateur local politics and entered the all-consuming responsibility of a front-line professional in the battle against federation.

The literature from which he drew his inspiration to perform what was often a lonely and always a hazardous task indicates his state of mind at the time. The Banda–Nkumbula memorandum guided his attack on federation, based on an analysis which established that federation would entrench the power of white settlers for the foreseeable future. He also had the use of material prepared for the struggle for independence in India, provided by a local Indian friend. Yet it was from more philosophical and frankly sentimental books that he drew his inner strength to carry out his work. He remembers reading a life of Abraham Lincoln, Ralph Waldo Trine's *In Tune with the Infinite*, and Arthur Mee. A strong and largely unsophisticated emotional vein has constantly run through his personality; it was clearly already dominant at this early stage of his life.

Again his family suffered. Whilst he was touring the northern part of the country for months on end, meeting chiefs, headmen, teachers, farmers, clerks, forming branches of Congress and explaining the significance of federation to Africans, his wife, mother and sister were left to care for the family and look after the farm. His wife has told how, although they could grow sufficient food for themselves, their clothes were becoming patched and tattered. The allowance of £10 a month, even when it arrived, which was not regularly, left nothing for buying new or even second-hand replacements.

At the beginning of 1953 an intergovernmental conference in London, boycotted by all Africans, agreed upon a constitution for federation. For the next few months the Congresses of Northern Rhodesia and Nyasaland feverishly tried every tactic to stave off the inevitable. In both countries bloodshed was predicted. Nkumbula symbolically burned the federal white papers in Lusaka and called for two days of prayer which would take the form of a national strike. But the miners' union would not co-operate and the strike turned out to be a failure. Petitions were sent to the local legislative councils and to the British parliament. A hundred and thirty chiefs in Northern Rhodesia petitioned the Queen.

Yet the federal band-wagon moved inexorably forward, apparently impervious to the arrows fired by the Africans. A referendum in Southern

Rhodesia approved the scheme by 25,570 to 14,729; only 380 Africans were entitled to vote. The two legislative councils in Northern Rhodesia and Nyasaland also approved; their membership included only two Africans in each, all of whom opposed federation. The House of Commons and the House of Lords ratified the enabling bill; it was given the Royal Assent. Federation legally came into force on 1 August 1953.

The failure of African opposition to halt the march of federation demonstrated the fact that Congress was still a weak organisation, with little experience, lacking authority in most parts of the country. The fact that it had been unable to hold a general strike exposed its lack of influence inside the trade union movement. This failure also proved that the government and copper companies, which had threatened to dismiss any striking employees, still wielded considerably more influence than any African organisation. Nevertheless, Congress opposition had not been fruitless, although its effects were not to be seen for some years. Certain sectors of British public life had been impressed by its lone voice. Determination to preserve important sections of policy in Northern Rhodesia and Nyasaland for the British government was stiffened, whilst Congress protests had both aroused many Africans to the dangers which faced them and moved groups of people in Britain to recognise their responsibilities in central Africa for the first time.

Naturally the mood in Lusaka when federation received the Royal Assent was one of despair. When 400 Congress delegates met in a Lusaka beer hall in the August, there were recriminations against some of its officials. Only Nkumbula of the main officials retained his office. The crucial election was to take place between two candidates for the post of secretary-general. A local journalist was asked to count the voting papers which had been collected in a hat. To considerable acclaim he pointed out the winner as Kenneth Kaunda. Within one short year since becoming a provincial organiser Kaunda had become recognised as a leading young Congress militant. In the circumstances of the Congress' traumatic defeat over federation, he was elected to the second most influential post in that organisation. He and Nkumbula were faced with the frightening task of pulling their party out of its grave, of devising policies capable of challenging the combined might of the new federal government, the colonial administration and the British government.

6

From Federation to Zambia (1)

In November 1953 Kaunda moved his family from the Shambalakale farm to Lusaka. As secretary-general of Congress, responsible for its organisation and activities throughout the country, it was essential for him to live in the capital.

The only accommodation which he could find in Lusaka was in the Congress office. By now the Kaundas had three children, all boys. So for the first few months the new secretary-general, his wife and three young children had to make do with the two small office rooms and a tiny kitchen. Each morning Betty had to be up early to clean the two rooms. For the rest of the day they were occupied by typists, clerks and visitors. Betty and the children had to spend the time in the kitchen, or outside sitting under a tree. She would prepare lunch for the staff who ate it in the same office. Often, too, there were important meetings held in the office at night, and often it would be midnight before Betty and the children could go in to sleep.

It was not until 1954 that the family was able to find their own house. This was in the same Chilenje district. It had a grass roof, cement floor and three rooms, together with a separate kitchen. There were no chairs, but one small table. Although it was larger and much more convenient than living in the office, the roof leaked badly. During the rainy season Kenneth and Betty often had to pile all the blankets on the children and spend the night standing in a dry corner. Another drawback was its infestation with ants. They would crawl all over the sleeping children, impervious to attacks of insecticide.

Once federation came into operation Congress was forced on to the defensive. Its activities were constantly harassed by Northern Rhodesian government officials, who were now, whatever their own opinions, compelled to support the federation. There were disturbances in the Luapula and Eastern provinces, with chiefs and people showing their resentment in the usual manner by disobeying agricultural regulations ordered by government officials. In a number of cases, the most notorious being that in the Gwembe Valley, riot police were used. It now became normal for the government and its officers to blame any resistance on Congress, trying to coerce the populace into accepting that Congress leaders could only harm them, that their welfare and safety depended on obeying whatever the government ordered.

Although Congress was weak and on the defensive, it was already too late for the government to consolidate its authority in many areas. The public debate on federation had aroused feelings of resentment which persisted independently of Congress activity. If there was one issue on which the people's emotions had been permanently roused it was that of discrimination. Once people begin to ask themselves why they should be treated as inferior on account of their racial origins or skin colour, they will never again accept discrimination as natural.

Federation was so clearly based on the principle of discrimination, irrespective of constitutional or legal niceties, that it could never be accepted by the majority of Africans. The Northern Rhodesian government, by associating itself with federation, became identified with racial prejudice. Thus the forms of discrimination which had been customary in Northern Rhodesian society now became subjects of popular resentment and objects of attack. As such, they provided constant opportunities for political action, even when national African political activities were under pressure from the government.

Once the issue of equality had been raised, local incidents took on a new significance. For instance, when three white men were only fined £5 each for an assault on an African which cost him an eye; when Nkumbula was refused a ticket at a railway station, also assaulted, and then fined for using abusive language; when Sokota, a member of the legislative council, was refused service with whites at a bank, or Yamba, another member, forbidden the facilities offered to whites at the airport, Congress did not need to employ propaganda. The evidence of its allegations of discrimination was supplied by the whites themselves. Debates on the issue in the councils became more frequent and more bitter.

Then there was the matter of discrimination in employment and wages. This mainly concerned the miners. The white miners, many from South Africa, had strongly secured their position in pre-war days when their services were essential to the industry. After the war they fought hard to preserve their monopoly of skilled, semi-skilled, highly paid jobs. Despite a report of the Dalgeish Commission in 1948 advocating opening more work categories to African miners, African advancement was entirely rejected by the powerful white union. A strike of African workers in 1952 was followed by an award by arbitrator Guillebaud. Professor Guillebaud commented on the embittering influence of the colour bar in the mines. The companies themselves began to recognise that it was in their interest to break this bar and tried to persuade the white union. It took them until 1956 to do so, however, and when the first promoted Africans went underground 1,000 white miners went on strike at Mufilira. Meanwhile, average wages in the industry, which affected the vast majority of African workers far more than the promotion of a handful, continued in the traditional ratio of 10:1 in favour of the whites.

Thirdly, there were the forms of discrimination which daily affected ordinary people. They were barred from cinemas and cafés, if they tried to attend church in a white area they were met with hostility and contempt, they were treated rudely in the stores, always having to wait until all white customers had been served, most of them could not get their children into schools; whereas the federal government spent £103 a year on the education of a white child, the Northern Rhodesian government allocated only £9 a year to each African child; and only a minute fraction were given the opportunity for secondary education.

These were matters which perhaps concerned the emerging urban elite more than the majority of rural inhabitants. But in Africa urban dwellers retain strong ties with their relatives in the country. News gets round and feelings spread. In the atmosphere of insecurity and resentment which had been created by the disputes on federation, the sense of affront grew rapidly in fertile soil.

As secretary-general of Congress Kaunda was now at the eye of each storm. He made his own and his organisation's position very clear almost as soon as he was elected and immediately after federation had been imposed. At the beginning of October, in a speech at Livingstone, he said: 'We do not hate the colour of the man, but his conduct . . . As long as power remains with the whites it is a police state and no peace can prevail . . . Unless and until the foreign power is removed, there can be no peace. We want the franchise and we want it now.' A week later he issued a press communiqué which read:

In central Africa a major constitutional change has been imposed against the expressed wish of some six million Africans in favour of a handful of reactionary white settlers. This imposition has only been possible because the imperialists count on the strength of the British troops which they are ruthlessly using in crushing down the national aspirations of the colonial peoples . . . They have only managed to shelve the inevitable racial strife in central Africa. Serious trouble lies ahead. The imposition of Federation has made this trouble more certain than ever.

This emotive language was new to Northern Rhodesian, although it had been used for half a century in India and over a lesser period in west Africa. It contained overtones of the phrases commonly heard in London's anti-colonial circles in the immediate post-war years when Nkrumah,

Kenyatta, Padmore, Du Bois and their British friends were organising the African nationalist campaign.

What is interesting and significant in these statements is the evidence they give that already Kaunda had linked the anti-federal cause to a specific anti-colonial policy designed to abolish colonial rule entirely, with the ultimate vision of an independent, majority-ruled Northern Rhodesia. Considering that the Colonial Office had been generally regarded as a paternalist protector against white settler domination, had been constantly reviled by white politicians, this demonstrated a lengthened perspective achieved with remarkable speed by the young man.

Despite the difficulties of family life, Betty Kaunda also became enthused with the struggle after moving to Lusaka. Traditionally African women had taken little or no open role in political life. Yet, as in west Africa amongst the market women and in Tanganyika, the new nationalist parties realised the importance of recruiting them. They recognised that unless they did so half the adult population would remain inactive during the struggles ahead. They also saw that women had a special part to play in their own contribution, in stiffening their husbands' resistance and in guiding their children into national consciousness.

So Congress established its own Women's League inside its structure. Betty was elected secretary of the Chilenje branch. She quickly took an active part in a campaign which directly affected most women. She and her colleagues organised a boycott of butchers' shops in order to force the shopkeepers to allow Africans to enter the shops and select their purchases. Up to then African shoppers had had to wait in queues outside the hatch windows where they were served. Often they would have to queue for hours. When their turn came they then had to accept whatever the butcher gave them, always the cheapest scraps, not even wrapped.

The boycott was enforced by the confiscation of any meat bought by Africans not participating. Kenneth himself went with the women when they tried to enter the shops; he was so moved by the treatment of the women that he vowed not to eat meat until his continent was free. He has kept his vow to the present, even after Northern Rhodesia gained its independence.

The boycott continued for ten weeks. But the butchers suffered financially, capitulated and from then on traded with the black women on equal terms.

Then the women turned to another form of discrimination. Traditionally African women brew their own beer. But this had been forbidden in many urban areas, including Lusaka. The municipalities insisted on their own monopoly, selling the beer through municipal beer halls. The Women's League organised a protest to the District Commissioner's office. The police were called out and the crowd subjected to tear gas. The women continued to brew their beer secretly, selling it at concealed places in the bush. A running war was waged between the women and the police. Although a good deal of humour developed in the conflict, the fines imposed on those caught in home brewing were not amusing. Although neither Betty nor Kenneth drank beer, Betty still brewed and sold it to supplement their tiny family income; Kenneth turned a blind eye, grateful for the small addition to their finances.

The first important decision which Congress had to take after federation came into force was on the attitude they should take towards the federal elections. It has always been a matter of argument in nationalist movements as to whether it is better to participate in elections held on a limited franchise or to boycott them. On the one hand it may be possible to use them in order to press for a broader franchise and increased democratic representation; on the other, this may appear to condone their current undemocratic features.

In the Northern Rhodesian case it was decided, after much discussion, to participate in the elections lest the federal parliament amend the constitution so as to allow the government to nominate its own African members who would then, by their dependence on it, accept government policies. Kaunda expressed his own view, and the majority opinion of Congress, when he announced, 'If we Africans are decided to continue fighting against human injustice, we will be well advised to link up our national movements with the established foreign parliamentary system. We must see to it that more and more of our men find their way to the parliamentary institution whilst on the other hand we intensify our national aspirations.' At that time it was becoming received policy amongst African parties to accept what limited opportunities of representation were offered and use them immediately to demand more. Congress was to discover that this tactic did not satisfy their needs in central Africa, for the political power of the whites was too great and British authority too weak.

The most remarkable aspect of Kaunda's experience in the post of Congress secretary-general is that it did not make him into a bitter anti-white racialist. Both he and Nkumbula were constantly harried by the federal and Northern Rhodesian authorities from the time that federation was imposed. Yet neither man has ever entertained racialist feelings.

In August 1954, for instance, they travelled to Salisbury in Southern Rhodesia to attend a meeting of the four federal members of parliament representing Northern Rhodesia and Nyasaland. They were both summarily deported as soon as they arrived at Salisbury airport. The deportation orders were applied under the Southern Rhodesian Deportation of Aliens Act. So, despite all the fine talk about 'partnership' in the new federation, two Africans were considered to be 'aliens' within its boundaries.

When they tried to start a cyclostyled Congress monthly newspaper they were both arrested on the charge of printing a newspaper without registering it. They had to be released when they proved that they had already written to the Postmaster-General who had explained to them that he could not register the paper as it was not actually printed.

In January 1955, came the ultimate harassment. In the early morning Kenneth was awakened by his wife who told him that two Europeans wanted to see him. They were policemen. They took him to the Congress office and produced a search warrant. Harry Nkumbula arrived at the office accompanied by other police. They searched the office and found copies of 'Africa and the Colonial World', a publication produced in London by Fenner Brockway, then a Labour member of parliament, and some of his friends. It had been declared a 'prohibited publication' by the Northern Rhodesian government. There were also publications of George Hauser's American Committee on Africa and some journals emanating from communist sources. None of these magazines had been solicited by Congress.

The policemen then returned to Kenneth's house where his wife in the meantime had hidden anything she thought might cause suspicion in a large pot in the kitchen and covered it with a sack. But she had been observed by police posted round the house. In the pot were translations into Bemba by Stephen Mpashi of Gandhi and Nehru's passive resistance campaigns for Indian independence.

Kaunda and Nkumbula were tried at the magistrate's court on a charge of being in possession of prohibited literature. They were sentenced to two months' imprisonment.

This kind of constant pressure on him by the authorities chafed Kaunda's sensitive nature. He felt the affront to his dignity as an equal human being trying only to serve his neighbours. He was particularly distressed by the indignities he suffered in prison as well as by the assault against the freedom he considered a natural, intrinsic right. It was especially offensive to him that, whilst serving his sentence, he had to appear in prison clothes and be accompanied by an armed warder when he went to visit his youngest son in hospital. His wife was only allowed to visit him once a month.

Paradoxically, however, the gaol sentences on Kaunda and Nkumbula strengthened their organisation. In the 1950s it became almost an essential qualification for a nationalist leader to have been imprisoned by the colonial authorities. The term 'Prison Graduate' was coined in the Gold Coast in reference to the experiences of Kwame Nkrumah and his colleagues in being sent to gaol for offences in pursuit of national freedom. The attitude was reflected elsewhere. Those who were imprisoned by colonial rulers were regarded as heroic martyrs by their own people. Nationalist movements gained a powerful stimulus on each occasion.

So the imprisonment of the president and secretary-general of Congress angered its members, spurring them to greater efforts, and at the same time provoked many ordinary people to show their resentment by joining the party. This did not, of course, compensate Mrs Kaunda and her children for Kenneth's absence. Not only was the youngest son so seriously ill that he had to be taken to hospital, but money was even scarcer than usual.

Both Congress and the Kaunda family were fortunate that at this time of need Simon Kapwepwe returned from four years in India. He was able to take charge of Congress whilst Kaunda and Nkumbula were in gaol, and he made sure that Mrs Kaunda and her children had sufficient to eat. Kapwepwe's return, indeed, marked the beginning of a new militant phase in Congress history. He was able to capitalise on the martyrdom of its two leading officials by channelling the consequent anger into support for the party. Subscriptions and donations suddenly increased; Kapwepwe himself dramatised the situation by setting the fashion of wearing a black armband; and he turned the imprisonments into a political rallying point by telegraphing all branches, 'This is the beginning of freedom'. In the following year, after Kaunda and Nkumbula had been released, Kapwepwe was elected treasurer-general of Congress. Henceforth he was to work closely with Kenneth, encouraging his radical instincts, sometimes to the disapproval of Nkumbula.

Congress at this time certainly needed all the resources it could muster. Once federation came into operation it soon became obvious that many of the fears expressed by Africans were fully justified. White power accumulated in Southern Rhodesia, the major companies moved their offices there and the federal government discriminated in favour of that territory. Salisbury was chosen as the federal capital, although Northern Rhodesia could have provided a more central site. The federal government used its budgetary powers to ensure that Southern Rhodesian economic interests were given preference. The federal leaders pressed on relentlessly towards their objective of independence, or 'Dominion Status', as they preferred to call it.

The most blatant act of discrimination was the selection of Kariba instead of Kafue as the site of a massive new hydro-electricity scheme. An agreement had been signed in 1953 for a dam to be constructed on the Kafue river in Northern Rhodesia. Eighteen months later the federal cabinet, headed by Godfrey Huggins, one of the signatories to the previous agreement, arbitrarily decided that the dam should be built at Kariba. The new site had the advantage, from their point of view, of allowing the power station to lie on the Southern Rhodesian bank of the Zambesi. Even the copper companies, now with their headquarters in Salisbury, preferred the Kafue plan. They were bludgeoned into acquiescence by Huggins' threat of an export tax on copper unless they supported him.

This flagrant discrimination of the federal authorities in favour of Southern Rhodesia, the home of the vast majority of whites, brought one slight new strength to the nationalists of Northern Rhodesia. The 'liberal' whites had been somewhat ambivalent about the federal issue to this point. Now Harry Franklin, a member for African interests of the legislative council, sounded a warning that if this was to be the attitude of the federal parliament, the future of Northern Rhodesia was in grave jeopardy. He was joined by Dr Alexander Scott, owner of the Lusaka-based *Central African Post* and an independent member of the federal assembly, who now became the most bitter white critic of federal policies.

Yet this was but small comfort to Kaunda, Nkumbula, Kapwepwe and their colleagues. They were faced with the undisguised hostility of the federal government, constant persecution by the authorities in Northern Rhodesia and complete lack of sympathy by the British government. They now knew that they had to rely on their own unaided efforts, occasionally assisted by local white liberals or members of the British Labour Party, to fight the war which had been declared against them.

For them the battle was waged in three main sectors: the rural areas, the towns, and the Copper Belt. The rural areas, where the vast majority of Africans lived, had always been considered by colonial administrators to be 'safe'. They were accustomed to work with respectful chiefs who would uncritically accept their authority and superior intelligence, mirroring the relations of a feudal Britain nostalgically imitated by many colonial officers. It was a cardinal principle of administration to 'keep politics and agitators' out of rural society, lest they disturb the peaceful authoritarianism of colonial rule.

Yet, as we have seen, political discussion and organisation had already begun to penetrate some country districts before the federal issue fanned the flames. After federation had been established, therefore, the Northern Rhodesian government and its administrators used all their authority to exclude Congress activities from rural communities. They expected the chiefs to assist them, constantly warning them against allowing dissident personalities to remain in their districts. Those chiefs who refused to follow this line were either removed by government or constantly harassed. This, in itself, aggravated resentment and provoked further political argument. On occasion it also incited action by Congress supporters against chiefs working with the government. There were numerous disturbances and clashes. Congress leaders found that they had a new problem to face. Their own officials, or those purporting to be Congress officials, would take arbitrary action in remote districts, thus allowing the government to blame

Congress for violent incidents which Congress itself had never sanctioned. The issue of party discipline, especially in the rural areas far from headquarters, remained a serious problem for Kaunda and his colleagues up to and after independence.

In the towns the boycott tactic continued to be employed. At the beginning of 1956 Kaunda announced that an all-out campaign was to be launched against the colour bar and high prices. In Lusaka, Broken Hill and the Copper Belt picketing of shops on the Congress black list raised the political temperature immediately. There were a number of cases of violence and intimidation. Europeans became increasingly apprehensive. Again the issue of party discipline had to be faced. Kaunda warned that pickets guilty of violent offences would be expelled from the party.

On the Copper Belt the conflict was principally conducted by the miners' union, with varying degrees of co-operation by Congress. Relations between the union and the party varied, partly according to the situation, partly influenced by personalities. Paradoxically, the success in modifying the colour bar gave birth to a new source of friction. The companies pressurised those Africans they promoted to leave the union and set up their own Salaried Staff Association. The fact that the president of the new association was none other than Lewanika, previously president of Congress and now an avowed supporter of federation, hardly endeared it to Congress or militant miners.

In 1955 and 1956 resentment grew against what was felt to be a deliberate attempt to deprive the union of some of its best members. Strikes and disturbances spread. There was also a two-month strike of 30,000 miners about a pay claim. The tension which had been mounting during this period culminated in September 1956 in the declaration by the government of a State of Emergency. About sixty Copper Belt leaders were arrested. Amongst them were many men who were not only trade unionists but also officials of Congress. Police reinforcements appeared from Southern Rhodesia and Nyasaland, troops and armoured cars supplemented police forces.

The government's action was directed principally against Matthew Nkoloma, the union's secretary-general, and the militant union members who supported him in his radical policies against the companies. Lawrence Katilungu, the president, kept away from the scene of action until the State of Emergency had been declared. This division in union counsels and leadership was to pose awkward problems for Congress, because they tended to be reflected from the union into the political party, many members being influential in both. But the industrial conflict, the State of Emergency and Commission of Enquiry which followed it, again increased the political heat and thus helped to increase the importance of the role of Congress.

In the meantime, the political temperature was continually being raised by the continuation of efforts by the white politicians to gain increased powers for the federation and to diminish the influence of the Colonial Office over the two northern protectorates. Huggins attended a Commonwealth Prime Ministers' Conference in London in 1956 – itself an omen for those who feared that the federation was to be granted independence, for only delegates from independent states were entitled to attend. He pressed the British government to grant his federation higher international status. Later that year he was succeeded by Roy Welensky as federal prime minister. He also immediately travelled to London to follow up Huggins' initiative. Lennox-Boyd, the Colonial Secretary, accepted his claim for greater authority, agreeing that the British government would never legislate for the federation except at the request of its government. Shortly afterwards the Colonial Secretary visited central Africa himself. He took the opportunity to re-state his support for federation and to reiterate the British government's determination never to allow any of the three territories to secede from it.

It became known during 1957 that a conference was to be held in 1960 to consider the possibility of the federation attaining Dominion Status, synonymous with independence, that the federal constitution was to be changed so as to give white electors even greater power, and that the Northern Rhodesian constitution was also to be amended. Congress realised that unless it could mount an offensive capable of impressing the British parliament in time, it would find itself at the mercy of white settler politicians as had occurred in South Africa in 1910. The political game had become a race as to whether white politicians could persuade Britain to grant them independence before the Africans were sufficiently organised to express national opposition to it.

It was at this stage that Kaunda and Nkumbula decided to fly to Britain in order to mobilise their support there and to prepare themselves for the decisive battles to come.

The occasion of this visit was a conference which I myself had organised as Commonwealth Officer of the British Labour Party. We invited socialist parties in the Commonwealth and various nationalist parties in the colonies to send representatives to Beatrice Webb House, a conference centre near Dorking in the woodlands of Surrey. Here for ten days representatives of parties from Africa, the West Indies, Asia, Australia and Canada listened to lectures from Aneurin Bevan, Hugh Gaitskell, Jim Callaghan, Barbara Castle and others. More important, we discussed amongst ourselves the issues, tactics and strategies of national struggles against colonialism, the roles we could each play in the transformation of the British Empire into a Commonwealth of sovereign, independent states.

It would be false to pretend that this was a wholeheartedly magnanimous gesture on the part of the Labour Party. Bitter hostility was shown to the venture by certain influential individuals in the Party and many snide comments were made about its conduct. Yet sufficient support was eventually forthcoming for it to be held and for the Labour Party to pay for hospitality, to arrange various visits for delegates and to subsidise a number of fares. The fact that the Australian delegation of four was led by Dr Evatt, leader of the Australian Labour Party, appeased some critics, although they continued to deride the calibre of colonial delegates, several of whom were later to become presidents, prime ministers or ministers in their own countries.

I had discussed my hopes of holding such a conference with Nkumbula at a meeting with him in Margate in 1955. He welcomed the idea, assured me that it would be of enormous value to his Congress and asked me whether his secretary-general could stay on in Britain to learn something of party organisation. Thus it was already agreed before the conference was held that Kaunda would not only attend with Nkumbula, but would stay in Britain afterwards for about six months in order to visit various parts of the country and study the organisation of the Labour Party.

Kaunda's visit to the Labour Party's Commonwealth Conference at Beatrice Webb House near Dorking was his first experience of leaving Africa. Indeed, apart from the few days he had spent in Tanganyika and Southern Rhodesia, it was his first time abroad. It was also on this visit that I first met him.

It has always seemed to me that the time Kaunda spent in Britain in 1957 formed one of the watersheds of his life. It was his first opportunity to test his ideas, oratory and beliefs on experienced politicians from other countries. It enabled him to widen his perspective by hearing of colonial problems from other Africans, Asians and West Indians. It showed him the workings of British political life and the organisation of a British political party. It introduced him to many ordinary British working men and women.

There was also a personal relationship involved in the visit which was to have profound effects on his future political career. For it was during his stay in Britain that Kaunda's suspicions of Nkumbula's private life were confirmed. He discovered that the 'playboy' side of Nkumbula's character could on occasion interfere with his political responsibilities. This discovery was to lay the foundations of mistrust which eventually led to a breach between the two leaders.

On arrival in London the two stayed for a few days at the Bentinck House Hotel. Already Kaunda was miserable. Despite his earlier frequent absences from his home, he found that in this strange city he was immediately homesick. But Nkumbula was very much at home, which aggravated Kaunda's unhappiness. He had lived in London when a student and visited the city since leaving. He had many friends, most of whom seemed shallow and frivolous to his companion. Nor could Kaunda reconcile himself to his president's extravagance. When Nkumbula enjoyed himself buying new shirts and ornate cufflinks, Kaunda was trying to remind him that they were in Britain on donations collected from poor members of Congress.

The relaxed atmosphere of the conference was in marked contrast to the tension-laden conditions of Northern Rhodesia. Kaunda certainly appreciated it, telling us how much easier he found it to talk with white people here than at home. This was his first international conference and he took it very seriously, but the friendliness and good humour of other delegates gradually reduced his solemnity. Before the end of the ten days he had made friends, was joining the evening visit to the local pub, and sitting up half the night participating in the endless informal discussions. Yet his commitment to the cause of freedom for his fellow-countrymen never wavered. He stood out as the most sincere delegate of the conference. In fact he became much more effective as the conference progressed, for as he relaxed he became progressively more persuasive.

From his arrival it became clear to us that he was a very shy man, anxious to avoid troubling anyone. He had not told us of his vegetarianism. He and Nkumbula arrived just as lunch was being served. He left his meat, contenting himself with carrots and potatoes. The housekeeper felt so maternal towards him that henceforth, without being asked, she prepared special meals for him.

His dedication to his nation was apparent even in social conversation. One lunchtime, for instance, he was telling us about his sons. Already he had planned their careers for them. His eldest, Panji, then ten years old, was to become a doctor; the second a lawyer and the third an economist. Northern Rhodesia was so short of professional Africans that Kenneth was convinced they should serve the country. In fact, Panji missed so much schoolwork that he did not qualify for medical school. He enjoyed the cadet force; the country needed trained soldiers, so he joined the army and went to Sandhurst. I remember with what pride Kenneth told me, much later, how his son had refused an invitation to dine with the Queen because it would interfere with his military studies.

During his time in Dorking it was interesting to observe his choice of friends. The most unexpected was Tawia Adamafio, who was representing Ghana's Convention People's Party. This was only about two months after Ghana's independence. Tawia presented a complete contrast to Kenneth. He openly admitted that corrupt election practices had been used in Ghana and never concealed his own roguishness. He was to become notorious in his own country for his part in the application of the Preventive Detention Act; then he himself fell foul of Nkrumah's establishment in which he had been one of the key figures, very close to the President himself. For a time he lay under a death sentence and some of us pleaded with Nkrumah not to allow the execution. It was eventually commuted.

The contrast to the puritanical Kaunda, with his Arthur Mee and scouting, could hardly have been sharper. Yet Adamafio was great company, full of good humour, a lovable rogue. I believe also that he was personally dedicated to African freedom, though hardly scrupulous of the means employed to reach the ends. Kenneth was appalled with his Machiavellian tactics. Yet he struck up a friendship with Adamafio. They saw much of each other in London after the conference ended, and kept in touch for several years.

Nor were the effects of this conference on Kaunda confined to the formal sessions or group discussions. In the evening, after the visit to the local pub, talk would continue in the bedrooms. That shared by Nkumbula and Kaunda was the centre for the most lively group. It consisted usually of the two Northern Rhodesians, Julian Compton, a lawyer from St Lucia who promised to help them with legal problems, Tettegah, a Ghanaian trade unionist, Adamafio, Dennis Phombeah and Oscar Kambona from Tanganyika, Imoudu, a veteran Nigerian trade unionist, and members of my staff from Transport House.

These informal discussions with active participants in nationalist movements from other African countries brought Kaunda a breath of understanding he could never have acquired at home. It placed the Northern Rhodesian struggle in a continental and international context which importantly widened his horizons.

Many famous British personalities visited the conference. Lectures were given by the Labour Party's leader and deputy, Gaitskell and Griffiths, by Jim Callaghan, Barbara Castle, Patrick Gordon-Walker, and Nye Bevan. The general secretary of the TUC, Sir Vincent Tewson, gave an address as did a director of the Co-operative Wholesale Society. The Australian Labour Party had sent a strong delegation, headed by Dr Evatt, the Leader of the Opposition and a former president of the United Nations' General Assembly.

Kaunda was thrilled to meet these personalities. He himself took a prominent part in the discussions, and was also selected as chairman of the session at which Barbara Castle spoke on economic aid. His fervour on the central African issue so impressed Dr Evatt, who had been totally ignorant of the African situation previously, that he wanted the conference to spend almost all its time on it and issue public statements about it. In his television interview at the end of the conference he, Kaunda and Nkumbula all made this their central issue.

During the conference a Declaration of Principles was unanimously agreed. These included a statement that:

Conference condemns the creation of the Federation of central Africa
. . . against the wishes of the African peoples. Conference demands that
they be given the right of self-determination and that all three territories
be granted a democratic constitution based upon adult franchise of one
man one vote . . . Conference states that in effect the problems of east
and central Africa lie in the concentration of power in the hands of the
minority European group, which gives them an opportunity to distribute
the wealth of the country as they desire. The solution lies in the establishment of a common roll, to be implemented as soon as possible, and which
should be based on the principle of universal adult franchise.

Kaunda left this, his first international conference, greatly enlightened
about political processes, stimulated by his success in impressing delegates
with the central African situation, and determined to use the rest of his
time in Britain in strengthening his political knowledge. He had been lent
a flat by Marjorie Nicholson, ex-secretary of the Fabian Colonial Bureau
and then an officer in the TUC. Shortly after the conference he was
awarded a scholarship to the Labour Party summer school and returned
to Beatrice Webb House for a further spell of lectures and discussion
groups. It was here that he first met Joan Lestor, later to be a prominent
figure in the Labour Party, a member of Labour governments and a
doughty fighter for African causes.

After the summer school he went to live in Highgate with Sadru
Rahimtullah, a Kenyan Asian who had been at the conference. This
enabled him to meet many colonial students, as Sadru was at the centre of
many student groups and had the previous year taken Nyerere to the
Blackpool conference.

Kaunda stayed in Britain until December. He attended the famous –
or notorious – Brighton Labour conference at which Nye Bevan recanted
his H-bomb views and was heckled by his own supporters. At that conference Kaunda spoke at an official party colonial meeting with Tom
Driberg and Jim Callaghan, again outlining the central African situation
and appealing for support. He also spoke at a public meeting organised by
the Movement for Colonial Freedom but, unfortunately, it suffered from
its usual fault of having too many speakers on a bewildering variety of
subjects. Nevertheless, this first venture into British public life gave Kaunda
valuable experience in finding rapport with a new kind of audience,
teaching him particularly the importance of basing emotion on rational
argument, for British listeners needed far more explanation of the issues
at stake than those he was accustomed to address in Northern Rhodesia.

Most of the rest of his time in Britain was spent in studying the Labour
Party's organisation, seeking to learn which techniques could be adapted
to his problems with Congress at home. In this pursuit he not only witnessed

how the annual conference was arranged, but visited regional, constituency and ward structures to see how the party was organised down to its grass roots. Apart from the time he spent in London and its environs, he visited Bridgewater in the west and Newcastle in the north-east. His investigations were thorough and by the time he returned home in December he had acquired a most detailed knowledge of party organisation and British political life.

Yet Kaunda had not come to Britain as a disinterested, objective student, examining party structure as an academic exercise. He was in the midst of a bitter, often bloody struggle. Only factors relevant to that struggle interested him; he had no time for anything outside this single-minded pursuit. Many colonial students he met at that time considered him temperate, not sufficiently declamatory against British politics, too concerned with parliamentary debates and the intricacies of party organisation.

The fact was that Kaunda was dedicated to the overthrow of the federation and the defeat of the British government which supported it. He was not interested in the self-indulgence of the kind of demagogy fashionable amongst many colonial students. He was concerned with changing institutions, not with composing phrases. He therefore took the opportunity to discover how the British political system worked, so that he might devise a strategy to combat its existing policies, to investigate its techniques, so as to strengthen his own organisation for the battles he was planning. Those of us who got to know him at this time realised that he was quite different from London's colonial students and, indeed, from the Nkumbula we had known for years. Here was a dedicated, single-minded man, who would either win his battle or be destroyed in it; there would be no compromise, no retirement from politics into law, academia or business.

During his visit an event occurred which presaged trouble. During the conference itself the Parliamentary Labour Party decided to initiate a debate on east and central Africa. I took Kaunda, Nkumbula, Phombeah, Kambona and Rahimtullah to the House to meet Callaghan for discussions on the points to be raised. Nkumbula told us that he and Kaunda were to see Lennox-Boyd, the Colonial Secretary, during their visit. It was becoming clear that the issue of federation was becoming a central factor in the colonial situation.

Yet when the time came for the meeting at the Colonial Office Nkumbula had returned home. Although he knew when the appointment was to take place, he insisted on flying back just two days previous to it. Kaunda was left to represent Congress alone. In fact, Lord Perth, the Minister of State, deputised for the Colonial Secretary and tried to lecture Kaunda on the need for patience, adopting a very patronising tone which revealed how far out of touch the Colonial Office was with the realities of the situation in Northern Rhodesia. Yet the significance of the event was not the interview but the fact of Nkumbula's departure. Kaunda, who had become progressively disillusioned with his president's preference for social life rather than political responsibility, was confirmed in his suspicions when Nkumbula chose to return home instead of keeping the appointment. For the Congress Executive had collected funds for his expenses on the understanding that an attempt would be made to meet the Colonial Secretary.

Kaunda returned home in December in response to a summons from Nkumbula as the Congress conference was due to meet in Lusaka. He did not hesitate when he received the telegram from his president, although his visit was not complete. But he arrived back in Lusaka with many more doubts concerning Nkumbula than he had felt when he left eight months previously.

7

Nyerere – Nationalist Leader

When Nyerere flew home in October 1952 he was met at the airport by the Roman Catholic Archbishop and a representative of the social services department of the government. But his fiancée, Maria Gabriel, was not there. She considered that it was not a woman's place to run after her man. In any case, she had sufficient perception to realise that people can change during a period of three and a half years abroad. She meant to make certain that Julius was the same man who had left his country in 1949, that his experiences had not so altered him that they no longer had sufficient in common to make a successful marriage. She was soon re-assured.

After their reunion in Dar es Salaam, Nyerere took the train to Mwanza and the steamer across the lake to Musoma where he was met by his family. From the lakeside they proceeded to his Zanaki home. There, with the assistance of his friends and relatives, he built a house for himself and Maria. Characteristically he took off his shoes and mixed sand and cement with his bare feet. To neighbours who wondered at a university graduate demeaning himself with such work he replied that 'everyone who has an education must work'.

During his absence Maria, advised by Father Walsh, had been preparing herself to be Julius' wife. She had spent some time in a school in Uganda, learning domestic science. Then she had taught for a time in Moshi. Finally she had gone to St Joseph's College in Dar es Salaam to study English. By the time that Julius returned from Edinburgh she was both widely travelled and well-read. She was ready to become the ideal partner for Julius, though she can have had no idea where that partnership was to lead the two of them. On 24 January 1953 they were married at the Musoma mission by Father William Collins.

Nyerere had already been appointed as a history master to teach in St Francis' College at Pugu, twelve miles outside Dar es Salaam. The Roman Catholic church had transferred the three top forms from Nyerere's old school, St Mary's College in Tabora, to Pugu to establish a secondary school which would serve the whole country. When Julius took me to the school some years later the Fathers showed us the spoors of a pride of lions which had rested on the grass in front of the buildings a few days earlier.

They also told me of a boy who had missed the bus from his village at the end of the school holidays. He arrived three weeks late, having walked the whole distance.

Before entering into his teaching duties, Julius had to combine bringing himself up to date in the political situation with building his connubial home. From the viewpoint of awakening national consciousness a considerable improvement was evident from the position when he had left the country. In particular, the Meru land case, although tragic from the point of view of those personally involved, had created an awareness of the menace of colonial rule which provided ready ammunition for those anxious to organise the ordinary people.

The Meru case arose out of a decision by the colonial government to consolidate lands which had been taken by European farmers. It involved moving a large number of Africans and their families from their homes and farms on Mount Meru. Although an alternative location was prepared for them, the evictions raised bitter resentment and many Meru Africans were arrested as a result of their protests. It provided another illustration of what has proved to be the greatest incomprehension of Europeans in Africa – the African's profound attachment to the land traditionally occupied by his community.

This incident occurred in 1951. It aroused passions all over the country as fear of loss of land spread. In that year a United Nations' Visiting Mission was in the country under the terms of the Trusteeship Agreement. An official of the African Association, Kirillo Japhet, had formed a Meru Citizens' Union to stop the evictions and eventually expel the European settlers. Japhet met the UN representatives who advised him to appeal to the Trusteeship Council. Collections throughout the country not only secured the money to pay fares to New York, but aroused feelings about the land issue amongst all the peasants who were asked to contribute.

Japhet faced Governor Twining before the Trusteeship Council in July 1952. In October the case went to the General Assembly, but did not secure the necessary two-thirds' majority. Nevertheless, it had become an' international issue. Moreover, the African Association had proved that it could take the government to the United Nations with the support of the ordinary people. The Meru case marked the beginning of adulthood for African politics.

Parallel with the seminal effects of the Meru case went a growth in political interest amongst the Sukuma in the Lake Province. After the war the government had helped to develop the production of cotton in this area. In 1949 Paul Bomani organised a Lake Province Growers' Association which grew into the Victoria Federation of Co-operative Unions, incorporating all the co-operatives. It aimed to gain control of cotton marketing which was monopolised by Indian businessmen who were considered to exploit the African farmers by paying low prices. By organising the farmers in the rural areas Bomani eventually secured a membership of 30,000. Inevitably this movement was seen to have its political overtones and when Bomani and his closest associates became full-time officers of the African Association in Mwanza also, it was clear that the TAA had become a serious political party, in Sukumaland at least.

In 1951 a constitutional committee had proposed a new constitution with an enlarged legislature composed of twenty-one members, seven from each race. In the same year the first African had been appointed to the executive council. He was the governor's favourite African, Kidaha Makwaia, mentioned above.

Thus when Nyerere returned home significant developments were already afoot in his country. Constitutional reforms were inviting political discussion and organisation amongst Africans on a national scale. In the north rural agitation on the land issue merged with the organisation of cotton farmers, both bringing the town-based African Association into intimate contact with the peasant inhabitants of the countryside.

It was Nyerere's genius to comprehend the national significance of these events and to recognise their potential for the future of his country. It was he who realised that the Association must become a fully fledged political party, rather than the amalgam of social and political elements it had been previously. This required a national headquarters, representing the whole country, together with a central direction of policy. But the foundations had already been laid, at least in Sukumaland.

Before turning to political activity, though, Nyerere had to settle into his new school and start his married life. Soon after their marriage Julius and Maria moved to Pugu where a house awaited them. Julius had been offered a salary of £300 a year but, after some argument, this was raised to £450, plus a 30 per cent cost of living allowance. This represented three-fifths of what he would have received if he had been a European teacher in Tanganyika. Yet, as he himself realised, it was more than he would have been paid in a similar post in Britain. He also considered that it was more than Tanganyika could afford. Already he was critical of the high incomes paid to the tiny elite in a country of mass poverty.

Whatever doubts Nyerere may have had as to what role he should play on his return from Britain, it was soon made quite clear to him that he was expected to play a leading part in the political drama. Hardly had he settled in Pugu when the newly educated young men who had taken over the African Association in Dar es Salaam began to pay him visits. They found a centre for their political discussions at the Arnoutoglu Community Centre where two progressive Europeans, Fraser Murray, a lawyer, and Jimmy McGairl, a community development officer, had formed an inter-racial discussion group. Among those who gravitated to the Centre were several men who were to be close colleagues of Nyerere, Amir Jamal, an Asian businessman educated in politics and economics in Bombay, Denis Phombeah, a Nyasa with experience in administration, Oscar Kambona, another teacher, Rashidi Kawawa, who became a social service worker, Zuberi Mtemvu, who was later to enter the lists against him. Within three months of arriving in Pugu, Nyerere had been persuaded to stand for the presidency of the TAA. He was elected in April 1953 and turned his mind to transforming the Association into a positive political party.

Nyerere had the advantage of coming from a small tribe, which saved him from any suspicion that he might be aiming at political dominance by a large community. On the other hand, this deprived him of the secure power base that, for instance, Kenyatta had amongst the Kikuyu. Moreover, he came from the far interior and was a Christian; this could have been a disadvantage to him in Dar es Salaam, the political centre of the coast, which was strongly Moslem. Yet the fact that he was an overseas graduate undoubtedly gave him immense prestige at a time when higher education was almost non-existent amongst Africans, but when education was highly revered as the key to the white men's secrets. A further advantage was that as a mission teacher he was not under direct government control. Nevertheless, the most common view of those who knew him or observed his effect on other people at this time is that it was his genuine humility and his sincere desire to serve which attracted followers and singled him out in their minds as a natural leader.

Shortly after his election as president of the TAA the governor, Edward Twining, banned civil servants from being members of the Association. Nyerere immediately protested that as most educated Africans were in the civil service, this was tantamount to banning the TAA and a serious blow to African political development. He did not even receive the courtesy of a reply. No more was needed to convince him that the administration was hostile to the new African politics. Nothing less than a fully fledged national political party would suffice to combat this hostility and establish that the African inhabitants of Tanganyika were seriously determined to gain control of their own society.

By now Nyerere had become convinced that the TAA as it stood could not become a political party. Its history was too redolent of the social tea-party atmosphere, of a dependent African elite patronised by European administrators. The exclusion of civil servants was likely to cripple its organisation.

So, at a meeting in October 1953, Nyerere and his friends decided to transform it into a new party which, it was hoped, would take over all the TAA's branches. But it was essential, before making any announcement, that the views of existing TAA members be sought. So Nyerere used his opportunities when attending teachers' conferences to discuss the prospects with local members of the TAA. He was able to visit the branches in Tabora, Dodoma, Iringa and Bukoba for this purpose, setting an early example of his constant concern that all parts of the country should participate in every major decision, rather than accepting that Dar es Salaam could speak for the whole nation.

As a result, by July 1954, plans had been prepared for the new party. At the annual conference of the TAA, held in the capital on the seventh day of the seventh month, it was announced that the Association was now to be renamed the Tanganyika African National Union. Nyerere himself, now thirty-two, was unanimously elected president and a national executive was also elected, though both were to be subject to re-election at annual conferences. Due to the difficulties of travel, it was decided that an executive central committee, composed of members living in Dar es Salaam, should also be appointed to meet weekly so that quick decisions could be taken in times of urgency. Ever since that historic date, 7 July has been celebrated in Tanganyika as Saba Saba, now a national holiday.

The 'Aims and Objects' of the new organisation illustrate the way in which Nyerere's mind was turning at this stage of his life. They included:

To prepare the people of Tanganyika for self Government and Independence . . . To fight against tribalism and all isolationist tendencies amongst the Africans and to build a united nationalism . . . To fight relentlessly for the establishment of a democratic form of government, and . . . to fight for the introduction of the election principle on all bodies of local and central government . . . To fight for the removal of every form of racialism and racial discrimination . . . To encourage and organise Trade Unionism and the Co-operative Movement . . . To oppose any move to join Tanganyika in a Union or Federation with the other East African Territories until the demand for Federation comes from the African inhabitants of these Territories . . . To co-operate with other nationalist and democratic organizations in Africa for the object of the emancipation of the people of Africa and the establishment of independent and self governing African States, free from any form of political, economic or social oppression.

Already, in deciding to create a political party and in composing its constitution, Nyerere and his colleagues had been influenced by the formation of Congress in Northern Rhodesia. Indeed, two of the group, Ally Sykes and Denis Phombeah, had tried to travel to Lusaka to attend a Pan-African Congress, but had been deported from Salisbury. They had also noted the experience of the Kenya African Union in their neighbouring country, whilst Julius had studied Nkrumah's Convention People's Party constitution when in Britain.

Nyerere was later to be challenged on the application of some of these

principles which had been laid down for his party. He was asked, for
instance, how it could be consistent to demand the 'removal of every form
of racialism and racial discrimination' when his party confined its membership to 'any African man or woman of the age of eighteen years or above'.
Nyerere was never content with rigid logic. He always explained that his
people had been the object of discrimination for so long that they had to
learn to run their own organisation entirely themselves before they could
gain sufficient self-confidence to allow others to become members. When
later he did apply the interdict on racialism as government policy, demanding an end to discrimination against non-Africans, he was attacked by
some of his own people for his non-racial policies.

It was significant that, from this starting point, the party was committed
to the objective of independence. At this time there existed a certain confusion in the minds of many colonial subjects over the relationship between
'self-government' and 'independence'. The former term was often considered to apply to a situation in which colonial inhabitants would control
legislatures and executives but still remain within the imperial ambit. For
a complete break from the British Empire demanded a revolutionary
mental leap too great for many colonially tutored subjects. Nyerere, however, had been accustomed to discussing this precise objective with his
fellow-colonial students in Britain. He had seen it taken by the inhabitants
of the Indian sub-continent. He realised that the Commonwealth was no
longer even partially synonymous with Empire, but an association of
sovereign states. He knew that Nkrumah in the Gold Coast and the
Nigerians were aiming at internal self-government as a stage towards a
complete independence which would be accompanied by membership of
the Commonwealth. These constitutional niceties might be too sophisticated to be grasped immediately by the mass of his people; indeed, they
were often confused by the British public and press; but if both objectives
were included in the party's constitution, the practical implications would
become apparent later.

Taken in conjunction with the other declared objects, this demonstrated
that the new party, TANU, had set itself the task of creating a national
consciousness over-riding all tribal considerations and embracing all
African individual and collective efforts. Its object was to establish a
Tanganyikan state in which every colonial chain would have been broken
and which would be governed by the elected representatives of the whole
population. Theoretically this was precisely what Britain was pledged to
accomplish under her United Nations' Trusteeship; but in most British
minds the objective existed in such a dim and distant future that it remained theoretical. The British prime minister himself, Winston Churchill,
had spoken of the British Empire existing for ' a thousand years'. He had
expressly excluded the Empire from the implications of the Atlantic

Charter. And he had categorically declared that he had no intention of 'presiding over the liquidation of the Empire'.

Nor did Nyerere himself envisage achieving independence in the immediate future. At the time that TANU was born no British colony in Africa had gained independence. The Gold Coast was in the process of becoming self-governing in her domestic affairs, but independence had hardly appeared on the horizon. It was generally believed that the long association of west Africa with Europe would enable her people to govern themselves much earlier than their cousins in east or central Africa. In reality this belief may have had more connection with the presence of European settlers in the east and centre of the continent than with African abilities in government. Certainly the west had the advantage of a greater number of formally educated Africans; it was to be discovered, however, that formal education was not a prerequisite for self-government. Nevertheless, after three-quarters of a century of imperial authority, people's minds were not attuned to the possibility of managing all the apparatus of a modern state in the near future. It took visionaries to contemplate even its eventual achievement. Nyerere himself talked in terms of gaining independence in twenty-five years.

Yet the goal had been defined. It now entered the political language. It became the focus of discussion. In itself, this fact brought its achievement closer. The Swahili word *uhuru* was soon to become the single popular unifying talisman of Tanganyikan nationalism.

Another significant aspect of the party's constitution was the bias it displayed towards mass participation. There had been some discussion in the preliminary stages of the advantages of organising the party as an elite group, spearheading a nationalist movement rather than involving all sections of the community in it from the start. Some felt that mass membership might dilute policy. There was also the danger that by including all sections contrary interests might arise from different interests. It could be, for instance, that conservative chiefs might clash with young militants who wished to abolish chiefdom, or wealthy members with those wedded to the idea of egalitarianism.

In fact these contrary interests were represented in the party from its beginnings and obviously introduced potential seeds of dissension. Nyerere was persuaded, however, that a genuine national movement must represent all interests. He relied on the single objective of uhuru attracting sufficient common loyalty to relegate sectional interests to a lower priority. So both individual and corporate membership were invited, including trade unions, professional associations, co-operative societies, farmers' associations and youth, women's, sports, cultural and tribal organisations. In short, the whole African population, either individually or through membership of existing organisations, was invited to join the new party.

These were desperately strenuous times for Julius. He had a full-time job as a teacher at a boarding school. Often in the evenings he would then walk the twelve miles to Dar es Salaam and the same distance back in order to attend a meeting. His party had no funds and none of its pioneers could afford the time to organise or collect fees. At first they were very dependent on the commitment of one of the few African businessmen of the time, John Rupia. He had a building transport business and, although he became the first treasurer of TANU, there were no funds to administer. So he used his own money to finance its earliest activities.

Yet, with or without funds, the party was immediately called upon to take action. The month after its formation the triennial visit of a United Nations' mission took place. If TANU was to substantiate its claim to represent the nation it was imperative that it be seen to do so by the mission.

Accordingly the National Executive met in August to draft a memorandum for submission to the members of the mission. The national character of the party was demonstrated by the presence of representatives from all its branches. The memorandum demanded immediate democratic elections, if necessary beginning in Dar es Salaam, and accepted the existing multi-racial parity in the legislative council as merely a temporary expedient. The objective must be a fully democratic African state. It complained of inadequate educational and economic opportunities, declared British economic aid to be insufficient and asked the United Nations to supplement it. So far this was conventional African nationalist policy; where it took a unique character was when it called for a freeze on wages and salaries. The balance saved from projected increases was to be used to raise the living standards of the masses. This was certainly a most radical concept for the new party to take almost at its inception. It could have been a mirror held to TANU's future originality.

When the mission met Nyerere in Dar es Salaam they were immensely impressed by his evolutionary, but determined, attitude to the future of his country and by his natural good humour. In their report they strongly criticised British policy, making a special point of the persistence of racial discrimination. They displayed considerable sympathy for TANU and its activities. Then they laid a time-bomb which was to be regarded by British and white settlers alike as the flashpoint of the report. They proposed that the British administration should work out a timetable with the local population for the attainment of independence within twenty-five years. This represented acceptance of the major demand put forward by TANU; but it was angrily rejected by the British government, the administration in Tanganyika, the local white settlers and whites throughout the continent, not least in neighbouring Kenya and the Central African Federation.

The publication of this report and the support it gave to the policy of

TANU marked the final breach between the governor and his administration on the one hand, and Nyerere and TANU on the other. Governor Twining had assured the mission that no organisation representative of Africans existed. This statement infuriated Nyerere who was naturally delighted to have his views publicly justified by a UN mission. Twining was as inevitably outraged.

The attitude taken by the governor and the colonial government over this report convinced Nyerere that he would have to fight them. He had no desire to do so, far preferring the traditional African method of discussion amongst those with differing opinions until a consensus view had been reached. Indeed, at this stage Nyerere had little criticism of the colonial administration, which had certainly progressed much farther towards African participation than any other in east or central Africa. The one issue on which he insisted, however, was that the principle of eventual independence under democratic rule be publicly accepted by the government. Once it had been, he would have welcomed the opportunity to work in harness with the governor and government to prepare his people to accept their responsibilities A detailed timetable was not essential to him. But neither colonial nor British government would admit the principle. With hindsight, it is perhaps fortunate for Nyerere that they refused; without some resistance against which to struggle it might not have been possible to attain such a degree of national mobilisation.

For the governor's part, he felt that he had given Nyerere his chance and been rejected. He had refused a government teaching post on leaving Makerere. He continued to insist on a mission appointment on his return from Edinburgh. Twining had even appointed him as a temporary member of the legislative council in May 1954, to fill Makwaia's seat during the latter's absence on a Royal Commission. Nyerere rewarded him by attacking the government's complacency on education, pointing out that by 1956 sixty-four per cent of children of primary school age would still not be at school. When he let it be known that he would also attack a report recommending increased civil service salaries, Makwaia was quickly brought back from London. The government could rely on him not to criticise the report for allocating too high a proportion of national resources to the elite. He did not do so, still further exacerbating relations between himself and Nyerere.

There are none so bitter as rejected patrons. Twining sincerely believed that it was his task to take the tiny number of educated Africans under his wing and guide them into increased responsibilities. When Nyerere refused his overtures he made the mistake of denigrating him. He did not realise and continually blinded himself to the evidence that Nyerere was quickly becoming a folk hero, attracting and enrapturing audiences wherever he travelled. The more Twining attacked him, the more popular he became. When the UN report found them on opposite sides the breach between them became so deep that it could never be healed. Twining was too proud a man to admit that he was wrong about a potential protégé who had rejected his patronage. He came from a generation to whom Africans, however intelligent or well-educated, were no more than children in comparison with Europeans, or at least with Britons.

The activity required to present a memorandum to the UN mission ensured that the new party quickly swung into action. Yet this could not directly solve its organisational problems. To run a national party amongst a population sparsely distributed over vast areas where very little previous experience of political organisation had been known demanded an enormous effort. The situation in 1954–5 was propitious, but the basic need was for funds and personnel.

Nyerere was fortunate in the colleagues who came to his support at this critical moment. The most important initially was Oscar Kambona. Kambona resigned from his teaching post in Dodoma in order to offer his services to the new party. He had a little money as he had just received a retrospective salary increase awarded by the same commission which Nyerere had wished to criticise in the legislative council. He was appointed as Organising Secretary of TANU and immediately began to build a mass membership. His method was to approach the chiefs and elders, interest them in TANU's objectives and suggest that they use their influence with their followers to join the party. In this way the party secured 10,000 members in its first six months. TANU's first mass appeal thus came through the agency of the country's traditional leaders, most of whom were decidedly conservative in outlook. Their support demonstrated how widely the current of anti-colonialism was running in Tanganyika at that time.

Paul Bomani was another who gave great assistance. His co-operative experience in the Lake Province, his leadership of the TAA in his own areas, and then his study of co-operative methods in England and Europe made him an invaluable ally. The TAA branches he had organised in the Lake Province quickly turned themselves into branches of TANU. He himself, with Nyerere's approval, was nominated to the legislative council at the end of 1954 and was thus able to act as the TANU spokesman there.

A third close associate in the early days of TANU was Rashidi Kawawa. He was another product of Tabora School, although he had already organised his fellow-schoolboys into a team of teachers in an adult literacy campaign before he went there. After leaving school he gained considerable prestige as a social worker. He also became a well-known star in Swahili films. He was a very active member of the Tanganyikan African Civil Servants' Association and became its president in 1954. As a fellow-pupil of Kambona's at Tabora he was naturally interested in the formation of TANU, but, as a civil servant, he was debarred from joining the party. Nevertheless, his position in the TACSA was to prove valuable to Nyerere and TANU, not least in collecting funds on their behalf.

There were others who played their part in sustaining the party during its early days of infancy. John Rupia has already been mentioned. There were the three Sykes brothers, one of whom Nyerere had defeated for the presidency of the TAA; Dossa Aziz, Phombeah, Patrick Kunambi, and Michael Kamaliza. Tanganyika was very fortunate indeed to have such a collection of dedicated, public-spirited young men ready to take prominent roles in her nationalist movement at the same time. Their teamwork was as crucial as Nyerere's leadership, as he himself has constantly emphasised.

Detailed knowledge about the new party may have spread slowly, but it soon became known that it existed. There was much writing of pamphlets and leaflets which were distributed to the various rail-heads by railway workers. The fact that the majority of the population was illiterate was not as desperate a handicap as it might appear. The African 'bush telegraph' is a powerful communicator. Nyerere's provincial visits, the delegate conference, the writings, the discussions of chiefs, the denunciations of the governor, all combined to spread news around the country. Much of it is certain to have been garbled; but it was news which spread. In fact, one of the early disciplinary problems of TANU arose because some of the Lake Province branches, which had been inherited by Bhoke Munanka when Bomani went to England, interpreted the formation of the new party too aggressively. Some gave the impression that it had replaced the administration. They were refused registration by the government for four years.

The composition of the memorandum to the UN mission and the subsequent mission's report, did not conclude the effect of the UN visit on the nationalist movement. At the beginning of 1955 a TANU meeting in Dar es Salaam decided to send Nyerere to New York in order to address the Trusteeship Council on the African point of view. Immediately the administration resolved to counter this move by despatching a multi-racial delegation to rebut Nyerere's case. They chose a European, an African and an Asian to form the delegation, but it was to be the European, Sir Charles Phillips, who was deputed to act as the sole spokesman.

It was one thing for TANU to take the bold decision of sending its leader to New York; it was quite another to arrange for him to go. He was a teacher and had his job to consider. It would also be a very costly business to pay for his travel and maintenance. The government urged Father Walsh to refuse Nyerere leave of absence for the month he would have to be away. Nyerere himself told Father Walsh that he would be pleased for someone else to take his place so that he would not have to neglect his pupils. But TANU leaders assured Walsh that no one else was suitable to send. So Nyerere was given permission, although the administration still complained to the Father that TANU was a subversive movement and that it did not make sense for a government to subsidise the salary of an employee who was trying to undermine its authority.

Then TANU had to find the money, about £600. Every possible source in Dar es Salaam was tapped. Some gave a few cents, Kawawa urged his TAGSA members to contribute, Rupia made a handsome personal contribution. The essential funds were eventually accumulated, though only just in time. There was a good deal of nervousness amongst them all as they prepared for this first international venture. Nyerere himself was infected by it. But he arrived in New York in time to address the Trusteeship Council on 7 March 1955.

Even after all this effort, Nyerere found that the British government could pursue him to America. At its request he was restricted by the United States government during his stay to eight blocks from the UN building and had to leave within twenty-four hours of his address.

Before the Council itself the British representative alleged that it would undermine existing political institutions to set a date for independence, stir up disorder, halt the capital inflow and destroy the civil service. Sir Charles Phillips argued that it was government policy to develop the country for the benefit of all inhabitants, emphasising policies designed to raise African living standards; that eventually the voters, with an African majority, would decide the country's future. But he could not counter the charge that he did not represent Tanganyikans as he had been appointed by the governor.

So far the reactions of the Council had been conventionally divided, the colonial powers supporting the British and Tanganyikan administration's case; the non-colonial delegates displaying scepticism. When Nyerere made his appearance the atmosphere changed completely. The roles were not simply reversed, as might have been expected. No one on the Council or in the public galleries had heard such a case before. They were accustomed to demagogic declarations from colonial petitioners or to confused, irrational arguments. They had never previously heard a calmly reasoned, logically argued conciliatory statement such as Nyerere now presented.

This slim, small-boned, neat little modest African astounded his listeners by claiming that his party desired non-Africans to participate in leadership side by side with Africans, that its policy was one of brotherhood, that he believed this to be also the policy of the administration. He added, 'As the Government seeks the same objectives, the members of TANU co-operate with it and it is our greatest friend.'

At the same time, Nyerere moderately proposed that further alienation of land should be prohibited, that immigration of foreigners should cease, that the trade unions and co-operatives should be encouraged, that education and technical training should be expanded.

Nyerere had deliberately adopted a tactic in New York. He took the professions of the British and colonial governments literally and professed to believe in their sincerity. They were thus hoist with their own petards; but within the velvet glove was a clenched iron fist. The crucial declaration he made in his address to the Council was contained in these words: 'What will satisfy my people is a categorical statement, both by this council and by the Administering Authority, that although Tanganyika is multi-racial in population, its future government shall be primarily African. Once we get that assurance, everything else becomes a detail.' That again may sound sensible and moderate; in a time when on Tanganyika's borders Mau Mau was at its height, the Kabaka had been banished from Uganda, Northern Rhodesia and Nyasaland had been forced against African opinion into a white-dominated federation, it presented a revolutionary demand. Nyerere had nailed his political colours firmly to the political mast. He had impressed his international audience and clearly pointed the way ahead to the Trusteeship Council under which Britain ruled. Now he had to compel the colonial and British governments to accept his terms for co-operation by mobilising African political action.

On his return from New York Nyerere stayed for a few days in London. At this time I had become the Commonwealth Officer of the British Labour Party and I was able to renew my Edinburgh acquaintance with him at Transport House. I took him to meet Jim Griffiths, then Opposition front-bench spokesman on Commonwealth and Colonial affairs, and Arthur Creech Jones at the House of Commons. Both had formerly been Colonial Secretaries in Labour governments. They were enormously impressed by Nyerere's quietly sincere demeanour, Griffiths in particular, being a warm-hearted man, showing a most fatherly affection towards the young man. He was then introduced to the Labour Party's group of MPs especially interested in colonial affairs and explained to them the aims and problems of his party. He was promised all possible support and left Britain with his confidence considerably augmented. He needed all the self-confidence he could muster, for on his arrival back home he was immediately faced by a severe personal predicament.

8

Nyerere's Battle with the Governor

Between 1954 and 1955 Nyerere was caught in a dilemma. He had been trained as a teacher and was very conscious of the Tanganyikan money which had been spent for this purpose. He liked teaching and believed that the profession had a high social value for the development of his people. He therefore felt it to be wrong to desert his pupils as he had to do when he visited New York. Yet he could not blind himself to the special contribution he had discovered he could make to the political progress of the country. He was quite sincere in telling Father Walsh that he hoped that TANU would find someone else to attend the Trusteeship Council so that he would not have to neglect his students; but he could not escape from the fact that he alone was capable of presenting the TANU case to its best advantage.

I know how troubled Julius was by this dilemma, for he asked for my advice in a letter and we discussed it during his visit to London. Father Walsh had gently suggested to him before he left for New York that he might soon have to give up teaching to become a full-time politician. His headmaster was becoming nervous because the governor had made it plain to the Catholic priests that he objected to any of their teachers participating in politics so long as the government was paying their salaries.

As soon as he returned home from his New York and London visits Nyerere faced this awkward situation and decided that he must resign from his teaching post. He did not want to cause any more embarrassment to his church or its school; and he agreed that his headmaster was reasonable in suggesting that he must choose between the two careers. So, rather more suddenly than he had anticipated, he found himself without a job or salary. He knew that TANU could not afford to maintain him as yet. So he had to find the means of providing for himself and his family.

Nyerere's reaction to this situation was characteristic. Whenever he has needed spiritual or emotional sustenance he has turned to the peasant communities. On this occasion he took Maria and their children to the house in Zanakiland which he had built before their marriage. It had been suggested that he might be employed by the Shell Oil Company and also that he could have the post of editor of a Catholic newspaper. But neither would have allowed him the time or flexibility to determine his next moves in the political chess match in which he was now engaged with the governor.

Nyerere had now reached another crossroads. After the exhausting experiences of the past two years he needed time for reflection, a pause before determining the next stage of his strategy and the proper role for himself in it. He had not lost the instincts of the scholar – in fact, he never has lost them – and personally would still have been pleased if an alternative leader had appeared, leaving him to read, write and philosophise. He was fortunate in finding employment which allowed him to indulge in these contemplative exercises for a few months.

It was the Catholic church which again came to Nyerere's rescue. He was offered employment by the Maryknoll Fathers in Musoma. They asked him to teach his tribal language, Ki-Zanaki, to Father Wille who was to establish a new mission in Zanakiland. He was also to translate some church readings into his language.

Julius eagerly accepted this offer. He moved to Musoma, where he stayed with his old friend, Oswald Marwa. All day he spent teaching Father Wille who was amazed and exhausted by his intellectual energy. Then they would talk about the future of the country and Nyerere was able to clarify his own mind by defining his ideas to his sympathetic pupil. He would spend the evenings in translation, preparing a reading from the Gospels for each Sunday of the year. Meanwhile he took the opportunity to study Gandhi's writings on non-violent resistance techniques.

These occupations suited this stage of Nyerere's life perfectly. He had not contracted out of the political battle. Indeed, he held a number of TANU meetings in the district in which he both continued to stress the single objective of uhuru and to insist that Europeans and Asians who accepted the democratic system would be welcome to stay after independence. Nor had the government forgotten about him. Marwa was an assistant district officer; he was asked to order Nyerere to report to him regularly! Apparently the official who gave the instruction did not know that the Nyerere family were Marwa's guests.

But during this period Julius was able to step outside the limelight for the first time since his return from Edinburgh. Fame, adulation and the constant pressures of administration, organising, travelling and speaking were foreign to the young man's nature. They left no time for contemplation. He needed the opportunity to re-charge his intellectual and emotional batteries. He found it amongst his own people.

One small incident proves that Nyerere was now aware that his destiny lay inexorably in public life. Recognising the implacable hostility he had aroused in the governor and his administrators and knowing what was happening in other parts of the continent, he believed that the time would come when he would be sent to prison. He was concerned as to what would happen to Maria and the children in that event. So he borrowed money from Father Wille to pay Marwa to put a corrugated iron roof on his house. The thatched-grass roof with which it had been built would need repairing constantly; he feared that this might cause difficulties for his wife.

Nyerere has always firmly believed in team co-operation in politics, rather than personal, individual charisma. The proof of his success in founding TANU on this foundation was shown in the fact that his party did not stagnate during his absence. Indeed, it grew rapidly.

I witnessed evidence of the effect which the party now had on the ordinary people. During our talks in London in March I had promised Nyerere that, as soon as possible, I would visit Tanganyika in order to give some assistance to his new party. The opportunity arose when I was deputed by the Labour Party to make a tour of Africa, the main purpose of which was to report on the situation regarding Seretse Khama, then exiled from his home in Bechuanaland. I wrote to Nyerere, saying that if it was of any use to him I could make a short stop in Dar es Salaam en route to southern Africa. He immediately welcomed the suggestion.

When I arrived at Dar es Salaam I was astonished to find a large welcoming crowd, most of them dressed in the TANU green shirts and blouses. To be honest, I had expected the party to be nothing more than a small group of dedicated enthusiasts who would quietly discuss tactics with me in a small back room or perhaps in a hastily rented schoolroom. That night I did, indeed, meet the small central committee in the Arnouto-glou Community Centre. But the following day, on the vast, sandy palm-fringed expanse of Mnazi Moja (now a national freedom memorial park) I was called on to speak to a crowd variously estimated between twenty and forty thousand. This vast throng of men in long white gowns and white plant-pot hats, veiled women in black biu biu, with a sprinkling of Asians and Europeans, had answered the TANU call to a public meeting. They had come from hundreds of miles around the capital. I met one old man of eighty-five who had travelled from Rufiji, 130 miles away, and a doctor from Tukuyu who had taken five days to reach Dar es Salaam.

The significance of this personal experience is that it occurred during Nyerere's absence. It was held on 1 June 1955, when he had been away from the capital for two months. Yet TANU was still less than a year old. Once could hardly have more dramatic evidence of both the tremendous popular appeal of the party or of the wide organisational foundations which had been built independently of its leader's presence.

One further curious feature of this event throws some light on the ambivalence of the governor and his officials. Some years later I was told on first-hand authority that in his despatch to the Colonial Office on the event Governor Twining had commented that he believed that my visit and the mass meeting had given TANU a new self-confidence. Yet immediately after the meeting had been held, Mnazi Moja was banned as a meeting place by the government!

By this time some of TANU's leaders in Dar es Salaam were becoming anxious about Nyerere. They sent Oscar Kambona to visit him with some money lest he were in need. Kambona returned to the capital soon afterwards, astonishing the central committee by bringing back much more money that he had taken with him. He had travelled on from Musoma by lake steamer to Bukoba where the local TANU branch presented him with a large sum for the party. Whilst in Musoma Kambona and Nyerere had also held a TANU meeting. But the news that most pleased the leaders in Dar es Salaam was that Nyerere had promised to return to them in two to three months.

During Nyerere's sojourn in the north TANU had another accretion to its strength. Tom Mboya was now becoming the foremost trade unionist in east Africa. The young Luo from west Kenya had spent some time in Ruskin College, Oxford, had been coached by the British TUC and Labour Party and then been taken up by the American trade union movement. He returned to Kenya in 1955 and, with the assistance of the International Confederation of Free Trade Unions, began to resuscitate the trade unions of his country. In July of that year he visited Dar es Salaam and met Rashidi Kawawa. At that time Tanganyika's few unions were fragmented and mostly organised on a localised basis. Kawawa learnt the technique of national organisation from Mboya and put it into practice in his own country. A Tanganyika Federation of Labour was established in October, with Kawawa as its first secretary-general. The following year he resigned from the civil service, freeing himself to join TANU. A series of strikes ensued which led Kawawa to visit the ICFTU headquarters in Brussels and the TUC in London. He was quickly becoming a fully fledged trade unionist. His leadership of the trade union movement in Tanganyika and his membership of TANU brought the party a wider influence, although it was also to raise problems of divided interest.

It was during Nyerere's absence from Dar es Salaam also that the newly constituted legislative council met for the first time. This was convened under a new multi-racial parity constitution which allocated ten seats to each of the racial groups, African, Asian and European. The government retained its majority by increasing its official members to thirty-one. The fact that 98 per cent of the population was African was not at this time considered inconsistent with the constitutional provisions.

Nyerere himself recognised that the new constitution marked a decided advance on previous arrangements. He would have liked at least the Dar es Salaam seats to be elective instead of being filled by the government's nominees. But where he and the governor differed most profoundly was in the length of time this interim constitution should last. The governor made no secret of the fact that he expected it to survive for many years in order to give Africans a long period in which to gain political experience. Nyerere considered it to be a very temporary arrangement. He contended that elections should be introduced quickly and that the African community should gradually see their numbers reflected in greater representation.

Despite his tacit acceptance of the new parity representation as a temporary expedient, Nyerere was greatly angered by the application of the same principle shortly afterwards to the division of a sum obtained from the confiscation of German assets. The governor announced that this would be divided three ways, an equal amount to be allocated to the education of the three races. This infuriated Nyerere by its unfairness, especially as African education had always suffered in comparison with the amounts spent on the education of the small European community. He made his trenchant criticism known, which angered Governor Twining even more as his decision was exposed as not only unfair but ridiculous.

Nyerere returned to Dar es Salaam in October. He had refreshed his spirit by living amongst his own people again, listening to them, realising what they were seeking. He now recognised that his role must be to organise the people to demand, secure and then use wisely their own government. This meant that he must devote himself to TANU, building it into a party based on the single objective of independence, but in such a way that independence could be used to change society so as to give the ordinary people the chance of a better life.

He had not yet solved the problem of how to make an income for himself and his family whilst he conducted his political work. When they returned to the capital Julius and Maria found a small house which was also used as a general shop. Maria took charge of it, selling various goods like flour, matches, paraffin, soap, bread, oil and the like to neighbours. In addition she began to knit a variety of woollen garments for sale. The Nyereres' family life was always simple, but for some years they had difficulty in providing regularly for even their basic needs.

The next year was one of intense organisation for Nyerere. It was too early yet to expect all his followers to understand his sophisticated attitude, nor to accept that uhuru was an objective to be achieved by patient effort. Some of the party members, especially in areas far from the capital, began to act as though they had already replaced the government. They even held their own courts. Twining and his administration were just, taking action against breaches of the law, but never banning the party nationally on account of the actions of a few of its members.

Nor was uhuru the sole immediate attraction of the party. It was essential at this stage of political organisation for TANU to use every grievance to swell its ranks. Thus it found itself supported by the ruling family of the Fipa trying to stave off the claims of a young, educated group of Catholics; by the enlightened radicals of the Kilimanjaro areas; by a Muslim minority group in Bukoba which believed itself persecuted; by the Sukumaland elite, using popular resentment against agricultural regulations to campaign against the power of the chiefs.

It was this multiplicity of motives and the lack of general understanding of political realities which made it essential for Nyerere continually to tour the country. He travelled in a Land-Rover, which became famous throughout the country. Before long he became the focus of a mass adulation which never pleased him. But he was persuaded by some of his sympathisers, white as well as black, that he must pay this price of political mobilisation.

On his return to Dar es Salaam from Musoma, Nyerere was faced by the loss of two of his most valuable lieutenants. Denis Phombeah had departed for Yugoslavia in July, much to the chagrin of Father Walsh. But when I had discussed the situation with the Father, he told me that he could not stand in the young man's way when he had a chance of a scholarship, for there were no British scholarships to offer him as an alternative. In fact, Phombeah only spent a few months in Belgrade. At the end of the year he was given a scholarship to Fircroft College in Birmingham.

Oscar Kambona was also offered a chance to study overseas, this time by the Tanganyika government. He was reluctant to accept it as it meant that he would be absent from the country for four years and he believed that the offer was Twining's method of undermining TANU. It is evidence of Nyerere's outlook at this time that he urged Kambona to go to London as independence was a long way off and he would be better able to serve his country if he had acquired further education.

The loss of these two important officials did not cripple the party. Nyerere was extraordinarily fortunate in the personnel of the team which he led. Steven Mhando, who replaced Kambona as organising secretary, was an unfortunate exception, having to be dismissed for profligate expenditure after about a year. But Nyerere found two stalwarts in Bibi Titi Mohamed and Elias Kisenge. I met Bibi Titi during my visit to Dar es Salaam in June 1955 and happened to mention the lack of women members of TANU, a universal weakness of all African nationalist parties in their early years. She was a woman of enormous energy; within four months she had recruited 5,000 members for her Women's Section; three months later there were more women than men members. Kisenge was another pupil from Tabora and had worked in the administration in the north.

He was also a member of the TAGSA but resigned from his job to become a district secretary of TANU in his home Pare territory. Having organised a strong branch there he moved to Tanga to repeat the process. In October 1956 he was appointed deputy organising secretary of the party, acting for Kambona during his absence.

Despite his own difficulties, Nyerere's party was growing rapidly, with most of the best African leaders coming to his assistance. He still sometimes encountered obstruction from chiefs, who felt their influence being undermined by the new young politicians, or were persuaded by the administration to oppose TANU; but usually the enthusiasm of their own people taught them that it was futile to try and halt the new movement. At the end of 1955 came a move which stimulated the progress of the party still faster.

It was certainly not the intention of Governor Twining to assist Nyerere or TANU when he instigated the formation of a rival party. Yet this was the consequence of his action. The new party was based broadly on the principles of the Capricorn Society, founded by David Stirling to preserve the concept of multi-racialism. It was named the United Tanganyika Party and secured the services of a British Conservative Party former organiser. It made great play of the fact that its membership was multiracial – Makwaia was a member – whereas TANU was confined to Africans.

Yet it was easy for Nyerere to point out that this concept of multiracialism would leave the whites in control for many years, that even blatant colour bars would only be gradually removed. Nyerere could not tolerate the continuation of discrimination, which he regarded as unChristian and an affront to the dignity of man. He was quite prepared to co-operate in an evolution towards independence, but would not admit the right of the whites to determine the pace.

The UTP, like so many white-dominated parties in post-war Africa, was born too late. If it had challenged colonial power at its height, it might have attracted admiration and support from the Africans. As it was only formed after TANU had shown its strength, when colonialism was in decline, it was regarded as irrelevant at best, at worst as a last-ditch attempt to retain white political influence.

Nevertheless, the UTP was just what Nyerere needed at that time. By presenting a challenge to TANU it forced his party's officers to increase recruiting and helped him to insist on discipline. Its appearance sharpened the political atmosphere, providing TANU with a rival which forced its leaders to mobilise all their resources, to devise those political tactics essential to combat a competitor.

From the end of 1955 to mid-1958 the future of Tanganyika was being determined by a gladiatorial contest between Twining and Nyerere. This was not of Nyerere's choosing. He was fighting the colonial system to transform it into self-government by Tanganyika's own inhabitants. The Governor, however, identified himself personally with the Empire. Consequently he felt Nyerere's attacks to be an assault on himself and his authority. If he had been a different sort of man he might have imitated the policy of Charles Arden-Clarke, Governor of the Gold Coast, who worked with Nkrumah to evolve self-government amicably, with careful preparation. Nyerere would have welcomed this attitude as warmly as Nkrumah; but Twining could not play that role.

Nyerere saw three strings in his bow. He had so to mobilise his own people as to mount an irresistible challenge to the governor's administration, forcing political changes which would ensure progressive representation for his own people. At the same time, because Tanganyika was a Trust Territory, he could use arguments at the United Nations to enlist support there for his demands. Yet he knew that, although United Nations' pressure could be useful, his main focus of overseas persuasion must be in Britain. British governments might pay lip-service to their responsibilities at the UN; but they always insisted that the final authority lay with them. Therefore Nyerere realised that he had to mobilise influential opinion in London to affect final decisions. By this means he would catch the colonial administration in a pincer movement between his own people and his supporters in Britain.

Nyerere had this strategy in mind when in 1956 he accepted an invitation from the Maryknoll Fathers to visit America for a second time to give some lectures and appear on television. Not only would this enable him to appeal to a wider section of the American public and make some money to repay his debts, but it would also allow him to appear before the Fourth Committee of the UN when Tanganyikan issues were discussed. But, equally if not more important, it gave him the opportunity to spend some time in Britain, exerting his influence on government thinking.

He arrived in Britain in September 1956. It was a fateful season, for this was the autumn of Suez. The British political atmosphere was charged with electricity. Nye Bevan and Hugh Gaitskell thundered against the government's duplicity and the ineffectual imperial nostalgia of its leaders. Anthony Eden shuffled and prevaricated. By the end of the year it could be seen that the days of the mighty British Empire, with its gunboat diplomacy, were finished.

Nyerere observed these momentous events in British history; but he had come for another purpose. Earlier in the year Twining had announced that the racial parity system would continue, but that some elections would be introduced in about two years' time. Nyerere had immediately protested that the committee to recommend electoral provisions was drawn from the existing legislative council, almost all of whose members had joined the UTP. In other words, one party was to be allowed to determine electoral arrangements for elections in which it would participate.

On his arrival in Britain Nyerere put this case to leading members of the Labour Party. He stressed that whilst TANU stood for equal rights for all men, the UTP qualified this by proposing that such rights be reserved for only 'civilised' men. He further emphasised this point in a memorandum which he submitted to the Labour Party. It included these words: 'Tanu's objective is democracy in Tanganyika under conditions in which the race of an individual is irrelevant to his participation in political activity. Our present proposals are designed as a stepping stone to this objective.'

His visit coincided with the Labour Party's annual conference. In that year it was held in Blackpool, the windy, raucous, honestly vulgar seaside Mecca of working-class holiday-makers in the north-west of England. Julius came to watch the conference in action. Blackpool is also famous for its illuminations, which draw hundreds of thousands of sightseers from all over the country. They are strung along the five miles of promenade, overlooking the sea shore. Julius insisted on seeing them all. Not for him the comfortable ride in the promenade tramcar. He must walk in the midst of the slowly shuffling crowd down to the south shore and back again. Not only was he fascinated by the illuminated tableaux, side-shows and amusement arcades; he loved to be amongst people, listening with affection to the broad Lancashire accents of miners, mill-girls, factory-workers, railwaymen, postmen, their wives, children, sweethearts, parents and grandparents. I could not help but contrast his natural, humanistic love of these ordinary British people with the superior attitudes I had recently heard adopted by some members of the Labour Party's Executive at the prospect of having to attend the conference in 'vulgar' Blackpool.

He listened to all the sessions of conference, held in the Winter Gardens. There he continued to impress Labour leaders and witnessed the background to the organisation of such a huge assembly. He had his photograph taken with Hugh Gaitskell and Jim Griffiths by the *Daily Herald*, useful evidence of his standing with leading British politicians. He also attended some of the 'fringe' meetings held in the evenings. At one evening meeting, officially organised by the Party Executive, he was a main speaker, along with Jim Griffiths, the Party's Deputy Leader, and Nye Bevan, the official front-bench spokesman on Commonwealth and Colonial Affairs. The meeting was a huge success, the hall completely full, Nyerere being received with great warmth. His quietly reasonable sincerity could charm and impress a British audience as effectively as an African.

After the week's conference Nyerere returned to London. In fact, following his exertions during the week he slept throughout the journey in the back of a Mini driven by a mutual friend of ours. He then spent a little time looking at the party's grass-roots' organisation in the south of England. During this time he stayed for a few days with Ron Hayward, then southern regional organiser, now general-secretary of the Labour Party. At this time organisation seemed all-important to him. He quietly observed ward and constituency meetings, office arrangements, party recruiting, financial supervision, propaganda planning. Everyone with whom he came into contact was impressed by his quietude, his desire to study every detail, his unfailing good humour and his dedication to the cause of his own people.

Another objective of his visit to London was to secure greater opportunities for Tanganyikans to obtain higher education in Britain. Already Denis Phombeah was in Birmingham and Oscar Kambona in London. He had several talks about this with Nye Bevan, who promised to help him.

Nyerere then travelled by ship to New York, where he was met by Maryknoll Fathers, some of whom had served in Tanganyika. He lectured in Washington, Chicago, Boston and New York and also appeared on a television show. It was at this time that he met Maida Springer, an organiser of the powerful Ladies' Garment Workers' Union, who gave him hospitality in New York. The following year she went to Tanganyika with a trade union mission, helping the young trade union movement there. It was with Maida Springer that Nyerere first saw something of the lives of American blacks. He noted that materially they were much more prosperous than his own people; yet, as a minority in a rich, white man's country, were faced by far greater problems in their search for emancipation.

In December Nyerere again appeared before the United Nations, this time at its Fourth Committee. As in the previous year, delegates were impressed by his moderation. He reiterated the demands he had made in London, progress towards a democratic state (which implied African control as the majority community), non-racialism instead of multi-racialism and voting rights for all adults. One significant change had been made in his presentation compared with that of 1955; whereas then he had called for independence to be granted in twenty-five years, this time he talked of it in about ten years' time. Such was the degree of change produced by TANU's efforts over the ensuing twenty-two months.

The Fourth Committee accepted the central principle of Nyerere's submission, as did the General Assembly when it came to vote. They called on Britain to state her policy towards Tanganyika and to include in it, in accordance with the terms of the Trusteeship system, the principle that 'the Territory shall be guided towards self-government or independence and shall become a democratic State in which all inhabitants have equal rights'.

Twining's government took the criticisms made by Nyerere at the UN so seriously that it published a leaflet refuting them. Apparently neither Twining nor his colonial administrators realised that this was bound to raise Nyerere's prestige still higher. The ordinary African reasoned that if the governor and his government were so concerned about this young man he must be important. They therefore listened to him with increased respect, providing further impetus for TANU's recruiting campaign.

The main English-language newspaper, the *Tanganyika Standard*, expressed approval of Nyerere's 'broadening attitude' in his speech to the Fourth Committee, and especially commended his recognition that all inhabitants were entitled to their rights. Yet when the UN resolution was published the European community loudly protested. It adopted the tactic which was to be increasingly employed against him over the next few years – that he and his party represented only a small minority of Africans, that the chiefs, elders, other African leaders and their followers held different opinions. With hindsight it is possible to regard this tactic as the last resort against TANU's leadership of a rising tide of nationalism.

The year 1957 witnessed the climax of the battle between Twining and Nyerere. The Governor used a variety of tactics, from coercion to blandishment. He detested the appearance of political struggle in his territory, believing that if he could only force or entice Nyerere away from his chosen course, Tanganyikans would revert to their earlier docile ways, content to leave Mother Britain to decide what was best.

Nyerere remained single-minded. Neither threats nor flattery affected him. He passionately believed in his people's right to freedom and was convinced that this could only be achieved through the creation of an independent state in which they would control every aspect of their own society. At the same time, his belief in freedom extended to all inhabitants of Tanganyika, irrespective of race. So that, whilst he abhorred the privileges which the colonial government had accorded to the tiny minorities of Europeans and Asians, he neither wished to force them out of his country nor to deprive them of their personal rights. He simply insisted that if they wished to stay, they must regard themselves as no more than equal to other citizens.

The government assault began almost as soon as Nyerere had returned from America. In January 1957 the registration of TANU's Korogwe branch was rescinded because one of its members had been convicted of sedition. Nyerere never criticised the government for applying the law against individuals who broke it; but he was infuriated when the error of an individual was vented on the organisation itself.

In the same month the government banned the wearing of all political uniforms, which was construed as another method of preventing TANU from organising its members and giving them a sense of party and national pride. The government's attack mounted. Nyerere was refused permission to hold two open-air meetings; a ban was placed on all TANU-organised public gatherings; several party branches were refused registration; and Nyerere was prohibited from entering Tanga province.

Yet, paradoxically, these government assaults aided the TANU cause. They strengthened the resolve of party members and, by proving that the government was trying to undermine African nationalism, they provoked a determination among the more resolute Africans to support the party. Moreover, Nyerere had become a past-master of turning adversity to advantage. As public gatherings were prohibited, but meetings of party members still legal, he spent the time in talking with people in their own homes and villages. This grass-roots' approach was always both pleasureable to Nyerere and advantageous to understanding within the party. Meanwhile, the government's renewed hostility to TANU could always be used as useful propaganda overseas. In July the Colonial Secretary had to answer several critical questions about it in the House of Commons. He declared that TANU 'had built up a general attitude of contempt for authority and a spirit of anarchy'. Dissatisfied with this statement and briefed by Nyerere, the National Executive and the Parliamentary Committee of the Labour Party sent a joint deputation, consisting of Nye Bevan and Arthur Skeffington, to make representations to the Colonial Secretary on the situation in Tanganyika. Nyerere had cards to play in London and New York as well as in Dar es Salaam. This hardly endeared him to Twining, who considered that authority in London should be his own trump card.

It was in 1957 also that a change in the constitution was agreed which could only sharpen the political conflict. The Legislative Council decided that in future its representative members should be elected. The constituencies were to be divided into two groups, elections taking place for the first group in September 1958 and for the second twelve months later. The parity system of equal members from each race was to be continued, with each voter compelled to use three votes in treble-member constituencies. Those eligible to vote had to satisfy certain qualifications based on education, income, office holding, residence or age.

TANU opposed the continuation of the parity system, by which the minority communities were enabled to secure an equal number of representatives to the majority Africans. It also strongly criticised the electoral provisions. Whilst it approved of a common roll instead of separate racial rolls, it pointed out that the compulsion for every voter to use three votes would result in electors being compelled to vote for candidates they did not support and perhaps had never heard of. What was going to be crucial to the political future of the country, however, was whether TANU would decide to participate in or to boycott an electoral system which it condemned.

It was at this stage that Twining made his final effort to draw Nyerere into his patronage. The Governor dissolved the Legislative Council in June 1957 and appointed a new one. He appointed Nyerere as a representative member for Dar es Salaam, at the same time nominating Rashidi Kawawa, then general-secretary of the trade union movement, as a member representing general interests.

Whether the Governor genuinely believed that he could thereby tame the young nationalist leader is a matter for conjecture. If he did, he was soon disappointed. Nyerere found himself in a constant minority amongst supporters of the government. Before the end of the year, following a debate on the electoral provisions in which his motion to drop the three-vote rule was defeated, he resigned. According to his statement, 'The Government has consistently, and for the most unconvincing reasons, rejected every proposal that I have made in the Legislative Council. I came to the Council expecting a little of the spirit of give and take. That spirit is not there . . .' He persuaded other TANU members and supporters to continue as members of the council; the party still needed the opportunity to air its criticisms and policies; but his tasks lay elsewhere.

It was typical of Nyerere that when, in July, I paid a short visit to the United States en route to the West Indies, he got up early in the morning to meet me. He and Maida Springer had to spend several hours waiting at what was then Idlewild Airport in New York as my plane was late. We then drove to Maida's house in Brooklyn to talk for the rest of the day.

In the stifling heat of a New York summer, we ate lunch in the backyard whilst Julius told me of his third appearance before the United Nations. He had again appealed to the British government for a simple statement that his country was to be developed as a primarily African state, that Africans be given half the seats in the Legislative Council and that adult suffrage be substituted for the qualified franchise. The main attack on Nyerere made by the government delegation, led by John Fletcher-Cooke, was that he was a racialist agitator. The multi-racial policy of the UTP was praised, with snide references to the exclusively African membership of TANU. It was also suggested that many TANU members wanted to drive non-Africans out of the country, that they opposed agricultural reforms and usurped the authority of government. The whole case was designed to give the impression that, however rational Nyerere might appear in New York, his organisation was racialist, disruptive and potentially violent.

Fletcher-Cooke failed in this objective. Some years later he told me that he had never met Nyerere before their encounter in New York as he had only been posted to Tanganyika a few months previously. But Nyerere related to me that afternoon that the government attack had failed not so much because Fletcher-Cooke was obviously speaking to a prepared brief which he did not really understand, but for two further reasons.

The first was that the British government representative on the Trusteeship Council was Sir Andrew Cohen. Cohen had been governor of Uganda, where he made the mistake of creating a situation in which he felt that he had to deport the Kabaka. But Cohen was a genuine liberal in colonial affairs. His mistakes were made from liberal motives. He reached an impasse with the Kabaka because he was trying to introduce democratic processes into traditionally feudalistic Buganda. He participated in the scheme for central African federation because he mistakenly believed that racial 'partnership' was feasible in the three countries and that Africans would progress only if economic development could be secured.

Cohen had been appointed as governor of Uganda as the last act of Jim Griffiths when he left the Colonial Office in 1951. The Conservative government which took office after the election of that year was highly suspicious of his liberal tendencies. So when he had completed his term in Uganda they tried to bury him at the United Nations where he would have to follow the briefs which they composed.

Cohen resented this appointment and the motive behind it. Yet he faithfully carried out his mandate as a civil servant. But his own judgement could not be entirely submerged beneath Colonial Office instructions. So when he came to speak about British policy in Tanganyika he did so in a positive rather than an intransigent manner. He drew from Britain's record, the UN Charter and the Trusteeship Agreement authority to declare that Tanganyika would be developed democratically. That implied that, as Africans formed the vast majority of the population, their participation in every aspect of national life would steadily increase. He also added that it was British policy to build a non-racial rather than a multi-racial society.

Nyerere told me that Cohen's words had satisfied him on the central issue, but that he feared that Cohen did not determine policy and he wondered whether these words fully represented the policy of the British government. He was right to feel suspicious. For Cohen told me himself later that he had been criticised for expressing his own interpretation, the sense of which, if not the actual words, were more in accord with Nyerere's demands than either the British government or Twining's administration would have wished.

The second factor was the attitude taken by Thomas Marealle, Paramount Chief of the Chagga. It had been expected that Marealle would take the government attitude, having been one of Twining's select circle.

But in fact his speech differed very little from that of Nyerere. He criticised the outlook of many Europeans in Tanganyika and warned them that they would have to recognise that the country would become primarily an African state. He expected independence to arrive in between ten and fifteen years.

Marealle's approach cut the ground from under the feet of those who were trying to divide the chiefs from the nationalists. Together with Cohen's conciliatory attitude it gave Nyerere sufficient cause for hope to prevent a confrontation.

He had complained about the government's repressive measures against TANU and himself and denied that he had ever made inflammatory speeches, which was the reason given by the government for banning his meetings. He also met directly the suggestion that his was a racialist party whilst the UTP was multi-racialist. In his counter-attack he was aided by the fact that a few months earlier TANU had adopted a British Labour Party document as its own policy. This was the policy statement entitled 'The Plural Society', one of a series of colonial policy documents issued at this time laying down the Labour Party's policies for meeting the major colonial problems of the time. 'The Plural Society' was addressed to the difficulties of transforming a society composed of different racial communities into a fully democratic society. It was based on an evolutionary approach, but culminating in unrestricted democracy. Nyerere and TANU fully concurred with its programme, including the possibility of providing special safeguards for minorities during the early period of independence. This made nonsense of the accusation that Nyerere or his party were tainted with racialism.

Nyerere told me that it had been agreed that after the elections a committee was to be set up to examine further constitutional advance. He seemed satisfied that events were still moving his way, although, wisely, he realised that there were several difficult hurdles to cross. He also told me that his party would participate in the elections, even though they disapproved of the methods of conducting them, and that he had informed the Trusteeship Council of this. His decision was apparently not reported in Tanganyika, which was to become very important at the next TANU conference, as we shall see.

We spent the rest of that sweltering day discussing the organisation of TANU and particularly of the administrative structure, which he considered its main weakness as membership was rising so rapidly. It was also apparent to him that there was always a danger of things going wrong when he was away. Of the past nine months he had been abroad for five. In his absence the government often intensified its repressive measures, whilst some of the party officers tended to take the law into their own hands. When we parted he was flying straight back to London to meet

Bevan and Skeffington who were due to see the Colonial Secretary on his behalf the following afternoon.

It should be remembered that this was 1957. In March of that year the Gold Coast had gained its independence as the sovereign state of Ghana with Kwame Nkrumah at its head. This event made a tremendous impression throughout Africa. It was the first time that any British colony in the continent had broken the colonial yoke and achieved full sovereignty. (The case of The Sudan was obviously different.) The fact that Morocco and Tunisia had achieved their independence from France in 1956 never had the same impact, for the Magreb and north Africa generally had few links at this time with countries south of the Sahara.

The independence of Ghana immediately raised urgent questions for all the inhabitants of the rest of the continent. Black, brown and white all wondered whether this should be considered as a precedent for colonial Africa or whether there were special circumstances making Ghana unique. West Africa found little difficulty in answering this question, but had no European settler community to complicate it. Even so, French West Africa took longer to recognise the implications. In the centre and south white determination to hold on to power and privilege was strengthened by added fear. In the east the whites still hoped to retain their position in Kenya, in Uganda it seemed obvious that only continued African disunity would retard independence, whilst in Tanganyika African morale was enormously raised, with increasing numbers of whites reconciled to the inevitable.

Yet there were those in positions of power who still refused to recognise that independence under African government had now appeared on the horizon. Moreover, there were Africans who could not grasp the perspective of history. Nyerere had to deal with both. If either defeated him bloodshed would become unavoidable.

The extent to which Twining's policies were controlled from the Colonial Office is still a matter of conjecture. Certainly I know that his successor became very angry with the amount of interference he suffered from the Colonial Secretary. And the motivation of Whitehall intervention in Tanganyikan affairs reflected the first important link between the problems of Nyerere and Kaunda.

To be frank, neither the Colonial Office nor British members of parliament were really concerned with Tanganyika. It was a very poor country, with few British settlers and no prospect of becoming important to any aspect of British policy. Thus much of their policy discussions on the territory concerned not the future of Tanganyika itself, but its effects on other territories which interested them more. The first was Kenya; but by the late 1950s this was becoming of less moment. Mau Mau had exposed the weakness of the Kenyan settlers. Unless the British government were prepared to station its forces permanently in the country, it had become obvious that Kenya could never become a white-ruled state. The second, and much more important, was the Central African Federation.

By the mid-1950s the Federation had become the corner-stone of British Conservative policy towards multi-racial Africa. Its fate was considered to be the major determinant in the future of all southern Africa, with overtones extending to Kenya. Britain's political and economic establishment, in alliance with the major economic forces in central and southern Africa, believed that it had discovered a new elixir in the magic word 'partnership'. This would allow it to preserve sufficient political power for the white community to develop central Africa along traditional Western capitalist lines to the mutual benefit of investors and settlers, but without the bitterness provoked by open apartheid. If this policy succeeded, it might attract South Africa to modify its ideology and provide a secure base from which to influence black governments farther north.

The Federation, therefore, formed a crucial focus for all British policy throughout east, central and South Africa. Everything else was subordinate and, if necessary, must be sacrified to the success of the Federation. One of these extraneous considerations was Tanganyika. As political momentum accelerated there it was feared in Whitehall and amongst the Federation's closest friends in Westminster that this might infect the Federation. Already African opposition to the Federation refused to wither away in the Rhodesias and Nyasaland. Suspicion mounted that events in Tanganyika were stimulating this opposition, that the nationalists of central Africa were drawing encouragement from the success of TANU, that the leaders of the two nationalist groups were forging links between their movements.

The stake in the success of Federation was inherited from Oliver Lyttleton by Alan Lennox-Boyd. He accepted it enthusiastically, using it as the foundation stone of his policy towards multi-racial Africa. Lennox-Boyd was really a very simple character. He showed no evidence of personal racialist feelings. In fact, on one occasion he offered the use of his yacht to Nyerere (he had been told that the young African needed a few days' rest). He was accustomed to live amongst the wealthy and simply assumed that money provided entitlement to political authority. As it was the whites of central Africa who owned the wealth and seemed most likely to increase it in that area, it appeared natural to him that their control should be entrenched.

In October 1957 Lennox-Boyd visited Tanganyika. His views on the situation there can best be gleaned from his own words. He declared that the constitutional development of the country was 'if anything in danger of being too rapid rather than too slow'; that Britain had no intention of handing over her trust to 'irresponsible people' or 'to any government under which responsible people of all races in Tanganyika would not feel secure'. Lennox-Boyd assumed that everyone would accept that 'responsible people' were those of any race with wealth, education or hereditary authority. As almost all such people were white, it was natural to protect their interests. But Lennox-Boyd visualised that progressively Africans would be added to them, as African society grew in the same direction as had that of Britain, with the emergence of a black middle class, rooted in property, bank balances and pensions, thus with a 'stake' in 'order'.

This attitude of Lennox-Boyd coincided with that of Twining. But the Colonial Secretary had a deeper motive than the governor. The opposition to federation of the Central African Congresses, especially those of Northern Rhodesia and Nyasaland, continued to threaten the white-dominated régime there. Lennox-Boyd realised that every success for Nyerere and his party strengthened the Congress movement. Whatever might be the consequences for Tanganyika, he was not prepared to jeopardise the Federation. Eighteen months later one of Lennox-Boyd's juniors was to assure Welensky's cabinet that progress towards independence in the colonial territories, including Tanganyika was being halted. In October 1957 Lennox-Boyd already had this clearly in his mind. He bluntly threatened that the British government would support any measures decided by Twining's administration 'to deal firmly with bodies that claim in some parts of the Territory to have assumed the function of government'.

Yet Tanganyika had moved too far along the road towards a constitutional transfer of power for a halt to be called without provoking serious dangers. Nye Bevan always used to advise colonial leaders that once representative opportunities had been gained, however imperfect, the British parliment would never allow their progress to full democracy to be halted. If the Tanganyikan government, under Colonial Office dictation, had been prepared to use force against those who protested against a curtailment of constitutional progress, a pause might have been imposed. But, as was to be seen later in Nyasaland and Northern Rhodesia, the British parliament would have ensured that the pause was only temporary. If the Africans had decided to boycott the electoral system which they considered fraudulent, there could have been disorder and consequent delay. But, despite Lennox-Boyd's inability to read history, the political momentum was now so strong that independence had become inevitable, with or without violence.

Nyerere, engrossed in day-to-day issues between himself and the government was not yet certain, but he was increasingly confident. Yet he had set his mind on gaining independence with a minimum of bitterness and without violence. He had to face his most crucial tests during the first half of 1958.

The first major issue was the decision whether or not TANU should contest the elections. It was not generally known that Nyerere had told the UN that he intended to participate. Most members of the party had become so hostile towards the electoral system, with its three-candidate constituencies, compulsory three votes and racial parity of members, that they assumed that the whole process would be boycotted. When TANU's annual conference met in Tabora in January 1958 this was the view of the vast majority of delegates. Led by Bhoke Munanka, virtually all the speakers took this line, embellishing their argument with the passionate denunciation of the electoral procedure they had learnt from Nyerere and TANU propaganda. The government's bannings of Nyerere and TANU branches, its blatant encouragement of the UTP, its attempts to use the chiefs against TANU and its opposition to all Nyerere's proposals in the legislative council, culminating in his resignation the previous month, all inflamed those attending the conference. Many accompanied their call for boycott with a demand for a general strike.

Yet Nyerere, though sharing all these sentiments about government tactics, had quietly thought out the issue of the elections. His reason led him to the opposite conclusion. He believed that if TANU remained aloof from the elections, the UTP would win all the seats. It would then have power to determine the pace and character of further constitutional advance. Meanwhile, TANU would be helpless to do more than protest. Above all, Nyerere feared that, whether or not a strike was held, such protests would almost certainly result in violence. This would be disastrous in itself, for people would be killed; it would also provide the government with further and more valid excuses to ban his party and decelerate political progress. Nyerere was not seeking the emotional satisfaction of denouncing his opponents or their tactics; he sought to build an African nation as quickly and surely as possible.

Nevertheless, convinced as he was that TANU should contest the elections, Nyerere knew that he faced a momentous task in persuading the conference. For it was largely due to his eloquence in denunciation of the electoral provisions that members of the party felt so bitterly hostile towards them. He realised that he would risk being called a traitor to the cause he had espoused, that some would suspect he had been bribed in some way by the government. Yet he did not flinch from the responsibility. He knew that he was fighting for his political life and ideals; that if he failed, he might well have to resign and leave public life, opening the door to those who preferred violence to reason to succeed him.

Nyerere made the closing speech at the conference. He followed Munanka who was completely opposed to participation. The vast majority of the delegates had already made up their minds that the elections must be boycotted. Nyerere first met the argument that if it participated TANU could only expect to win the ten African seats, therefore condemning itself to becoming a permanent minority. He argued that there were sufficient European and Asian supporters of TANU to hold out hopes of capturing all thirty seats. That would enable TANU to mount a two-pronged attack, from inside and outside the legislative council, to demand a new constitution. He could see the possibility that such tactics would bring self-government within a few months, followed shortly afterwards by full independence.

This was an appeal to reason against the emotional atmosphere which had gripped the conference. Nyerere followed it by relating his argument to a metaphor which he took, as he has frequently done, from a common African experience:

Imagine that you have a shamba and that in front of it there is a pond, with a lot of mud around it. If you want to harvest your crops and carry them out of the shamba you must step into the mud and dirty your feet. What would you prefer? To lose your crops and keep your feet clean? Or to harvest your crops and dirty your feet? Now think about what we want. We want that house in which Twining is now living. In order to get into it, we must dirty our feet by walking through the mud of an unfair election. What would you rather do? Keep your feet clean and not get the Twining house, or dirty your feet and get the Twining house?

Such logic, allied to shrewd political strategy, carried the day. The majority of the delegates were immediately won over from their previous convictions. Amidst an enthusiastic clamour it was resolved to contest the elections, to demand an increase in the number of unofficial members in the council, responsible government with a majority of elected members and ministers in 1959. TANU delegates worked off their emotions by declaring that if the government refused this demand, 'more positive action' would be considered.

This was probably the most direct challenge Nyerere had met to either his leadership or his policies. If his touch had been less sure he could have been driven from his office, his influence destroyed. His triumph proved the immense depth of his hold on the party. He lost Zuberi Mtemvu, who broke with TANU to form his own Tanganyika African Congress, standing for complete African control with no influence being granted to non-Africans. But very few TANU members defected.

Yet Nyerere's historic feat proved something else. It showed that the leader was in sophisticated strategy far in advance of his followers. This had been his personal success, not the result of teamwork or collective leadership. Nyerere had no desire to become a charismatic leader above all his colleagues in the style of an Nkrumah. The victory itself gave him cause for renewed concern about the need for increased political education, for the creation of a stronger team of leaders, that the mass of his followers should raise their awareness of the necessity to participate in decision-making.

During the next few months Nyerere had two main tasks. He had to try and tighten discipline in the party lest the temptation to intimidation in certain areas spill over into the violence which he realised could thwart constitutional progress. He had also to find Europeans and Asians sufficiently sympathetic to TANU's aims for the party to support them in the elections of September.

Interference with such government schemes as cattle dipping continued amongst certain party officials in the countryside. The Iringa branch had been closed on these grounds. Some African members of the UTP were also being intimidated by supporters of TANU. This was understandable in a country alight with political expectation, in which a new party was trying to block the nationalist advance. But TANU expelled those found guilty of interfering with agricultural reforms and Nyerere himself condemned intimidation, urging party members to act responsibly.

Yet it was impossible to prevent violence everywhere. The worst case was in Geita, in the Lake Province. The government was trying to introduce Europeans and Asians into district councils which previously had been confined to African members. Nyerere and Bomani had visited Geita in April, after the local TANU branch had been refused registration in the previous month. They were not allowed to hold a meeting. In May all TANU activities in the district were banned for six months. In July about a thousand African protesters camped in Mwanza, the provincial capital, for several days. The police used tear gas to disperse them and arrested their leaders. Here was clear evidence of a popular uprising against the imposition of multi-racialism on chiefs and people, demonstrating the degree of antagonism now prevalent between the administration and the ordinary African.

It was this kind of grievance which Nyerere exposed in his articles in the party newspaper, *Sauti ya TANU*. One of his editorial articles, however, created a situation in which the very violence he was trying to prevent could have broken out.

Writing at the end of May 1958, Nyerere again warned his followers against provocations to violence, which, he said, were a sign that the enemy knew he was losing the argument. He then went on to attack two district commissioners for falsely putting a chief on trial and trying to undermine TANU. He wrote, 'These same officials would have people committing perjury in court if only to vilify TANU. These same people who intimidate and punish innocence, cajole and reward crookery, have the temerity to invoke law and order.' The government prosecuted him for criminal libel.

This was an extremely rash action on the part of the administration. The government simply could not win. If it won the case Nyerere would become a martyr; if it lost, it would be considered that it had been beaten by Nyerere. It is true that Nyerere's choice of words was uncharacteristically harsh. But he was in the midst of an intense political struggle with a government he believed was using unfair tactics, which was determined that his party, however representative of the people, should not be allowed to gain political control. He had also been to Geita and was convinced that the local officials of the area were ignoring justice in their obsession with destroying TANU. Twining later tried to excuse the government's prosecution by claiming that it was the responsibility of the attorney-general, with whom the governor could not interfere. But it seems more likely that the action was that of a governor and government recognising their waning power in the struggle against Nyerere, employing desperate measures to avoid humiliating defeat by the young nationalist whom they had chosen to regard as the symbol of defiance to their authority.

The denouement of the struggle for independence had now been reached. The party was angry, some of its members eager for a violent confrontation. Many of the chiefs who supported TANU's nationalist objectives were under extreme pressure from the government. The unions had already tested their strength in a beer boycott against scab labour earlier in the year, cementing their alliance with TANU, which had supported them. The party felt that after Lennox-Boyd's intransigent words in Dar es Salaam and at Westminster, the British government was hostile to it and to its objectives. The strategy of moderation on detail combined with firmness on principle appeared to have failed. It seemed certain that within a few weeks the party leader would join that band of 'prison graduates' stretching from Gandhi and Nehru to Nkrumah, Kenyatta and Makarios. This would certainly light the beacon calling party and nationalist followers to arms. The future of Tanganyika for peace or war, the fate of constitutional transition from colonial rule to democratic independence throughout east and central Africa, appeared balanced on the judgement of an obscure magistrate in Dar es Salaam.

9

Struggle to Victory

That the 1958 crisis in Tanganyika was resolved without disaster was due to an accident of fate juxtaposed to the sensitive perception of two men. It was fate which decreed that Twining should come to the end of his term of office in June. If that had not been the case Nyerere's trial would almost certainly have provoked a confrontation between government and nationalists. The trial actually started, early in July, in the absence of a governor. But a new kind of man was on his way to take Twining's place.

When those of us in London concerned with African affairs heard that the government had appointed Sir Richard Turnbull to succeed Twining we were appalled. We knew that Turnbull had been chief secretary in Kenya during the height of the Mau Mau rebellion and had acquired a reputation for 'toughness'. This meant that he had been one of the hard-liners, determined to stamp out rebels rather than seek a political solution. If he were to see the situation in Tanganyika as similar and apply the same methods, all chance of peaceful devolution in that country would be finally destroyed.

I had a long talk with Turnbull in London before he left to take up his new appointment. To my surprise and gratification I found him to be a shy man, very anxious to learn anything which could help him to succeed in his difficult task. Others who talked to him at the same time found the same. So far as my advice was concerned, it consisted of a single point: 'Make friends with Nyerere.'

As soon as he arrived in Dar es Salaam Turnbull demonstrated that his administration and his personal attitude would be entirely different from those of his predecessor. He took his oath during the course of Nyerere's trial. He did not even wait until the trial was over. He invited Nyerere to Government House nine days after he had taken office, whilst the trial was still proceeding.

Nyerere appreciated this break with convention and the desire it revealed of the new governor's determination to co-operate with him. Turnbull's first words to Nyerere were prophetic: 'I am glad to meet you, Mr Nyerere. You and I have a great responsibility in this country.' The two men, both with an innate sense of shyness, felt that they could work together. The character of colonial government had suddenly undergone a radical change.

When the trial was over and Nyerere given the alternative of paying a £150 fine or spending six months in gaol, the young nationalist was able to reciprocate the governor's gesture. He had been determined to go to prison, believing that the charge was unfair and that the political situation demanded that he should not be seen to succumb to government coercion. Now he realised that Turnbull had inherited problems not of his own making. After talking to him Nyerere felt confident that the Twining era was ended. He therefore considered that it would be foolish to precipitate the crisis which must arise from his imprisonment, that it would be unfair to the new governor and destroy any chance of genuine co-operation with the new régime. Nyerere has always possessed a very strong strain of fairness, whether it concerns himself personally or others, including his opponents. To the astonishment of his supporters he decided to pay the fine and avoid imprisonment. Turnbull recognised the gesture as brave and generous. A new partnership between governor and party leader was thus forged. After that all TANU had to do was to demonstrate its national support; the governor had still to resist the braking power of the British government.

It only took three and a half years from Turnbull's appointment for Tanganyika to attain independence. The constitutional details have been recorded elsewhere, but certain features of the process were important to an understanding of Nyerere and significant for his future.

In the first batch of elections, held in September 1958, TANU had set itself the task of capturing all the African seats and indicating those Asian and European candidates most sympathetic to its policies. The symbolism of non-racial Tanganyikan citizenship for which Nyerere had always stood was amply demonstrated when he addressed an election meeting in the northern town of Moshi, on the slopes of Mount Kilimanjaro. He was flanked by the TANU African candidate, Solomon Eliufoo, an Asian, Sophia Mustafa, and Derek Bryceson, a European. Moshi was in the midst of European farming country, so that the election appeal was made to a genuinely multi-racial electorate.

Nyerere and TANU were fortunate in their inter-racial support. The rationality of Nyerere had begun to appeal to the younger minds amongst both Asians and Europeans. This attitude sharply contrasted with that shown in neighbouring Kenya or Northern Rhodesia. Asians such as Amir Jamal and Mahumud Rattansey had guided their Asian Association close to TANU, leading Asian opinion away from the wealthy Karimjee family which had been inclined to support the government and the UTP. Derek Bryceson, Lady Chesham, Miss Johanasson, a Swedish missionary-teacher, were influencing many politically conscious Europeans in the same direction. In short, TANU policies, if not TANU membership, were becoming non-racially national under the widely accepted leadership of Nyerere.

This was clearly evidenced in the elections themselves. Twelve seats were actually contested, the other three returning unopposed candidates. Every candidate supported by TANU was elected, polling 67 per cent of the votes cast. The UTP was annihilated. Mtemvu, who stood for his Congress, could only secure fifty-three votes. TANU had proved that as soon as even a limited number of the people were allowed to vote – only 28,500 were registered – they unhesitatingly chose TANU candidates.

Turnbull had already earned himself wide acclaim by bringing forward the second half of the elections from September 1959 to February. By the time these were held TANU had so demonstrated its invincibility that only three of the fifteen seats were contested. Again TANU-supported candidates won them all. Henceforth there was no more question that TANU represented the only coherent political force in the country. It would determine the character and pace of all future constitutional progress.

In the meantime, Governor Turnbull had been consolidating the sympathetic initial impression he had made on the nationalists. Opening the new session of the legislative council in October, he made exactly the speech for which Nyerere had been waiting over the past four years:

In terms of population the Africans always will be an overwhelming majority in Tanganyika, and, as the country progresses, it is right and proper, as indeed it is natural and inevitable, that African participation both in the legislature and in the executive should steadily increase. It is not intended, and never has been intended, that parity should be a permanent feature of the Tanganyika scene.

As he had started his speech by insisting that he intended to use the phrase 'non-racial', instead of 'multi-racial', and that this form of policy would not 'in some way or other prevent the Africans of Tanganyika from reaching their full political stature and from playing their proper part in the government of this country', Nyerere was given all he had ever asked. No one could ever imagine Twining making such a speech; yet it was only three months since Twining had left the country.

Nyerere thus realised that he had won his crucial battle: against colonialism as represented by the governor and his administration. He was delighted that it had been a bloodless victory. The path of constitutional co-operation to full independence was now cleared. He had to turn his attention to the character of that independence and the objectives for which it could be used.

His first problem was the old one of discipline. Nyerere never deceived himself that independence would cure all the ills of his society. He realised that Tanganyika was basically a poor country, that even after colonial rule had been removed poverty would remain. It would then become his responsibility to mobilise the efforts of his people to increase their wealth. He coined the slogan, 'uhuru na kazi' ('freedom and work'). But such mobilisation would require popular discipline and firm leadership in a country which, by colonial standards, was lightly administered, was very large and whose population was scattered.

An immediate instance of this problem faced Nyerere after the September elections. The trouble in the Lake Province had only temporarily abated after the Geita incident. The results of the election led some TANU supporters to believe that self-government had virtually arrived. They renewed their defiance of the local government's authority, again campaigning against cattle dipping. It required considerable sophistication for people who had been encouraged to regard the government as their opponent now to recognise that they must accept its authority.

Yet Nyerere realised that unless this change in attitude was quickly achieved, respect for all government could crumble, with disastrous consequences once African government was established. So he flew to Mwanza to speak to a crowd of some 10,000. He told them that law and order must be maintained, that TANU instructed its members to obey the laws of the country, that countries must all have laws which citizens obeyed, irrespective of who was in power, that they should not continue the practice of swarming into Mwanza every time one of their number was arrested. He added that they must not think that a TANU membership card excepted them from the processes of the law and, significantly, added that the 'TANU of today' was quite different from the 'TANU of yesterday'.

Nyerere was much praised for this speech. Both the governor and the newspapers commended his courage. But to Nyerere the importance of the incident was the shadow over the future. In victory TANU and its supporters could be more difficult to control than in the years of hard struggle. For it must be remembered that at this time TANU still had very little money and only a flimsy administrative structure. Outside Dar es Salaam organisation was very rudimentary. The kind of disciplined mobilisation essential for success after independence had still to be created.

Another factor which worried Nyerere was the small proportion of the population which participated actively in the elections. Allowing for the restrictions placed on the right of franchise, by no means all those qualified took the trouble to register as voters. In the 1960 election, for instance, where the franchise had been widened, 885,000 electors registered. But this was estimated to be only half those entitled to register. In the event, less than one-seventh of the registered voters actually used their votes, because so many candidates were returned unopposed. So under one-fourteenth of the qualified electorate went to the polls. This pattern was to recur to an even more extreme degree after independence. Already, though, three years before independence, Nyerere was concerned at the meagre participation in active politics which reflected TANU's weak organisation and a dangerous lack of involvement by the populace. Nyerere was again looking and listening to discover the people's real needs and responsibilities.

There were further shadows over the future in the racial situation. Mtemvu and his Congress colleagues had split from TANU because they did not consider it to be sufficiently committed to Africanisation, because they believed that Nyerere was too concerned with his European and Asian friends, because they did not want non-Africans to be allowed membership of TANU or given the right of Tanganyikan citizenship. Mtemvu and his Congress could not compete with the immense popularity of TANU nor with the tremendous momentum it had acquired. But their words could cause trouble in the party and in the unions, because they sometimes struck a sympathetic chord amongst those with grievances. Nyerere knew that the hard tasks to be faced after independence would be accomplished quicker and more efficiently if most of the skilled Europeans and Asians could be persuaded to stay in the country. He also sincerely held the ideal of a genuinely non-racial society in which all committed to the country would be eligible for citizenship, regardless of race. He noted the growth of racialist feelings in the party with alarm. He recognised that the years of discrimination against Africans made this almost inevitable; but it raised a dangerous barrier to the creation of the kind of society which he wished to build in Tanganyika.

It was at this time that Nyerere was able to turn his attention to wider African affairs than previously had been possible. He had, of course, always been a pan-Africanist. He deplored the racialism of southern Africa, as he hated racialism anywhere. He had opposed the Central African Federation from the start. He was worried by the violent conflicts in neighbouring Kenya and by the divisions in Uganda. Yet his energies had been so concentrated on the struggle within his own country that he had found little opportunity to participate personally in the affairs of the rest of the continent.

Now he found that opportunity. Just when he felt he was winning the battle at home, he began to take an active part in the wider scene. Nyerere was never an unrealistic idealist like Nkrumah. He knew sufficient of the nature of nationalism to recognise that any early attempt to create an all-African parliament or government, even on a federal basis, was bound to fail. He was just as convinced as Nkrumah that such an institution was the ideal, but for the time being it was purely Utopian.

President Nyerere with his wife Maria

The scene at the end of the April 1961 Constitutional Conference at which the date for Tanzanian independence was announced. Nyerere is seen with Iain Macleod and, on his right, Sir Richard Turnbull, the Governor

Nyerere with John Rapia (Vice-President of the Tanzanian African National Union) during a triumphal drive through Dar es Salaam after the Governor's address

The President being saluted by rapturous crowds in the capital
following the announcement

President Kaunda making his speech at the 1965 Commonwealth
Conference in London

The two Presidents celebrating the completion of the Tanzam railway

President Nyerere's first Cabinet. Sir Edward Vasey is on Nyerere's left, Amir Jamal on Vasey's left, and Oscar Kambona (who defected) is third from the right in the back row

Mrs Betty Kaunda, the President's
wife, with their family

Mrs Helen Kaunda, the President's mother, being interviewed in 1965
at her home in Chinsali

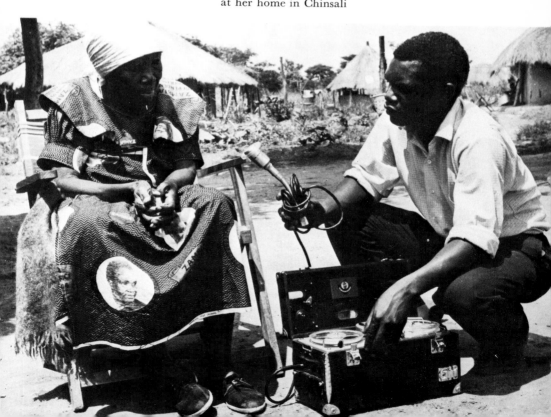

Iain Macleod, President Kaunda and S. L. Katilunga (the High Commissioner) at a reception to mark the opening of Zambia House in London

President Nyerere with Dag Hammarskjöld

When he turned his mind to the future of Africans outside Tanganyika and to the part which his own country could play in it, he gradually became convinced that the only realistic approach was to attain unity through regional federation. As a start, a conference was hosted by TANU in September 1958, just after the first batch of elections. It was held at Mwanza (which led the local provincial commissioner to blame it for further arousing political passions in the Lake Province) and attended by delegates from Kenya, Uganda, Tanganyika, Zanzibar and Nyasaland. Northern Rhodesia was subsequently included. Nyerere was elected chairman, and was accompanied by Kawawa and Munanka as representatives of TANU.

The conference itself did not produce anything new. Colonial rule was condemned, Pan-Africanism and democracy lauded, discussions held on the rights of non-Africans, co-operatives, trade unions and the press. One local issue was raised, the suppression of political activity in Sukumaland, following the Geita disturbances.

But two factors which were to be important to Tanganyika and to Africa as a whole arose out of the conference and stimulated further thought in Nyerere's mind. The first was the preparation for the first All African People's Conference to be held in Accra the following December; the second was the question of an east African federation. The Accra conference was designed to co-ordinate the efforts of nationalist parties throughout the continent in their battles against colonial rule. It also enabled efforts to be made to heal the divisions within those nationalist movements where schisms had appeared. TANU was sufficiently strong and united not to need assistance from the conference; but its awareness of the problems facing other nationalists without its advantages was enhanced.

The federation issue was much more directly relevant to Tanganyika. The concept of federation in east Africa had been prejudiced by the efforts made by Europeans, particularly those from Kenya, to form some kind of federation which would have entrenched white power before the Africans could mobilise their political potential. At the time of the Kabaka of Buganda's deportation a rumour about this kind of federation spread throughout east Africa, no doubt fanned by hot breezes from the newly created Central African Federation. The idea was indignantly repudiated by Africans throughout the region.

Nyerere, however, was thinking in deeper and longer terms. He had joined in the denunciations of federation in central Africa, not because of any antipathy towards federation as a concept, but because in central Africa it was designed to perpetuate white domination. In that region the political power of the Europeans was so deeply entrenched that any accretion of constitutional authority was bound to result in a consolidation of opportunities for the whites to deny Africans their rights as citizens. The same situation prevailed in east Africa during the early and mid-1950s.

Yet by 1958 it seemed to Nyerere that Tanganyika had progressed so far along the road to genuine democracy that within a short time it could be expected that Africans would take control of their own country. In Uganda similar prospects were apparent once the various African communities could agree on the form which a self-governing constitution should take. Zanzibar was also developing along similar lines. So the only major problem obstructing African majority rule throughout east Africa was that of Kenya, and even here the Mau Mau emergency seemed to be coming to an end.

The prospect for federation had therefore taken a radical turn in the second half of the 1950s. Nyerere was the first to appreciate the change which had taken place. He was also very conscious that the chances of real development would almost certainly be retarded if each of the four countries set up its own state apparatus and conducted separate economic policies. Already the East African High Commission provided the means for important joint efforts in such fields as postal services, railways, airways and harbours, in fiscal policy and currency. Was it possible to persuade other east African leaders and the British that some form of federation between the four could avoid the drawbacks of separate statehood?

Two years later, in Addis Ababa, Nyerere put his thoughts on paper and mooted his idea to a gathering of African leaders. His paper was unwittingly released to the press. It could have acted on his career like dynamite if he had not been so widely trusted, for his ideas had not been cleared with his colleagues; and they certainly demanded an extreme degree of sophisticated patience from TANU and its followers if they were ever to be implemented.

For Nyerere proposed no less than a postponement of Tanganyika's independence. His thesis was that it was essential for east Africa to become one country. The best chance for a federation to be created was for it to be established at the moment of independence. This would enable a spirit of achievement to be engendered, whereas if the attempt was made after independence the states would have to be asked to sacrifice their sovereignty. He concluded with the words, 'We in Tankanyika will delay our independence until Kenya and Uganda get popularly elected governments.' The three countries could then become independent simultaneously and federate immediately. But the British government was not helpful, despite their fervent commitment to the Central African Federation; and the other east African leaders never showed the enthusiasm to seize the initiative Nyerere had offered them. In the event, the fears Nyerere felt for the dangers presented by separate sovereignties were justified. The prospect of federation steadily declined once each country had secured its independence and created its own state apparatus, raising new vested interests against any surrender of sovereignty. So Nyerere never had the opportunity to discover whether his own people would have supported his bold initiative.

Once TANU had again demonstrated its overwhelming support by winning the second batch of elections in February 1959 the way was really clear for the march to independence. It could have been halted when TANU tried to insist that domestic self-government, which implied a majority of elected members in the executive, should be achieved during that year. The governor could not accept this. Indeed, he was under pressure from Whitehall at this time to slow down constitutional progress. He had announced after the elections that he would invite four elected members to become ministers. Under TANU's pressure he increased this to five, three Africans, one Asian and one European. There were members of TANU who were not satisfied. There was talk of a strike and the governor prepared for a state of emergency. But Nyerere's counsel of compromise was again accepted and another danger-point was safely passed.

Nyerere himself did not accept ministerial appointment. Indeed, he was increasingly concerning himself with building a united team and increasing the discipline of the party. He had formed an Elected Members Organisation so as to ensure that the new TANU members of the legislature worked to a common policy. Before any elected members were appointed as ministers the whole body had to agree. Once this common view was expressed Nyerere encouraged his closest associates, Jamal, Kahama, Bryceson, Eliufoo and Fundikira, to join the Council of Ministers. He himself continued to organise the party, lobby Westminster and wait until there was a majority of elected members in the Council which would mark the real transfer of powers.

It was during this formative period that Nyerere also gave his definitive view of the future role of the chiefs in Tanganyika. There were still those in the administration who thought that the chiefs could be used to provide a conservative counter-balance to TANU's radicalism. It was suggested that a Territorial Council should be created, composed of chiefs and other dignatories, rather like a House of Lords. Nyerere made it plain that for him independence was to be a means to modernisation. He said, 'We tell the Chiefs quite frankly that their authority is traditional only in the tribes, which were the traditional units. Tanganyika is not a traditional unit at all, and if the Chiefs want to have a place in this thing we call Tanganyika, they have got to adapt themselves to this new situation. There is nothing traditional in the Central Government of Tanganyika today.' This attitude sharply contrasted with that in Kenya, Uganda or Nigeria.

It was not a rejection of ancient values, for Nyerere has always retained a strong affinity for the morality of tribal society. But it was a clear declaration that the new state itself could not be based on traditional forms of authority. The state must be directly subject to the will of the people who would delegate their authority to their own elected representatives, irrespective of heredity or age, the usual determinants of tribal authority.

The other issue which might have retarded independence was the fear of the British government that swift progress towards non-racial democracy and a transfer of authority in Tanganyika might prejudice developments in Kenya and central Africa. As mentioned earlier, Lennox-Boyd had demonstrated the danger of his obstruction in October 1957. Lennox-Boyd was still Colonial Secretary in the early months of 1959. It has since been revealed by Roy Welensky that on 19 March 1959, two days after the new Tanganyika Legislative Council was opened in Dar es Salaam with Turnbull's promise of a Council of Ministers including elected members, Lord Perth, Minister of State at the Colonial Office, spoke to the Cabinet of the Central African Federation in Salisbury. He told it that, 'So far as our general colonial policy is concerned, a halt is being called to the rapid advance of colonial territories to independence. For Tanganyika, for example, we are proposing a long-term programme.'

This secret brake by the British government on Tanganyika's apparently smooth constitutional progress was directly linked to issues raised by the appointment of a post-elections committee. Turnbull had announced in March that he would appoint such a committee in order to recommend what changes should be made in the electoral system. He had also promised to forecast when responsible government could be introduced.

TANU submitted a memorandum to the committee. It proposed an enlarged legislature, with a majority of elected members; an elected majority in the Council of Ministers; universal adult suffrage on a common roll; abolition of parity representation. On Nyerere's insistence the recommendations for increased representation included blocks of reserved seats for Asians and Europeans as a means of reassuring them of their participation in governing the country and in the hope that it would provide a bridge to full democracy.

There was very little objection to these proposals inside the country. Indeed, the Asians declared that they did not need reserved seats. It was from outside Tanganyika that opposition was mounted. In particular, the prospect of adult suffrage and an executive dominated by elected Africans directly threatened the assumptions on which both Kenya and central Africa were being built.

The context in which this conflict of interest was fought should be recalled. Early in 1959 central Africa had begun to erupt. Disturbances in Nyasaland and Northern Rhodesia, a state of emergency in Southern

Rhodesia, the deployment of troops and mass arrests had begun to teach the British government that, as they had learnt in Kenya, it was impossible to govern against the will of the majority. In Kenya itself, the Hola scandal only added to the mounting tensions between Whitehall and African nationalism.

Yet Lennox-Boyd still remained adamantly wedded to the concept of white privilege, to the support of European domination of government. It was not until he was replaced by Iain Macleod after Britain's October election that the collision-course between Britain and Africans was diverted. By that time the Prime Minister, Harold Macmillan, had realised that his government's colonial policy could bring him disaster.

In the meantime, however, Turnbull was engaged in bitter arguments with the Colonial Office over what he saw as the danger of bloodshed in Tanganyika. He feared that if his policy of evolutionary constitutional progress was obstructed because of appeasement of white interests elsewhere, resentment amongst the Tanganyikan people would spill over into violence. In that event the trust he had evoked amongst the nationalist leaders would have been destroyed, he would probably have resigned and almost certainly Nyerere himself would have been overthrown as leader.

Turnbull just managed to hold the line. Although the Ramage committee on electoral reform was not allowed to consider adult suffrage, Nyerere was able to restrain the militants, who suspected that this indicated obstruction to full democracy, on the understanding that responsible government would be considered and the next elections expedited.

It so happens that I saw a lot of Nyerere during the middle of 1959. I visited him in Dar es Salaam during June and in the following month he spent some weeks in London. It was my first visit to Tanganyika since I had worked with TANU four years previously. Again there was a TANU crowd at the airport, but this time in the official green uniform of the TANU Youth League. The party had now acquired a fleet of Land-Rovers and it was in one of them that Julius and I were driven into town. It was obvious that the intervening four years had seen TANU become a mature, structured organisation. Its popularity and that of its president was amply demonstrated by the cheers and waves of crowds beside the road on the drive from the airport. My travelling companion, Werner Holzer, editor of the *Franfurter Rundschau*, was tremendously impressed. It was his first visit to the continent and, although he had toured west, South and central Africa, he told me that he had seen nothing like this good-humoured, disciplined, enthusiastic party.

I had just come from the turmoil of central Africa. It was delightfully relaxing to sense the contrast. As we sat in Jamal's house to discuss the situation it was immediately evident that both men felt that the battle was almost won. Nyerere was content to allow things to develop slowly, provided that the ultimate objective was guaranteed by the government. He saw very clearly the need for his colleagues to acquire experience and for a definite strategy for the independent state to be thought out. The proposals put by TANU to the Ramage Committee he described in a typical phrase. 'A solution containing the barometer of feeling within the cobweb of the constitution.' Jamal, who was to become one of the five ministers in a few days' time, was equally sanguine. In fact the discussion at Jamal's, and later that evening outside the New Africa Hotel, was more of the problems of independence than of hurdles still to be crossed.

The New Africa had become the forum for inter-racial discussions, accompanied by much laughter and gaiety. It had been built at the beginning of the century for a projected visit by the Kaiser and faced the old, spired German Lutheran Church. From its central square courtyard a palm tree thrust its heavy leaves against the midnight blue sky. The terrace beside the road was our favourite meeting place; everyone visiting Dar, from up country or abroad, who wished to take the political temperature would drop in there to join the noisy arguments.

Yet, at the time of my last visit in 1955 the New Africa was reserved for Europeans only. An African could not even be served with a beer outside. The only places at which my TANU friends and I could eat together then were the Cosy Café or Rex Hotel. When I was in Dar in 1951 the issue had never been posed. No European thought of eating or drinking with an African and when I mentioned it even a United Nations' representative smiled in a way which showed he considered me mad. What a revolution in eight short years! What a transformation TANU had made in the shorter four years! Nothing could illustrate, for me at least, the extent of the emotional change as that social contrast as I sat with Africans, Asians and Europeans outside the New Africa.

Another revealing experience on this visit was to accompany Nyerere to a football match. Tanganyika were to play a visiting side, the Middlesex Wanderers. Nyerere is not personally involved with sport as Kaunda has always been, but he felt that on this occasion he ought to participate in the interests of his people. There was no question about the degree of that interest. The ground was crammed on every side, every palm tree surrounding it provided a supplementary grandstand and so many crowded on to a nearby roof that it collapsed during the match.

What was most impressive, however, was the manner in which the people treated Julius and Maria. The couple could not have been shown more affection if they had been royalty, but there was no hint of obsequiousness in the crowd's attitude. They and their friends were given the seats of honour, but the greetings were good-humoured and friendly. They were obviously regarded as 'of the people'.

Later that evening the Nyereres and I visited some Asian friends. Here we discussed two projects dear to Nyerere's mind. He wanted to establish a national newspaper outside the control of the wealthy group which owned most of east Africa's English-language papers; and he hoped to create a workers' college where Tanganyikans without the advantages of higher education could study and prepare to serve the party and the nation. We examined a draft trust deed for the college, removed the prohibition against alcohol from it, and discussed a possible site. When it was suggested that the Bel Air Hotel, previously known as the Dolphin, across the bay from the town, could be taken over, Nyerere made one of his characteristic comments. The hotel had fallen on bad times (I could never understand why; I had sat outside it with UN representatives in 1951 delighting in the fairyland of shore and ship lights, and again with TANU officials in 1955), and it was suggested that it could be acquired cheaply. Julius argued that it was unfair to buy it for less than it had cost! Before long the old hotel had become Kivukoni College, based broadly on the lines of Ruskin College in Oxford.

At this time Julius and Maria were living with their five children in small rented rooms, though they were preparing to build a house in the capital. They had no car and Julius has always refused to learn to drive. Having just visited most of the other British African territories of the time, both Holzer and I were profoundly impressed by the complete contrast in life-style between Tanganyika's leader and the prominent Africans we had met elsewhere.

Before I left, Julius had a private and serious talk with me. I had seen Turnbull and felt certain that he was being held back by strings from the Colonial Office. He was desperately anxious to prepare Tanganyikans as fast as possible for the responsibilities of independence. He was still apprehensive about some of the anti-European statements being made in some parts of the country, was not yet confident that order could be maintained and felt that the whole situation was dangerously dependent on Nyerere's health. It was when he talked about future progress, about the limitation of the franchise and the prevention of discussion on adult suffrage in the Ramage committee, that I was sure that the governor was being shackled by the Colonial Office.

Nyerere entertained the same fears. He spoke to me of his 'abiding faith in humanity' which would allow him and his colleagues to change the consciousness of race within five years; of the committee on integrated education which had already been set up; of the recognition that rapid education and training was essential as a preparation for self-government – and all these opportunities for rapid progress towards a successful nonracial society were dependent on keeping at bay the fears of the Colonial Office for their effect on neighbouring territories.

The following month, within a couple of days of returning to London,

I was with Nyerere again. He had come to press the Colonial Office to grant responsible government in that year. He declared to the press, 'We are impatient for responsible government. We are not impatient about independence. We want to handle the education of our people, economic development, improvement of communications, and so on. When we are doing the job independence can take care of itself.'

He was still apprehensive about the prejudice which the Colonial Office seemed to be showing in favour of the white régimes. He was in London when parliament debated central Africa, the Devlin Report and the Hola incident. He spoke to the Labour Party's Colonial Group on the example which Tanganyika could show to the rest of Africa in setting up demo-cratic government in a multi-racial society. The following week Roy Welensky spoke to the same group, defending the policies of the Federal government.

Nyerere also was a participant in a crucial meeting which took place later in July. In the midst of all the bitter arguments about the future of central Africa the position taken by the Labour Party was one of the critical factors. Its attitude had been somewhat ambiguous since it was under Attlee's Labour government that the federal scheme had first been designed. That government had left office before any decision had been taken as to whether it was to be implemented. Yet, although the Labour Party had officially attacked the methods used by the Conservatives in establishing federation, the party had never entirely rejected federation itself. Indeed, some members of the party, including former ministers, openly supported the concept. When the issue of its future arose from the disturbances and deaths in central Africa, the Devlin Commission's report and Welensky's demand for Dominion Status by 1960, the Labour Party found itself in an equivocal position.

It seemed to some of us that it was essential, both for the future relations of the party with Africans and for peace in central Africa, that the Labour Party should unreservedly oppose federation; that it must support the right of the three territories to pursue their separate progress towards an independence based on full democracy. The key would be the attitude taken by Hugh Gaitskell, the party leader. Gaitskell tended to be wary of committing himself to substantial changes in the status quo, dubious whether he would be able to carry out such pledges when in office. He had never taken a personal interest in the affairs of central Africa, nor, indeed, of other Third World matters, although he felt deeply the injustice of the economic imbalance between rich and poor worlds and was to become a doughty opponent of racial discrimination.

When central Africa came to the forefront of British politics Gaitskell characteristically set up a special committee to advise him on the issue. Those on the committee whose judgement he most trusted were inclined to support the federation and to oppose any proposal that the party should take a publicly critical attiude towards it. The only member who consistently supported my own uncompromising hostility to it was the late Lynn Ungoed-Thomas, who had been Solicitor-General under Attlee and was later to become a judge. But Gaitskell was suspicious of us both.

Ungoed-Thomas and I felt that the committee was moving towards advising Gaitskell to give the government almost uncritical support in its sympathy with Welensky and his federation. We also believed that this would be fatal. So, for the first and only time, I made use of my acquaintance with Gaitskell's brother, Arthur, architect of the Gezira scheme in The Sudan, and an experienced economic adviser to several Third World countries. I arranged for Nyerere and Ungoed-Thomas to have lunch with Arthur Gaitskell, who was a great admirer of Nyerere. Over that lunch, although at first reluctant to interfere in politics or to influence his brother, which he told us he had strictly refrained from ever attempting, Arthur became convinced by Nyerere's arguments. He recognised that this was a crucial moment of history, when the racial situation in Africa could take a fatal wrong turning. He saw Nyerere's argument that if Tanganyikan democratic progress were halted in order to appease the central African whites it would be impossible to create the non-racial state which was Nyerere's objective; that if the federation were allowed to develop along modified South African lines the future for Africa and for inter-racial harmony anywhere was bleak; and that if the Labour Party were to associate with such developments, Africans, Asians and West Indians would conclude that all British politicians were alike, that Britain herself was an implacable enemy of democracy in multi-racial societies.

When next I saw Arthur Gaitskell he told me how much he had been impressed by Nyerere's calm, good-humoured, rational arguments; that if only he could retain his leadership Tanganyika might well set an example to the whole of Africa and beyond. He had approached his brother who had given the case serious consideration. I knew already that Hugh considered his brother to be his conscience on Third World issues, for he had told me so himself. I got the impression from him that he regarded Arthur with some awe, the older, wiser brother. I was quite content and did not pursue the matter further. Hugh Gaitskell most unusually rejected the views of his closest advisers and became a most perceptive critic of the federation. His and the Labour Party's opposition strongly influenced the Macmillan governments of 1959–61.

On his return to Tanganyika, almost satisfied that the main dangers to progress had been removed, Nyerere turned his attention to preparing his people for the responsibilities of independence. He held meetings in various parts of the country, explaining the difference between responsible government and independence, assuring them that freedom had almost been won, that the necessity now was for hard work. He emphasised that the Asians and Europeans would be staying after independence, that their capital and skills would still be needed.

The governor announced in October that the next election was to be brought forward from 1962 to 1960 and that the parity system would be ended. Nyerere was so delighted that he made his famous declaration, 'We would like to light a candle, and put it on top of Mount Kilimanjaro, which will shine beyond our borders, giving hope where there was despair, love where there was hate, and dignity where there was humiliation.' When deeply moved, as he was now as he saw the end of the battle, the dawning of his vision, Nyerere could become lyrical. Yet I believe that this poetic exhilaration was caused at least partially by relief. Nyerere has never been a fighter by temperament. He prefers to construct rather than battle to destroy anything, even colonial rule. He was vastly relieved at the prospect that the end of his struggle was in sight; now he could turn his energies to building a nation, a much more congenial task for him than fighting against institutions or the people who governed them.

By December, Turnbull was ready to publish the Ramage report and to announce that, provided nothing unexpected happened, responsible government would follow the next elections. Nyerere's suggestion of reserved seats for the minorities had been accepted and the franchise was to be widened. By this time Macmillan had learnt his colonial lesson. He had replaced Lennox-Boyd by the much more liberal Iain Macleod.

There was wild jubilation when the governor's news was heard. Nyerere himself was carried shoulder-high by the crowd, garlands round his neck, as thousands gathered round Karimjee Hall set off in spontaneous procession through the streets of the capital.

Yet the excitement did not divert Nyerere from the task he knew ever more clearly he must now pursue. At the TANU conference early in 1960 he had these stern words to say to his party : 'I have seen some TANU officers getting drunk with power, and scheming to undermine one another. Some officers are too interested in finding ways of dominating others and in seeking to eliminate their friends from their posts . . . There is a great danger that many of our leaders are working for responsible government to provide themselves with high positions.' This criticism could have been levelled at any nationalist movement in Africa. The unique feature in Tanganyika was that the leader recognised the dangers well before independence and brought it to public attention. It was to provide a continual theme after independence, eventually resulting in specific action, laying down rules to be observed by all leaders. Already Nyerere was clearly indicating his determination to steer a unique course in national life. Leaders were not to become separated from the people they represented. They were responsible to the people who had elected them, not their rulers. Ostentation, obsequiousness, power-pride and power-seeking were to be repudiated in Tanganyika, to be publicly regarded as morally objectionable. Few other countries, if any, have sought this form of ethical humility.

From the time of the governor's promise of responsible government constitutional progress moved smoothly towards complete independence. By this time Nyerere had persuaded a noted liberal European from Kenya, Ernest Vasey, to join him as Minister of Finance. This appointment re-assured the business community that investment would be safe in a self-governing Tanganyika. For, at this stage, Nyerere's economic thinking was largely conventional. He considered that, at least for some years, external as well as local investment was essential for the kind of development of the country which he contemplated after independence. Vasey was also useful to him because of his international experience.

After another tour of America early in 1960, Nyerere, Vasey and Turnbull held discussions with Macleod in London on the future structure of the Council of Ministers. So well was Macleod impressed by Nyerere that he told the UN visiting mission that he was anxious that Tanganyika should remain a showpiece among territories developing towards indepen-dence . . . that Tanganyika would not be held back because of possible repercussions in other territories. The Lennox-Boyd bogy was laid. Tanganyika's Chief Secretary, Fletcher-Cooke, went even further when he told the Trusteeship Council that 'in Mr Nyerere we have an outstanding political leader – indeed a great African statesman.' It seemed that by this time Nyerere had convinced everyone of his integrity. No longer were there doubts about whether Kenya or central African prejudices should take precedence over the multi-racial experiment in Tanganyika; Nyerere had ceased to be considered by the administration as an 'agitator'. Yet neither Nyerere nor the situation had changed, except in so far as Nyerere's con-sistent policies were seen to be successful.

In the elections of August 1960 TANU again swept the board, winning all seats but one captured by a TANU member rejected by the party's executive committee. Nyerere was then called on to become the country's first Chief Minister and to form his first government. He included all his closest colleagues: Kawawa, Jamal, Bryceson, Swai, Fundikira, Kahama, together with Vasey and two officials. In the new Legislative Council were fifty-two Africans, sixteen Europeans, eleven Asians, one Arab and one Goan, a striking example of multi-racialism in practice.

By the following March it only took Macleod two days to agree with Nyerere and his colleagues that full internal self-government would be achieved in May, with the withdrawal of the governor and officials from the Council of Ministers, and complete independence by December. In the interim between the two events only defence and external affairs would be left as responsibilities of the governor. The announcement at the end of the conference was again greeted by wild enthusiasm inside and outside the conference hall. In his speech Nyerere demonstrated the high regard Turnbull had won for himself when he declared that the governor's chairmanship of the Council of Ministers had never been a burden; the whole hall rose to him when Turnbull himself rose to speak. The mood of the conference itself and Nyerere in particular was displayed in Nyerere's words, 'This is a day of triumph for Tanganyika . . . I rejoice to say that it is not a day of triumph *over* anybody. It is a happy victory for a good cause in which we all are winners.' When the Council of Ministers became the Cabinet in May, and Nyerere became the first Prime Minister, nine of the ministers were African, two European and one Asian.

The period between TANU's definitive success in the 1960 elections and the achievement of independence at the end of 1961 was not without difficulties. The first was the effect of the violent chaos which broke out in the Congo immediately following Belgium's sudden grant of independence to her former colony in 1960. The Congolese had never been given a chance to prepare themselves to govern their state and had virtually no experienced people to carry on the business of administration. The violence which erupted between ethnic groups, regions and political factions inevitably provoked fears of a repetition in other African states as they attained sovereignty.

Nyerere knew that the non-Africans in his country were naturally fearful of a similar fate overtaking them when they heard of the attacks made on Europeans in the Congo. He reacted immediately. He re-emphasised that TANU respected all human beings, regardless of colour or race, and added, 'Changes are going to take place in this country, but there will be no change in TANU's attitude to law and order, except to enforce even more respect for law and order.' His assurance calmed non-African nerves, but the effects of events in the Congo were to disturb the political atmosphere for several years.

The second threat was even more menacing because it affected the mass African movement. Nyerere had always been wedded to the full nonracial concept because of his complete absence of racial sense, his profound belief in the unity of the human race and his conviction that his destiny was to establish a state in which race or colour were treated as of no significance. Yet he recognised that because Africans in his country had been treated as lesser human beings, they would need to build their confidence before they could live on equal terms with those who had been accustomed to denigrate them. It was for this reason that his party was confined to African members. This began to change soon after responsible government had been granted. Asians and Europeans were first introduced into the executive of the parliamentary party.

But Nyerere's view was not universally accepted in the party. We have already seen how Mtemvu revolted against it. Although he did not take many members with him when he left the party, he certainly exposed the opinions of many members who remained inside.

The first overt attack came from the trade unions. They criticised Bryceson, Minister of Labour, for adopting the principle of localisation in place of Africanisation in his employment policy. Nyerere unhesitatingly supported Bryceson and reminded the unions that they were part of TANU and must accept its policy.

It was the same principle which was at stake when objections were raised in the National Assembly over citizenship qualifications. The government proposed that dual nationality be allowed for two years, at the end of which period each individual would have to choose whether to retain foreign nationality or renounce it to become a Tanganyikan citizen. The second provision was for all citizens of Commonwealth countries who had lived in Tanganyika for five years to be eligible for citizenship of the new country by registration from independence day onwards. When Nyerere heard members of the Assembly disputing the right of non-Africans to citizenship his anger flared. He compared their attitude to the racialism of the Nazis. He declared to them that 'this government has rejected, and rejected completely, any ideas that citizenship, with the duties and the rights of citizenship of the country, are going to be based on anything except loyalty to this country'. He made the issue one of confidence, announcing that although there would be a free vote, his government would resign if defeated. He secured an overwhelming majority; but it is doubtful if many of his critics were convinced by his arguments.

Nor was all peaceful on the economic front. Nyerere made it plain that he recognised the danger presented by the gross inequalities of wealth within the country, especially as they tended to coincide with racial groups. This could endanger attitudes, especially towards the Asians, many of whom had become successful businessmen. All Jamal's exhortations to his community to realise that those with privilege must identify with the efforts to raise general living standards did not avert harassment of some Asian shopkeepers, especially in the Lake Province. When threats of strikes were heard from the teachers' and medical workers' unions, Nyerere showed the iron fist within his personality. He declared that the country could not afford wage increases, well aware that they came from people whose standard of life was far above the average. He then threatened to dismiss any government worker who went on strike after the claims had been considered. Trade union leaders trained according to the British system by the TUC did not expect such a reaction. It angered them, causing relations between the unions and the government to reach a depth of bitterness which boded ill for the post-independence period.

Nyerere did not wait until independence before using his country's influence on the international community. His appearances at the United Nations had already kept the racial issue and the whole question of colonial rule constantly in the limelight of international attention. His initiative in trying to build a federation of east African states had failed because of British indifference, Uganda's disunity and the slow political progress of Kenya. But in one sphere his impact was immediate, perhaps decisive.

When the Commonwealth Prime Ministers met in London in March 1961 they had to face a new situation in South Africa. The South Africans decided by referendum to cut their ties with the British monarchy and become a republic. There was no prima facie reason for this action to prevent them from continuing as members of the Commonwealth. But because of their new constitutional situation they had to ask the other members to accept their continued membership. This gave those members most critical of apartheid the chance to try and remove South Africa without having to force the issue simply on the grounds of her domestic policies.

Nyerere, although not yet Prime Minister of an independent country and therefore ineligible to attend the conference, made his views quite clear to those who did attend. He pointed out that the young nations of Africa were anxious to join the Commonwealth but only provided that it observed those principles of equality and justice for which it stood. In this perspective the attitude they took to South African membership was crucial.

Not content with the powerful effect this message had made, Nyerere then wrote an article for the *Observer* in which he clearly spelt out his position. He could not have been more explicit than when he wrote:

We believe that the principles of the Commonwealth would be betrayed by an affirmative answer to South Africa's application for admission as a republic. Inevitably, therefore, we are forced to say that to vote South Africa in is to vote us out . . . The apartheid policies now being practised in the Union of South Africa are a daily affront to this belief in individual dignity. They are also a constantly reiterated insult to our own dignity as Africans . . . The Tanganyika government cannot afford to have any relations with the South African government, and it must within the bounds of international law lend support to those who struggle against the system of apartheid . . . We fear the evils of racialism and its consequences on the minds of majorities and minorities alike. We believe that the dignity of man is the idea which can defeat racialism; but we know that any action of ours which appears to compromise with the evil we are fighting must weaken the execution of our own policies.

This means that we cannot join any 'association of friends' which includes a state deliberately and ruthlessly pursuing a racialist policy.

This enunciation did far more than state the Tanganyika government's policy towards apartheid and racialism. It contrasted sharply with the frequent demagogy of anti-apartheid spokesmen. It formed the quietly reasoned, logical philosophy of its author, revealing in public the certain convictions he held. It had a profound effect on members of the Commonwealth Conference; South Africa left the institution.

What was Nyerere thinking about as his country moved rapidly through the last few months towards independence? Fortunately I have some specific evidence of the manner in which his mind was working. In March 1961, when the issue of independence was virtually settled, I sat with him in his hotel room in London and we agreed that a part of our conversation would be recorded on tape. Portions of the conversation subsequently appeared in the *New Statesman*. The following extracts are reproduced verbatim :

Question: To what would you ascribe the exceptionally smooth transition to independence by Tanganyika?

Answer: I think the explanation is historical; many things have combined to give us in Tanganyika the success we have achieved. One is the fact that, being a Trust Territory, we did not attract large numbers of settlers; and so, although we are classified among the so-called multiracial societies, the settlers did not have actual power. Thus when we began organising for independence, we could direct our struggle against the colonial powers as such and not against a European minority in Tanganyika.

Q: But you did have trouble with the Europeans at one time.

A: Yes, we did have trouble; but, as it became clear that we were succeeding and that all the time were emphasising that our struggle was not directed against any European settler in the country, the Europeans were able to accept what was happening.

Q: Do you think the Europeans in Tanganyika have fully accepted African majority government now?

A: I think they have. If you went to the Northern Province now, you would find it the province with the greatest confidence in the country. Yet that was the province which used to have diehard European settlers.

Q: And what about your economic problems?

A: Our economic problems, I think, are going to be more difficult, and again for the historical reasons which I will explain. You see, Tanganyika has been of all the east African countries the most backward in every respect, except that now we are leading politically. But economically

we are still undeveloped. However, with the political stability that we
have, I have no doubt that we shall get the assistance that we need from
outside and that you will see an economic activity which will change
the face of our country in a very short time.

Q: What about your hopes for federation between the three east
African territories?

A: The furthest we have gone so far is to make the argument about
federation public; and, as far as I know, there is nobody in east Africa
against the idea of federation, except perhaps the Baganda; but the
rest of the countries in east Africa accept the federation, at least in
principle, which is a step forward. I think they have also accepted the
argument in principle that we should achieve federation before the
separate countries have achieved complete independence.

Q: What are the main advantages of such a federation?

A: Many. First, a negative one. You stop the permanent Balkanisation
of east Africa. If you look at the map in west Africa at present, I think
it is terrifying that these tiny little units have achieved their independence
as separate units – and the chances of re-uniting them and stopping
permanent Balkanisation have thus been reduced. If we in Africa really
want to have a say in the councils of the world, the bigger the units, the
better. And economically too, I think we can develop these countries
much better if we combine our resources in bigger units.

Q: Do you think the prospects are good for federation in east Africa?

A: I think at present the chances are 50:50. My own argument is that
we should move on to a federal structure now, so that we come out of
colonial status as one unit. But I say 50:50 because it all depends upon
what happens in Kenya and Uganda. I couldn't possibly be expected
to sit down with the *Governor* of Kenya and the *Governor* of Uganda
to talk about the federation of east Africa. I would sit with the two
Chief Ministers to discuss it. But I don't know when we are going
to have Chief Ministers in Uganda and Kenya. When we get them,
then we will try to meet as quickly as possible to find out whether
the others accept the principle of federation as much as we accept it in
Tanganyika.

Q: How long are you prepared to hold up independence in Tanganyika?

A: I have no intention of holding up the independence of Tanganyika –
I should like to achieve independence now.

Q: Before federation?

A: Before federation. But if we move on to a federal structure at once,
I am not going to lead a secessionist movement in Tanganyika. In that
event east Africa would become one country, and I should not act like
the Baganda and rush to declare independence. So the date of independence of east Africa will be determined by east Africa. I am not going

to determine it in Tanganyika. It may come this year, it may come next year.

Q: But if you don't move on to a federal structure before any of the three territories becomes independent, you will still pursue federation after independence?

A: Yes. But I feel that after independence it is going to be much more difficult.

Q: You have already had talks with Dr Banda and with Kenneth Kaunda and Harry Nkumbula. Do you see the possibility of extending your federation to central Africa, at least to the British protectorates of Northern Rhodesia and Nyasaland?

A: If my arguments are accepted. I would use the same principles not only in east Africa, but in central Africa too, that you have got to have democratically elected governments before their leaders can meet and talk about federation.

Q: Looking ahead, a federation involving the east and central African territories might solve a lot of economic problems.

A: Well, that is one advantage of federation. Frankly, if you could have a freely entered federation from Nairobi to Salisbury, you would have the biggest and most highly developed unit on the African continent, with the exception of South Africa.

Q: Yes. And then, of course, South Africa would be even more isolated?

A: And then South Africa would be in real trouble.

Q: Have you any general views about developments throughout the continent of Africa – any hopes for the future?

A: I think we may commit the same silly mistakes that have been committed by the other nations of the world. First, we are in danger of becoming the most Balkanised continent of the world. Unless we are careful, we are going to find ourselves, after the present wave of nationalism which is temporarily binding Africa together, entering a period of eighteenth-century nationalism. The mistakes which have been committed in Europe are obvious. If we don't avoid them, we shall get into trouble; and what is more, we shall lose the opportunity of helping the progress of history. We are not, for instance, an armed continent. We come to independence when the world is frightened and talking about disarmament and all that. Now, one thing Africa could do, which could be very helpful, is to refuse to arm. And there are very good reasons for such a refusal. If we arm in Tanganyika, no one would believe me if I said we were arming in order to defend Tanganyika from possible aggression by Britain or America or India or China or the USSR, because I could never defend Tanganyika against these world powers. So why should we arm? We could only be arming against Kenya or Nyasaland or Uganda. It is madness for Africa at this stage to arm against Africans. One contribution I think we could make to the present history of the world is to refuse to arm – and really set an example to the other continents of the world.

Contemplating these visions, Nyerere prepared to face the hazards of independence. He had achieved the first task he had set himself; he realised that the second, using his influence in an independent Tanganyika to build a new and better society, would be the more difficult.

From Federation to Zambia (2)

Kaunda returned from Britain with two convictions beginning to take priority in his mind. He had realised in his study of British politics that British governments and the political establishment only recognised power in the colonies when it emanated from well-organised, mass groups, led with dedicated discipline. This he believed demanded the non-violent approach of a Gandhi, although he also recognised that even Gandhi was unable to restrain his followers on all occasions when they were provoked by force used by the colonial government.

Some time later Kaunda was to write to Nkrumah, 'You have set for us in Africa a goal which we must work for; you have set for me a standard of behaviour or personal discipline exemplified in your famous three "S"'s: Service, Sacrifice and Suffering – with which we must equip ourselves before we can even hope to start on the great task before us.' Impressed by his experiences abroad with the strategy which had led India and Ghana to independence almost without bloodshed and which was leading Tanganyika along the same path, Kaunda had become convinced that any hope of breaking from the federation depended on the existence of a disciplined national party. His observations equally convinced him that such a party could only be led by men committed to the ascetic way of life. In this he was entirely supported by two other Congress stalwarts, Kapwepwe and Sipalo. Both had spent some time in India, where their conviction was reinforced. In 1958 Kaunda also spent some months in India as well as visiting Dar es Salaam where Nyerere preached and practised the same doctrine. These influences on the view held of the importance of leaders' personal lives were to affect the future of Congress as crucially as policy issues.

As this belief in the importance of ascetic dedication rose in Kaunda's perspective of priorities, so the fitness of Nkumbula to lead the liberation movement increasingly came into question. On his return from London and during Kaunda's continued stay in Britain, Nkumbula became progressively more dictatorial. Whilst the two leaders were absent Sipalo, Kapwepwe and Makasa had increased the tempo of Congress activity, reviving its action groups and trying to start a youth movement. On his return Nkumbula sensed that his position as leader was being undermined. He dismissed Sipalo and had frequent altercations with Kapwepwe over control of the party's finances.

As we have already seen, Kaunda had become worried about his president's personal commitment during their stay in Britain. Before he left for home he was urged by Mainza Chona, then studying law in London, to assume the leadership himself on his return. Indeed, his arrival home was greeted with some acclaim by a section of the press. This caused Nkumbula further concern for his own position, but Kaunda assured him that it had not been done at his instigation.

The fact was that, although Kaunda was increasingly doubtful as to whether Nkumbula could give nationalism the kind of leadership he believed essential, at this stage he was equally convinced that unity was crucial. He had seen that in other African countries such as Uganda, Kenya, Southern Rhodesia and South Africa, division within the nationalist movement had led to weakness which had been taken advantage of by colonial rulers and white supremacists. It seemed vital to maintain the unity of Congress if it was to have any chance of winning the battle against federation. So, despite his misgivings, he continued to work in harness with Nkumbula.

Yet he found that already the Congress president had caused antagonism within the party by his policy attitudes, irrespective of his private behaviour. During Kaunda's time abroad a new party had been formed named the Constitution Party. It was founded under the inspiration of Colonel David Stirling whose Capricorn Society tried to present a multi-racial approach in east and central Africa. It was this same Society which had been instrumental in establishing the UTP in Tanganyika. Despite its multi-racial approach, it always attempted to wean Africans away from the nationalist movement, trying to unite 'moderate', privileged, Africans with the more liberal Europeans. (David Stirling was later to re-emerge as an organiser of security forces for various governments and as one of the proponents of 'private armies' in the Britain of 1974.)

In the case of Northern Rhodesia Stirling attracted two prominent Africans, Lawrence Katilungu and S. H. Chileshe. But, of greater import, his ideas were taken up by Dr Alexander Scott, an independent federal MP and newspaper promoter who had been sympathetic to Congress, and by Harry Franklin, another liberal. Nkumbula became very close to Franklin, even taking him to meetings of the Congress executive. It was thought that it was Franklin who influenced him in trying to call off boycotts and eventually persuaded him to favour participation in the territorial elections to be held under a constitution which Congress had condemned.

When this vacillation on policies was added to Nkumbula's increasingly dictatorial attitude to the management of Congress, it was inevitable that, from the time of his return from Britain in 1957, the Congress president had to face increasing criticism within the party.

Nevertheless, Kaunda loyally co-operated with Nkumbula during the first few months after his return. Within a few days of arriving home he was plunged into the party's annual conference. There had been a move towards deleting the clause in the constitution insisting on non-violence. Kaunda, with his total commitment to non-violence, was able to stem the tide of frustration, arguing that violence would play into the hands of those who would use any excuse to destroy Congress.

A few weeks later he and Nkumbula visited the Governor, Sir Arthur Benson. This was Kaunda's first visit to Government House; six and a half years later he was to make it his home. On this occasion he took with him Congress' proposals for the new Northern Rhodesian constitution. They were based on full adult suffrage, and were rejected by the Governor. During the interview an exchange took place which was to become famous in Zambian history. When Benson suggested that if the Congress proposals were accepted the Europeans would paralyse government, Kaunda riposted, 'Are you implying, Your Excellency, that for our demands to be met we have got to be in a position to paralyse government?'

Significantly, during the first four months of 1958 Kaunda spent most of his time in the rural areas. This was a chore which had little appeal to Nkumbula, but Kaunda realised that a truly national party must be based in the countryside where most of the people lived. It was also tactically important, for the government, as in Tanganyika, continued to regard the rural population as its natural allies. It characterised the nationalists as a tiny group of political agitators misleading a section of the small proportion of the people who inhabited the towns. Yet the government was not sufficiently confident of its case to allow the rural population to decide for itself. It constantly coerced the chiefs, whom it appointed and paid, to exclude Congress organisers from their districts and to harass local sympathisers.

During this period Kaunda's health began to give cause for concern. He had serious trouble with his lungs which was aggravated by long journeys on unpaved roads in the midst of clouds of dust. On one occasion he had to spend some time in the hospital at Chikankata where the Salvation Army doctor, Dr Gauntlett, was very kind to him. Nor was his health improved by a terrifying experience which occurred to him in the Congress office. As he was telephoning during a thunderstorm the machine was struck by lightning. He was unconscious for fourteen hours and his left leg was badly burned. This was the fourth time that his telephone had been hit by lightning, some evidence of the hazards of life in the tropics.

It was becoming increasingly recognised on all sides that the fate of the federation and of its constituent territories would be determined during the next two years. From the time of the Suez fiasco in late 1956 British power and self-confidence had visibly waned. The federal government had taken advantage of this by claiming that as it supported the British government at the time of Suez it was entitled to British support in its plans for constitutional advance. Welensky had convinced Lord Home, the Commonwealth Secretary, that his revised constitution was viable. The Colonial Office took no stand on behalf of the two Protectorates which were its responsibility. The African Affairs Board protested, its protests were rejected and it sank into the insignificance for which the whites had hoped. Britain promised not to legislate for the federation without a request from its government. Above all, the conference to review the constitution scheduled for from seven to ten years after federation had been established in 1953 was to be held at the very earliest moment, at the beginning of 1960. It would be at this conference that the federal government would demand Dominion Status, which meant that it would be free to legislate without interference from Britain; it would become a sovereign state. Once that occurred, the Africans would be left without protection from outside the country. They would become as subject to white power as their cousins in South Africa.

So time was short. The nationalists knew that they had barely two years to mount an offensive capable of avoiding this fate. The whites knew the same; if they were to achieve their objective they had to stem the nationalist tide until they had rid themselves of the last vestiges of British authority.

Kaunda certainly shared this sense of approaching climax. In a letter to a friend at the beginning of 1958 he revealed his feeling of desperation. He wrote, 'Every day leaves me with the impression that I have not done anything to further the cause for which I try to work so earnestly – it is a terrible thought you know and indeed very heartrending.' Later in the same letter he expressed his sense of impending crisis when he explained, 'There is so much that is happening here and all of it at once . . . all I can tell you is there is plenty of trouble breeding here and you should expect an outburst at any time. What shape this will take I don't know. The thing is the white man is going ahead with his mad schemes while the African is getting out of his deep slumber of trusting him [the white] and wants to look after his own in his own way – naturally the conflict is bound to come some time.' He was also apprehensive that the government intended to remove him from the public scene. He declared that 'we are doing all we can to keep ourselves out of Her Majesty's Hostels and also avoiding receiving a free ticket from HMG to travel to some remote island in the Atlantic . . . In fact I have already been reliably informed that I am

topping the list of those likely to answer a call from HMG's representatives
... All I can say is I am still as determined as I have ever been to see this
thing through at all costs.'

In view of this obvious consciousness of the critical nature of the period,
why did Kaunda choose to be out of the country from the beginning of
June to the end of September, particularly as he had been abroad for
most of the previous year? I believe that within the answer to this query
lies an important clue to his state of mind at this time and to his whole
conception of his role in life.

He went first to Dar es Salaam at the beginning of June, the day he was
discharged from hospital. First he had had a shock over his health. He
later realised that he had not paid enough attention to the warning signs.
He wrote at the time, 'I have received so many letters showing annoyance
at my carelessness with my life – some of them going to the extent of telling
me I have become a coward and so would like to die early to get away
from it all – that I am now taking care of it.' He had treatment in Dar es
Salaam for his lung trouble lasting up to the day of his return home. A
few weeks later he was in India, where he was supposed to have an operation. But the doctors told him that his lungs were healing and the operation
unnecessary. Yet he stayed in India for another two months.

Determination to repair his health was one reason for this long absence
from the scene of battle, but it was only part of a larger one. In Dar es
Salaam he met TANU leaders and other leading Tanganyikans. In India
he was appalled by the conditions he saw, identifying them with what was
on the verge of happening to his own country. 'India,' he wrote, 'has
shown me more clearly my own problems than I have ever seen them
before and I am very grateful to her.' He added, 'My heart is more
than full as I see India just getting out of this house of disorder –
IMPERIALISM – while we are getting in from the other side.'

The fact was that Kaunda had begun to visualise the struggle in a
historical context. He was looking not just to an immediate victory over
the federation and the British government, but to the issues which would
arise after independence. In this he was unconsciously following the same
mental path as Nyerere, whom he first met on his visit to Dar es Salaam,
although there is no record of their first encounter. But it took much more
imaginative effort and sheer faith to assume that the battles against
federation and Britain could be won or that he would be in a position of
influence after these wars had ended. Nyerere at least could see his foe and
was virtually unchallenged as Tanganyika's leader. Kaunda had two
enemies, both of which often seemed shadowy; and he was still only second
in command, with many potential rivals surrounding him as well as the
constant danger of being removed from the struggle either by imprisonment or by assassination; he had received death letters at this time.

Nevertheless, Kaunda showed his historical sense in taking his opportunities to go abroad at this crucial time. He had gained experience of international politics, a close view of his British antagonists and training in political organisation when in Britain. Now he saw the struggle in Tanganyika at first hand, and was able to gain knowledge of TANU methods. Thence, in India, he experienced the effects of British rule on a country a hundred times the size of his own, absorbed the inspiration of his hero Gandhi, and was able to place his own nation's role in the historic perspective of the global anti-imperialist drama. He was convinced that he had a part to play, though not necessarily as the supreme national leader, for he had no concept of personal charisma. But he was steadily preparing himself for whatever role to which he might be called. This seemed more important than the immediate power struggle in central Africa, although it was always related to it.

On his return from India Kaunda was again faced with a crisis. During his absence criticism of Nkumbula had increased. He had again been sent to London to meet the Colonial Secretary. At the time of his appointment he was still in bed at his hotel! He had continued to dismiss Congress officials arbitrarily when he found their support for him waning. Kapwepwe, Sipalo, now expelled from Congress, Justin Chimba and Reuben Kamanga started consulting with each other about the problems raised by the president's conduct.

Kaunda's attitude was dictated by policy rather than personal considerations. He had considerable affection for the man who had led the nationalist movement, although he increasingly recognised that his personal outlook on politics would no longer suffice in the kind of battle which had been joined. It had now become obvious that Nkumbula was interested neither in mass organisation in the rural areas nor in responsible deployment of funds collected from the ordinary people.

But it was the president's flirtation with Harry Franklin and the Constitution Party which convinced Kaunda that the nationalist movement would fail if Nkumbula were left in charge. For this led the president to defy Congress decisions and, instead of supporting the agreed boycott of the new constitution, to propose an electoral alliance with Franklin. For the next few years Nkumbula flirted with one group after another, after Franklin with the government, then with the settler party and even with Tshombe in Katanga.

The first objective of Nkumbula's critics was to replace him as president. When this failed at the Congress conference of October 1958, Kaunda, Kapwepwe, and a small group of supporters left the meeting. Two days later at Broken Hill they held the inaugural meeting of the Zambia African National Congress. Over a thousand members of the ANC attended a public meeting, surrendered their ANC cards and joined the new party.

So the battle had to be started all over again. Kaunda was elected president of the new party, Kapwepwe treasurer-general and Sipalo secretary-general. But they started with nothing. On the day that the party was founded Kapwepwe and Kaunda had just two shillings between them to buy food for their families. And it was back to using the Kaunda home in Chilenje as the party office, despite the fact that Betty Kaunda was expecting their sixth child.

Moreover, the split in the nationalist movement occurred at a time when the federal flag was flying high. In February of that year Garfield Todd, who had liberal sympathies, had been deposed as prime minister of Southern Rhodesia. This made it easier for his successor, Edgar Whitehead, to take his party into a merger with Welensky. The new federal constitution had been approved, increasing the assembly members from thirty-five to fifty-nine with all but four dependent on European votes. The African Affairs Board had been exposed as a useless institution for the protection of African interests. The new Northern Rhodesian constitution, based on one of the Colonial Office's 'fancy franchises', consolidated white power. It seemed that the tide of white supremacy was running strongly towards the high water mark of Dominion Status by 1960. The division in Northern Rhodesia's nationalist ranks looked like a collapse of the principal breakwater.

Kaunda and his colleagues had two immediate tasks to perform. First they had to convince those whom they had previously recruited into nationalist ranks that the split was caused by policy rather than personality factors; secondly, they had to implement the boycott of the Benson constitution. The two tasks were clearly linked; indeed, the future of their new party would largely depend on their success in combating Nkumbula's new-found willingness to fight elections under the new constitution. If the ZANC persuaded most Africans to refuse to register for the elections, this would establish the policy difference between the two parties and substantiate the claim that policy, not personality, divided them.

Kaunda, Kapwepwe and Sipalo possessed one crucial advantage over those who remained with the ANC. Because of their earlier organisational work they were closer to the people in most rural areas. Thus a great deal of their initial support came from the north and the east. The south, which was Nkumbula's home territory, remained mainly loyal to ANC, the west was still to be won, in the towns the battle continued to rage, though Kapwepwe's Bemba allegiance gave ZANC an advantage on the Copper Belt.

Before the end of the year another external event drew Kaunda away from his home, again demonstrating his self-confidence in leaving the eye of the storm. In December Kwame Nkrumah called an All-African People's Conference to Accra. This reflected his determination to use

Ghana's independence as a base to assist the rest of Africa to freedom from colonial rule. Both Kaunda and Nkumbula attended, this being Kaunda's first experience of west African life.

At the conference the need for unity in the anti-colonial struggles was continually emphasised. The split in the nationalist movement of Northern Rhodesia was especially deplored, as it was recognised that central Africa had become the key area in the immediate strategy of fighting white supremacy.

Various individuals tried to persuade Kaunda and Nkumbula to bury their differences whilst they were in Accra. Hastings Banda, who had returned to lead the Nyasaland nationalists a few months earlier, and George Padmore, then heading Nkrumah's Pan-African Institute, had preliminary discussions with the two. Then Nkrumah himself saw them. It was really too late. Already the ANC, after a period of some indecision, was preparing to fight the elections; the ZANC was organising a national boycott of them.

Once again Kaunda demonstrated his determination to take every opportunity to prepare himself for what he visualised as a long struggle for independence and nation-building. He stayed on in Accra for a month after the conference ended, attending an Extra-Mural School at Legon, the university college of Ghana, seeing something of how the country was being run, visiting Togoland, and endlessly discussing African problems with everyone he met.

On his return to Northern Rhodesia, encouraged by his Ghana experience of the total African assault on colonial rule, Kaunda threw himself into the struggle to build his new party and the battle to persuade Africans to boycott the elections due in March. By now the ANC was committed to fighting those elections, Nkumbula himself being a candidate. Indeed, there was some evidence that the government was helping Nkumbula, now regarding him as the moderate, with the ZANC representing the militant wing of nationalism.

Kaunda and his party won that battle. Despite ANC encouragement to Africans to register as voters and desperate government efforts to the same end, under 8,000 were persuaded to place their names on both electoral rolls open to them. The government target had been 25,000. But the battle was won at a cost. On his return from Accra Kaunda told his supporters in Lusaka, 'Whatever the consequences, we are prepared to pay the price of freedom in this country.' He was soon to experience those consequences. The government could not afford to have its new constitution flouted.

By now the political temperature was rising rapidly throughout central Africa. Welensky and his colleagues in each of the territories, together with the governors of Northern Rhodesia and Nyasaland, were frightened by the news they had of the Accra conference. They recognised that the African nationalists in central Africa now had support in other parts of the continent. Banda in Nyasaland and Kaunda in Northern Rhodesia had publicly declared war on the federation itself. The white leaders believed that either nationalism must be crushed now or prospects of an independent federation might disappear forever.

At the end of February a State of Emergency was declared in Southern Rhodesia, a few days later in Nyasaland. Hundreds of Africans, including Hastings Banda, were arrested. The removal of their leaders led to violent protests from African followers, accompanied by counter-violence from the security forces with considerable loss of African lives.

Northern Rhodesia could not be exempt from this reign of intimidation, although it took a slightly different form in that territory. Kaunda and Sipalo were in the eastern province at the time, meeting some of the Nyasaland Congress. On their return to Lusaka it was immediately apparent to them that they were about to be arrested. Kaunda himself has vividly described the scene in his autobiography, *Zambia Shall Be Free.* He relates how ten people were sleeping in his two-roomed house in New Chilenje, he and his wife, their five sons, two nieces and a nephew, one stiflingly hot night in March. At 1 a.m. the police burst into his bedroom, gave him a paper to sign, made him pack a suitcase, gathered all his books and papers and drove him away handcuffed in a Land-Rover. Police vehicles were all over Lusaka that night, eventually converging on a quarry six miles out of town off the Great North Road. All the ZANC leaders had been picked up. Finally they were driven at high speed to the airport, which was also filled with security forces. With two companions Kaunda was flown deep into the remote north-west province where they were 'rusticated' at Kabompo. Each of the leaders was detained in some remote district, always far from their home area. The Zambia Congress was banned.

It is still impossible to comprehend how the minds of the men who ordered this or similar detentions operated. With the example of the consequences of incarcerating men like Gandhi, Nehru, Nkrumah, Bustamante, Burnham, Jagan, Makarios, already before them, it seems incredible that they could still close their eyes to historical logic. No contrary data existed; when has detention of a nationalist leader resulted in the destruction of his movement?

The rigours of first detention and later imprisonment certainly did not crush Kaunda's spirit. It was typical of him that he sought to find new opportunities in his predicament instead of dwelling on the injustice of his fate. This was particularly difficult in his case for he immediately suffered from dysentery and then from malaria whilst at Kabompo. Throughout his period in detention and prison he also experienced stomach trouble, for the authorities made it difficult for him to purchase the foods he was accustomed to eat. Nevertheless, during his time in Kabompo he not only gained the confidence of the local people and studied their life, for he had never been in the district before, but found time to gain some inspiration from meditating on the beauties of the natural environment in which he was confined. But he was very worried about the drunkenness of the young men of the district and wondered how they would face the task of nation-building which continually agitated his mind. He was particularly incensed to hear that the government was going to bring a bottle store to the neighbourhood.

Kaunda's attitude to his detention can again be gleaned from his letters from Kabompo. In one he humorously described the place as 'a St Helena on the mainland'. It was again characteristic that he wrote asking for a book entitled *A Guide to Confident Living and the Power of Positive Thinking.* He was worried about his family, which could not travel the great distance from Lusaka to see him. His wife was also troubled, both about his health and by the fact that she had no money to pay for her sons' school fees. But he was greatly encouraged to learn that, despite virulent government propaganda about the evils of his party, people throughout the country were demonstrating that they still had faith in its future.

That Kaunda did not lose his sense of humour, even under the provocation of deliberately harsh treatment, is attested by the way in which he described one of the heartless deprivations to which he was subjected: 'You know I get 4/6 per day. I got my supply of eggs from a Government Development Centre here for the first two weeks at 2/– per doz. But you see all fowl here heard of my "rabid" politics and so right in revolt they went "until the principal there could stop supplying me with their eggs – no more laying!" So that the poor fellow gave in and had to sell me no more eggs. I have now to get my supply of eggs at 4/6 per doz. [400 miles away].'

In a further letter from detention Kaunda reiterated his refusal to become anti-white, at the same time revealing a touching faith in the Labour Party which had given him hospitality. He wrote:

Settlers here are shouting night and day at the 'irresponsible Labour Party'. A new era has been reached if only the rank and file and leaders of both the Labour Party and African nationalist organisations can use it to the advantage of mankind as a whole . . . As for me I think it is a healthy sign. It is an effective measure in stopping African nationalism from becoming rabidly anti-white which I believe to be wrong. There is no moral strength in Africans preaching against racial discrimination by whites and then replacing it with one of their own. And when on the political plane you remove morals from the scene, I believe your politics will be dead.

With typical thought for his colleagues, he listed the location of those he knew to have been detained and asked that newspapers, periodicals and letters be sent to them. Then he summed up his own perspective on the significance of his detention in these succint words: 'It is a test examination for us to see if we are ready to face the tempests of what we lightly refer to as LIFE.' The spirit of his missionary father was still alive.

During the few months of 'rustication' Kaunda and his companions were free to wander around the district, meet the people, and work from their improvised office. But 'rustication' was not sufficient for the government. No doubt it was uneasy over the detention of men against whom no charge had been made. So it decided to charge Kaunda with 'conspiring to effect an unlawful purpose' and 'authorising to be held an unlawful meeting'. The government's desperation can be witnessed from the vagueness of such charges. But Kaunda was arrested in Kabompo, flown back to Lusaka and sentenced at the court there to nine months on the first charge and three months on the second, the two sentences to run concurrently. He was sent to Lusaka Central Prison, to the same cell he had occupied with Nkumbula in 1955. He worked as a cook in prison and, although lodged in the European, Asian and Euro-African quarters, received according to the regulations four ounces less of sugar, cheese and fish than the white or brown prisoners.

I was in central Africa at this time. Having just talked to Hastings Banda, Henry Chipembere and Dunduza Chisiza who were detained in Gwelo gaol, I proceeded to Lusaka where I also secured permission to see Kaunda. He assured me that his health was now improved, but told me that he still could not get the foods he needed, about which I made a strong complaint to the governor. Although he had now despaired of Nkumbula, he assured me that splinters from the ANC would join him and that he aimed to build a united nationalist movement. He was as relaxed and earnest as I had ever known him, quite determined to maintain his non-violent methods and the democratic principles he had observed when in Britain. He explained that the violence of which the government accused his followers only started after the leaders were removed into rustication, an inevitable reaction but one which he deplored.

I spent some time during that visit with Nkumbula, whom I had known longer than Kaunda, and for whom I had much affection. But I had no doubt that it would be Kaunda who would lead his people into nationhood. It was an emotionally unpleasant experience to have to leave him in prison. I was also left in no doubt on this visit of the appalling tensions which had been provoked by the detentions, nor of the gross mismanagement of justice which was being perpetrated in the crisis. And my informants were not politicians but a number of lawyers and magistrates. It was at this time, too, that I first heard of Alice Lenshina, the African prophetess who was to figure in one of the country's major tragedies. Already, she had been assaulted by the police and her church desecrated.

Kaunda did not have long in the kitchen in Lusaka prison. He, Sipalo and Wilson Chakulya, secretary of the Broken Hill branch and a trade unionist, were handcuffed and driven to Salisbury. Thus once again the federal influence was being impressed on the nationalists. They were not to serve their terms in their own country, but in the capital of the federation.

Despite some harassment from junior prison officers, Kaunda was reasonably happy during his stay in Salisbury gaol. He spoke especially warmly of the consideration he received from the superintendent. He also enjoyed working in the book-binding department and was able to use some of his time in correspondence study of economics from Ruskin College. Letters and books from friends in many countries enabled him to feel that he was spending his time usefully.

In December came a re-transfer back to Lusaka for the last three weeks of his sentence. On this occasion he was driven by Sir John Moffat, with a corporal in the back seat, as the plane was full. The sight of December green fields after five months with no view but prison walls brought an emotion Kaunda has never forgotten. At the end of the first week in January he was released from Lusaka gaol. He immediately made a statement which included these declarations:

> Freedom! All I am asking the Africans of Northern Rhodesia is that they should remain calm and patient; and should prepare themselves for the real non-violent struggle that lies ahead. The Zambia African Congress was banned, but there is no power to ban our desire to be free, to shape our own destiny. In this struggle for freedom, we will tell the present rulers to realize that the colour of man should not count; what should count is his behaviour . . . I am determined more than ever before to achieve self-government for Africans in this country. Detentions, imprisonments and rural-area restrictions will only delay, but will not stop us from reaching that goal, which should be reached this year, 1960.

During Kaunda's absence from the scene events had moved swiftly and he emerged from prison into a maelstrom of political developments. The Northern Rhodesian elections had been held peacefully, but with such frustrating results for Africans that the constitution was now acceptable to only a tiny minority. Even Nkumbula and the ANC now realised that almost every member of the new Council depended on white voters. In the previous July the Devlin Commission, appointed to report on the events in Nyasaland, had come out with the devastating judgement that Nyasaland had become virtually a 'police state'. Shaken by this finding and by the simultaneous Hola incident in Kenya, the Macmillan government in Britain had belatedly recognised that its colonial policy in Africa could become an Achilles heel. After it had won another term of office in October 1959, much to the Africans' chagrin, the government had been re-organised. Lennox-Boyd was retired to the Lords and replaced by Iain Macleod, who, despite lack of experience in colonial matters, came from the liberal wing of the Conservative Party.

By this time, too, the Monckton Commission had been appointed and was about to visit central Africa. Its appointment had caused great argument in Britain. The Commission was to investigate the federation prior to the 1960 review. In order to persuade Welensky to accept it, the terms of reference were to exclude the issue of the right of secession by any constituent territory. Its membership was also heavily weighted in favour of the whites and of the preservation of the federation. In these circumstances the British Labour Party refused to nominate members to it, alleging that its purpose was to whitewash the federation.

In practice the Monckton Commission was to report an almost total hostility towards the federation from Africans. Even those Commission members favouring the federation could not escape this conclusion from their investigations, even though the African nationalists refused to give evidence. The fact that no opponents served on the Commission only strengthened the effects of these findings.

This was the time, also, when Harold Macmillan, impressed by the importance which Africa was assuming in British politics, was starting an African tour. He travelled to Nigeria, Ghana, the federation and South Africa. So impressed was he with the temper towards colonialism and white supremacy of the Africans he saw, that he made a remarkable statement for a Conservative politician. In Cape Town at the beginning of February he was moved to declare, 'The most striking of all the impressions I have formed since I left London a month ago is of the strength of this African national consciousness . . . The wind of change is blowing through the continent . . . Our national policies must take account of it.' Such a statement from a British Prime Minister whose government was wedded to the white-dominated federation demonstrated that the 'wind of change' was blowing through Whitehall as well as in Africa. It made it blindingly obvious that the kind of federation which had been created could no longer rely on uncritical support from the British government – provided always that the African nationalists maintained their pressure.

One final factor in this changing balance of forces should be mentioned. The Belgians had just reversed their traditional policy in the Congo. That

country was to become independent at the end of June. No one doubted
that the Africans of British central Africa had much more experience of
politics and were far more capable of running a state than those of the
Congo, who had been starved of experience by Belgium. The Congo had
a long frontier with Northern Rhodesia; indeed, it was only European
partition which had artificially divided the peoples of the frontier area,
who had previously been members of the same communities. It seemed
unlikely, at least, that the Africans of Northern Rhodesia would be content
to remain under white rule, whether federal, territorial or colonial, whilst
their cousins on the other side of the border controlled their own state.

In fact it had become apparent in London during 1959 that Welensky's
chances of getting Dominion Status on the agenda of the 1960 review
conference had disappeared. The mood of British politics after the emergencies of February and March altered radically. The change was confirmed by the Devlin Report. The period of fantasy which had lasted
from 1953 was concluded. British politicians realised yet again that a
democratic country cannot be ruled against the will of the governed. Once
that will had been clearly demonstrated, parliamentary approval for
suppressing it could not be sustained for long. Welensky and his colleagues
had sealed the fate of their plans by their authoritarian actions in all three
countries. Once the impact of those actions was felt in Westminster the
federal case for independence under continued white domination was lost.
Just as the British parliament had realised that the Mau Mau emergency
in Kenya demonstrated that the Africans could only be subdued by force,
so in central Africa the emergencies proved that the federal government
was opposed by the weight of African opinion. The mistake of giving
independence to the minority whites of South Africa in 1910 had been
learnt by now, whilst, in the meantime, British political life had become far
more democratic.

This did not imply that the whole battle was won. Indeed, when in
central Africa in 1959, it seemed to me that the greatest danger which
faced the nationalists came from various liberal schemes rather than from
Welensky and the white supremacists. Whilst they might have reduced the
more obvious injustices of the existing federal and territorial constitutions,
the schemes would have blurred the central issue of confrontation between
white supremacy and majority rule. They would have preserved the
federation under an elitist system, which could only have delayed the final
decision and would have led to an aggravated frustration amongst the
Africans that might well have resulted in further violence.

Yet although independence for the federation by 1960 was now virtually
impossible, the future of its three constituent territories was the immediate
issue at stake. Welensky and the pro-federationists might have won a
Pyrrhic victory over the nationalists in the emergencies of the previous

year; now a more realistic battle was to be joined between the two forces, with this time the crucial difference that Westminster had entered the lists as adjudicator.

During Kaunda's period in gaol a number of new parties had been formed, partly to replace the banned Zambia Congress, partly through splits in Nkumbula's ANC. In November they had all merged to form the United National Independence Party, with Mainza Chona as interim president. By the end of January Kaunda, Kapwepwe and Sipalo were all free again. So the interim officials of UNIP stood down, allowing the trio to take up the positions they had held in the ZANC. It was to be this new party on which the main responsibility for fighting Welensky was to fall. Their immediate task was to organise and build the party to become a genuine national organisation.

Although it decided to boycott the Monckton Commission because of the absence of secession from its agenda, the visit of the Commission to Northern Rhodesia gave Kaunda and his colleagues an excellent opportunity to mobilise support. Both Kaunda and Nkumbula had met Macmillan during his African tour, both telling him firmly that their parties would not give evidence to Monckton and were implacably opposed to a continuation of federation. When the Commission arrived in Northern Rhodesia the campaign against it enabled the party to talk directly to the people throughout the country on a subject about which feelings were now rapidly rising. The release of Hastings Banda in April and Macleod's willingness to hold discussions with him, also gave UNIP a spur to greater effort. If Nyasaland's Africans could inspire confidence with the British government, there was no reason why Northern Rhodesia's should be treated with less respect.

In their efforts to extend their party membership from their strongholds in the north and the Copper Belt to the rest of the country Kaunda's reputation as the man who had been martyred by the government gave UNIP a great advantage over the ANC. The contrast between the leader who had spent over nine months in detention and Nkumbula who had become a member of the Council provided a sharp contrast before African opinion. Yet this raised one major problem. As the party rapidly expanded, discipline became more difficult to maintain. Amongst the thousands who flocked to join there were bound to be many hot-heads who had little concept of the strict self-discipline essential in the tense atmosphere of the time.

Kaunda steadfastly continued to emphasise the importance of non-violence. It became a central point of each speech he made, continually reinforced by articles in the party newspaper. What he was trying to devise was an amalgam of Gandhi's non-violence and Nkrumah's positive action, a desperately difficult balance to attain.

The dangers of violence were aggravated by the slogan 'Independence by October', which had been coined before Kaunda left gaol. There was really no chance of this objective being attained and, although Kaunda knew this, he had to walk the tightrope of avoiding misleading his followers without disavowing his predecessors who still served alongside him.

The tension continued to rise as it appeared that all hope of constitutional progress was blocked for the next three years which the Benson arrangements were designed to cover. Trouble started in certain schools, there were a number of outbreaks of arson, petrol bombs were thrown, cars stoned and railways obstructed. None of these violent protests was sanctioned by UNIP, but the party was blamed by the government which banned its meetings in certain places. It was becoming increasingly clear to all concerned that the trial of strength had started. The government made ready by enlarging the police force, preparing detention camps, and setting up a network of informers.

It may again seem curious that at this tense moment Kaunda once more chose to leave the country. Yet he realised that in this battle with the government overseas' opinion would probably be decisive. His party was also desperate for funds. He hoped to combine lobbying with fund-raising.

In April he made his first visit to the United States on a lecture tour. He stayed in Britain for some time on his way back, speaking at meetings, talking to members of parliament, discussing his tactics with a number of us in the political world, and having a discussion with the Colonial Secretary. He then visited some African countries, culminating in being deported at an hour's notice from Kenya, an occurrence which gave him even greater popularity at home.

Whilst he was in London, however, Kaunda received news which, for a moment, shattered him. In May a young white woman, Mrs Burton, was burned to death in a petrol bomb attack on her car in Ndola following disturbances between police and crowd at a banned UNIP meeting where a hundred people were arrested. Kaunda was horrified. He saw all his efforts for inter-racial understanding destroyed, his policy of non-violence flouted. It caused him to wonder whether it was safe for him to leave his country when such acts were perpetrated in his absence, especially as some of UNIP's other top officials were abroad at the same time. UNIP and its officials, including Kaunda, were banned from Western Province. The incident tempted the governor to flirt with the idea of using it to undermine UNIP and encourage the ANC.

The Burton murder certainly raised inter-racial tensions, but it speaks much for the underlying bonds that it did not provoke an outburst of racial violence. Acts of violence did continue, however, but suddenly decreased the following August. It was at this time that the governor, now

Sir Evelyn Hone, began to have discussions with various political leaders. This marked success for the nationalists in the first phase of the battle. Although the constitution had still three years to run and Macleod had stated that any review would have to wait until after the federal conference at the end of the year, it was clear that consideration of a new constitution had started. At the end of September the Colonial Secretary announced that constitutional changes were to be made, with a conference on them being held at the same time as the federation was reviewed. As Banda had just been promised a constitution providing for an African majority, it was expected that Northern Rhodesia would be granted something similar. Kaunda was spared the awkward choice of admitting that the people had been misled by UNIP into expecting independence in 1960, or declaring all-out war on the government. The first round had been won by UNIP and lost by Welensky and his white settler supporters.

The backcloth to Macleod's conversion was the copy of the Monckton Report which he had in his office. It was not published until the next month, but Macleod had read his advance copy. He knew that, despite the white-biased nature of the Commission, it had been so impressed with the hatred of federation amongst Africans that it recommended that a new constitution should be offered to Northern Rhodesia before the federal review was completed, and that it should be similar to that given to Nyasaland. With such testimony published, the British government would be unable to withstand pressure to grant Kaunda's demand for some form of majority rule.

When Kaunda came to London at the end of the year, along with Nkumbula and Katilungu of the ANC, Banda from Nyasaland and Nkomo from Southern Rhodesia, he was more relaxed than on any previous visit. All appearances suggested that the major battle was won. He was treated in Britain as the leading African, having clearly won his contest with Nkumbula. After the Monckton Report he had reason to believe that the federation would not survive much longer; and the Nyasaland precedent strongly suggested that he could expect a more democratic constitution for his own country in the near future. In private conversation and in talking to the various groups which all the delegations lobbied interminably, he exuded a new-found confidence, although he never assumed that the whole war was over. He was not to know that almost two more years of storm and strife faced him in the next phase of the battle.

Lancaster House, scene of the gradual dismemberment of the British Empire during the 1950s and 1960s, became the stage on which the final drama of federation was acted. The federal review conference with which proceedings opened, was simply a farce. There was no common ground between the African nationalists and the supporters of federation. The week was punctuated by prepared speeches which did no more than finally convince the British government that it would have to choose between African nationalism and continued violent imposition of white rule. At various points the African delegations staged walkouts, partly jockeying for position, partly ensuring that their supporters at home recognised that they would not compromise. At the end of a week the conference was adjourned. It was never to reconvene.

By now it was realised that the crucial area of negotiation lay in the constitutions determined for the two Rhodesias. Welensky and his closest colleagues were reconciled to the secession of Nyasaland. They had never wanted the territory included in the first place, their main objective being to combine the copper wealth of Northern Rhodesia with the industrial base of Southern Rhodesia, the combination to form the foundations for a comfortable, prosperous white community. Thus the crux of the London negotiations was the fate of Northern Rhodesia. Behind the scenes Welensky was deploying every available weapon to defend a continuation of white rule in the north. He realised that if African government came there, his federation was doomed.

Discussions on the issue of a new constitution for Northern Rhodesia were brief, but again demonstrated the absence of common ground between the nationalists and the white delegates. Kaunda and his colleagues were determined to accept nothing less than majority rule. At this time he was supported by a similar attitude from Nkumbula and the ANC delegation.

Now began a year almost entirely taken up by a bitter struggle between those who believed that the time had come for majority government for Northern Rhodesia and those who, convinced that this would bring death to the federation, were determined to prevent it. On the one hand Macleod and his supporters in the British government and parliament, were trying to devise means of clearing an evolutionary path through the jungle of racialist antagonisms; on the other, Welensky, with the support of British right-wing politicians like Lord Salisbury, were resolved to defeat his plans. On the sidelines the African nationalists, Northern Rhodesia's white politicians, and various liberal forces in Britain, led by the Labour Party, supplied the ammunition.

The bitterness and intensity of the contest can be judged from the fact that at one time Welensky called up battalions of territorials in both Rhodesias, whilst the British government moved troop carriers from Aden to Nairobi. It seemed for a moment that Welensky was on the point of declaring the federation independent in defiance of British authority. But the moment passed; probably Welensky realised that he could not count on the large number of Africans in his army and in the police forces if he should try such a desperate gamble. Moreover, although Welensky was passionately angry at what he saw as British betrayal, it was not really in his character to make war against Britain.

For Kaunda this was a year of unremitting nervous tension. He had been assured by Macleod at the first talks in December that he could expect a constitution on the lines of that granted to Banda in Nyasaland. Yet, although he did not know the details of the battle being waged between the British government and Welensky, he was well aware that it was taking place. When the situation reached its first climax in February 1961 he declared that if Britain yielded to federal pressure over majority rule the reaction in Northern Rhodesia 'would make Mau Mau look like a child's picnic'. He quickly qualified the impression given by this statement by reiterating his continued commitment to non-violence.

Eventually, in February, Macleod published a White Paper which contained a framework of his proposals. It was based on a legislature of forty-five members, divided into three equal sections. There would be two electoral rolls, one mainly white, the other largely African. Each roll would elect fifteen members. The other fifteen would be elected by the two rolls combined. But the crucial issue was the conditions which would be laid down for the election of this third section of members. For they would inevitably determine which political group could command a majority. These members would have to secure a percentage from each roll; on the size of that percentage would depend who could expect to win the seats.

It was clearly the intention of the British government at that time to devise a scheme which would allow John Moffat, Harry Franklin and their Liberals to win most or all of these fifteen 'national' seats, hold the balance between white and black nationalists and form a government. At the height of the crisis with Welensky John Roberts and his white settler party members had resigned from the Northern Rhodesian government. Their places had been taken by Moffat's Liberals and civil servants. Macleod's calculation was that with the Liberals winning the fifteen 'national' seats, and perhaps a few of those on the upper roll, they would be in a position to steer a 'moderate' course between the rival nationalists, bringing in 'moderate' Africans and Europeans to establish a strong centre. Even Macleod was under-estimating the powerful ground-swell of African nationalism. With a typical British viewpoint he equated 'moderation' with rational policies capable of forging inter-racial co-operation. But Africa was in the midst of revolution. It needed strong, principled policies if bloodshed was to be avoided. Centrist approaches could only frustrate both contestants, increasing the provocation to violence.

Nevertheless, Kaunda and Nkumbula were prepared to consider operating this constitutional device as a temporary expedient. They calculated that it would probably provide a majority opposed to a continuation of federation, allowing them room for further manoeuvre in the future.

Nkumbula had another reason for considering acceptance. Although Welensky had railed against Macleod's proposals, his party in Northern Rhodesia, the United Federal Party, was already planning to use them in order to return to office with the increased executive powers which the new constitution would provide. The tactic of John Roberts, its leader, was to make a bargain with Nkumbula whereby his UFP would supply the necessary white votes to ANC candidates, Nkumbula securing African votes for the UFP. When, in the midst of this bargaining, Nkumbula went to prison on a driving charge and was replaced by Katilungu, the chances of accommodation were improved.

Yet the battle was far from over. The federalists were not prepared to accept defeat by Macleod. They enormously increased their campaign after the White Paper had been published, concentrating on the conditions for election to the decisive 'national seats'. Immense propaganda was unleashed in Britain, directed by a public relations firm and aided by right-wing Conservatives and business interests.

Kaunda was not content to leave the defence of African interests to Macleod and his British supporters. He intensified his campaign at home, telling one Copper Belt rally that he had prepared a 'master plan' which could paralyse the country. He also visited Britain again, adding his warnings to those already delivered by the governor and Moffat that any surrender to federal pressure would provoke serious trouble in Northern Rhodesia. By this time Kaunda was tense and anxious once more when he came to us in London. He knew that Welensky was throwing in every resource he possessed in a final effort to coerce the British government into modifying its proposals in his favour. The atmosphere in London itself was electric. Delegation after delegation lobbied us, pressure after pressure was applied to politicians, press and public. The most violent threats were made – one delegation from the white copper-miners, for instance, assured us that they had guns and ammunition stored, that they would be on the streets if ever African rule were proposed. Some of us were receiving telegrams and cables, often couched in obscene language.

Kaunda's fears were justified. The burden of pressures was beginning to have effect inside the Conservative Party and its government. It was sufficient to coerce Macleod to produce proposals in June which would clearly deny the nationalists their majority. The requirement for election in the 'national' seats would necessitate securing a number of white votes which no nationalists could attain without an alliance with the UFP; but there would be so many Africans on the roll that European candidates would need only a small proportion of black votes to secure election. The whole constitution was so complicated that virtually no one could understand it clearly and there was constant argument over its interpretation. Jo Grimond, then leader of the British Liberal Party, perhaps made the most telling comment when he pointed out that demands for electoral reform in Britain were continually rejected on the ground that they were too complex for the electorate to comprehend; yet the British government was offering this complicated constitution to people whom it alleged were not yet fit for universal suffrage. There was general agreement amongst critics of the government that it could well bring democracy itself into contempt.

It was the consequences, not the details, of the new proposals which angered Kaunda. He had been virtually promised a majority constitution similar to that granted to Banda; now he had seen that promise broken as a result of Welensky's pressure. He believed that unless he could mobilise sufficient counter-pressure, the British government would reprieve the federation, forcing Northern Rhodesia to remain within it. That would give Welensky and his friends the opportunity to remove it as far from British authority as South Africa had placed herself. In that event, nothing short of civil war could establish African constitutional rights.

Once more Kaunda had to face the dilemma of violence and non-violence. He knew that in the desperately tense situation which had now arisen any form of protest would certainly provoke some of his supporters to take violent actions. Yet to desist from protest at this moment would be to admit defeat of all he believed. He had already been given emergency powers by his annual conference, had announced that the elections would be boycotted and declared that 'we shall not let the constitution survive'. When he was searched by federal officers on passing through Salisbury airport it appeared to his followers that the federal government was determined to make war on them. They were ready to counter-attack.

Kaunda now made an extensive tour of the whole of the north. He had adopted the toga type of dress made famous by Nkrumah, emphasising the African, non-European nature of his leadership. He added a further dramatic effect by training his hair to stand up as though electrified. During his tour he continued to emphasise that non-violent measures only should be used, that his party was fighting the government, not whites or individuals. His influence prevailed. Although white farmers and their families were as isolated as those in Kenya, there were no attacks on white settlers. The followers of UNIP interpreted Kaunda's instructions as freedom to sabotage the government's material possessions, whilst refraining from harming people. Roads, railways, bridges, telephone wires, schools and workshops were attacked. Riot police and troops were sent in massive numbers to the disaffected areas. There were many African deaths, injuries and arrests. UNIP was banned in the north, which once again removed Kaunda's moderating influence from the scene of violence.

Once again the British government bowed to pressure. For the third time in a year it changed course. By this time, of course, British colonial policy had been reduced to withdrawal at any cost from the Empire, handing over authority to whoever appeared in the ascendant at the time. Its difficulty in Northern Rhodesia from 1960 to 1962 was that it could never make up its mind where ascendancy lay.

In September 1961, after an intensive campaign in which UNIP, the British Labour Party, the churches and sections of the British press all participated, the British government announced that it was re-opening discussions on Macleod's 'final' constitution. It is possible that their own constitutional proposals had been so convoluted that they had not been fully understood by members of the British government itself. I had a personal discussion with Macleod at this time. He was convinced that his June proposals would produce an African majority, especially if UNIP and ANC co-operated. Significantly, he assured me that if he was shown to be wrong, he would try and amend them.

Inevitably, the new announcement infuriated supporters of federation. For a second time they considered themselves betrayed by the British government. Amongst the militant whites in Northern Rhodesia plans were made for a rebellion, but nothing came of it.

The new situation caused significant changes in the political situation. In place of the rebellion visualised by the hot-heads of the UFP, that party renewed its efforts to secure co-operation with the ANC. With Nkumbula in prison, the white politicians found his successor, Lawrence Katilungu, much more efficient and amenable. He had suffered opprobrium from many Africans for agreeing to serve on the Monckton Commission, but his experience in the trade union movement and his rejection by militant nationalists and trade unionists made him the ideal figure for the whites to project as the 'moderate' alternative to UNIP. The fact that he was tragically killed in a car accident in November 1961, together with the return of Nkumbula, weakened but did not destroy UFP–ANC collaboration.

The other side of ANC manoeuvres was an association with Tshombe in Katanga. Tshombe had plenty of money available to help the ANC, was friendly with Katilungu and saw the advantage of having African allies in Northern Rhodesia whose support for Katanga secession could be bought.

Meanwhile, although the disturbances in the north subsided after the British government's latest change of mind, the constitutional issue remained the core of the political battle. Kaunda and his colleagues had to devote all their efforts to impressing the new Colonial Secretary, Reginald

Maudling, with the necessity for changing Macleod's June proposals so as to allow a majority-elected government to take office.

In the course of this political battle the question of party discipline again became important. One instance illustrates both the dangers and Kaunda's authority. At the Belgrade conference of the non-aligned nations a number of UNIP leaders issued a statement. It accused the European settlers, with the sanction of the British government, of 'a well-planned genocide operation'. Kaunda realised that this grossly exaggerated claim would antagonise his supporters overseas. He publicly repudiated the 'genocide' accusation and apologised to the British government. Nothing could have more clearly demonstrated his stature in his tension-ridden country than this ability to repudiate the words of less rational colleagues.

All through the final months of 1961 and into the following year the battle of contending pressures mounted. Maudling visited Northern Rhodesia towards the end of the year – immediately before Tanganyika's independence. He listened to all sides, but when I met him in Government House it was obvious that he had no idea what to do with the situation he had inherited. He talked to me about the 'thousand years' it had taken universal suffrage to evolve in Europe, clearly ignorant of Africa's history of democracy. It was equally obvious that he and the government were impressed with the virtual unanimity of African opinion. Even important chiefs told him that he must ensure an African majority.

Those in the government and amongst the whites who were seeking an evolution of multi-racialism in Northern Rhodesia realised the damage done to their hopes by the federal intervention. Even John Roberts told me that he had always sought a gradual extension of African representation until a majority was attained. During the earlier part of the year, when Macleod had indicated his intention of granting majority government, many of the whites had accepted the *fait accompli*. During this time Kaunda addressed many white clubs and received quite a warm reception from them. The interference of Welensky and his supporters had turned back the clock, thereby damaging the prospects of inter-racial confidence by holding out a false hope that white power would continue for a lengthy period.

It would have been madness to raise African hopes again only to dash them by new proposals on the lines of those suggested in June. Yet Maudling and the British government almost did just that. When the new provisions were announced at the end of February, the qualification for national seats had been slightly amended in the Africans' favour, but did not appear to guarantee the crucial African majority. In fact, although the amendment appeared likely to prevent the UFP from gaining the national seats with ANC help, it seemed almost certain that the new decisions would make it impossible for anyone to win them. The

British government had tried to avoid facing the challenge of either side, arriving at a conclusion which rendered the constitution almost entirely unworkable.

Kaunda saved the British government's face on this occasion. There was a long and heated debate in the UNIP national committee between those who thought it best to fight elections under the new constitution and those who believed that the constitution should be rejected and further protests organised. The former view narrowly prevailed. With profound distaste, the party decided to fight the elections. The decision brought a sigh of relief to Whitehall, which had been holding its breath lest the disorders of the previous year be repeated.

The election was to be held at the end of October, to be completed before the rains broke. Before the campaign proper started, it became obvious that deep hostility existed between UNIP and the ANC, for violent clashes broke out between supporters of the two parties on the Copper Belt, several people being killed. The suspicion of collusion between the ANC and the UFP aggravated the bitterness created by the original split.

Yet the real campaign took place between the two racial communities. If UNIP was to aspire to majority government it was essential to attract European votes. The reputation for violence arising from the events of the previous year militated against their chances. In any case, most Europeans felt that the UFP was their party and that they should give it all their support.

Kaunda worked harder during this period than ever before. For two months, during September and October, he was speaking, organising, talking privately for eighteen hours a day, seven days a week. He gambled everything on the creation of inter-racial harmony, on the concept of a new, non-racial nation. He collected an impressive team of candidates, including one of the country's oldest settlers, Sir Stewart Gore-Browne; a lawyer, James Skinner; a missionary, Merfyn Temple; an Asian business-man, T. L. Desai and a Cypriot businessman, Andrew Sardanis.

The gamble failed. The European press, the whole weight of federal political organisation and the alliance between UFP and ANC were aligned against Kaunda and his party. Racial polarisation was obvious from the results. UNIP polled 78 per cent of the votes on the lower roll gaining twelve seats, whilst ANC attracted 21 per cent of the voters which gave it three seats. The UFP took thirteen seats on the upper roll, with 70 per cent of voters and UNIP one seat from 20 per cent. The election for the national seats was a farce. For example, Gore-Browne polled 11,264 African votes, but only fifty-five European; so he was not elected. The UFP secured two further members, as did ANC, as a result of their alliance. In by-elections for seats not filled UFP took one further seat and

ANC two more. Yet eight seats could not be filled even after by-elections; UNIP, which had polled the vast majority of African votes, could not win a single national constituency. Maudling's constitution was exposed as the comic tragedy which had been forecast.

The result therefore left UNIP with fourteen seats (which included the Eurafrican–Asian seat), UFP with sixteen and ANC with seven. Once again the country teetered on the brink of revolution. Was the UFP–ANC alliance to construct a coalition government in defiance of the massive African poll secured by Kaunda's party? If it did, violent revolt was certain. The mass of Africans would not see their judgement flouted in this way by constitutional complexities imposed by the British government. Were all Kaunda's hopes of non-racial nationalism to be dashed by a phoney constitution? If so, he would probably leave public life and his reins would be taken up by the apostles of violence.

The tension lasted for a month. All African opinion was united in demanding that the two African parties should form an alliance. The chiefs intervened by appealing for re-unity; even those members from each party who had most bitterly fought their rival nationalists were appalled at the prospect of the UFP returning to office. Nkumbula himself, although prepared to use the UFP to secure seats and bargaining power, had never relinquished his hostility to federation or his demand for universal suffrage.

By this time 'Rab' Butler had been given responsibility for the future of all central Africa. Kaunda and Nkumbula travelled to London in December to discuss the situation with him. They returned home ready to form a coalition government. Kaunda was perhaps the one man who recognised the significance of the situation. The constitution had been proved spurious. It would have to be amended soon. The form of amendment would depend on the character of the government in office. He agreed to give Nkumbula half the six ministries, despite the difference in votes and seats between UNIP and ANC. It was essential to secure a nationalist, anti-federation government. Once that was established and the danger of another Welensky-backed government averted, African majority power, secession from the federation and independence would follow. Nkumbula, for his part, recoiled from the brink of betraying his anti-federation principles. A UNIP–ANC coalition was formed in the middle of December; but Kaunda knew that this was simply a transitional measure. The real battle against federation was won. It would not be long before genuinely representative government would follow and that would bring independence. The birth pangs of the infant Zambia had become brisk and rapid.

It was John Sokoni, the third of the youthful trio with Kaunda and Kapwepwe, who declared, 'Zambia is born – December 14th, 1962.' Yet, if the agreement between Kaunda and Nkumbula to form a coalition African government presaged the collapse of the federation and the independence of Northern Rhodesia, there were still two years of hard work to realise the opportunities which had now been forged.

The coalition was always unstable, with Nkumbula unable to change his way of life in order to accept the constant responsibilities of ministerial office, frequently tempted by seductive offers from Kaunda's enemies and often making threats of resignation. Kaunda drove himself and his colleagues even harder than previously, determined not only to prove their capacity to govern the country, but to destroy both the remnants of federation and the shackles of colonial rule as quickly as possible.

By the end of the first quarter of 1963 the first of these objectives had been achieved in all but name. At yet another London conference, this time on the future of central Africa, Kaunda and Nkumbula walked out on the opening day, claiming that they would not discuss the federation until the right of secession was granted and a new constitution promised for their country. By now Butler recognised that the federation had virtually collapsed. Banda in Nyasaland had been given the right of secession and was certain to take it. The Africans of Northern Rhodesia had shown that nothing less would satisfy them. Welensky had even lost control of Southern Rhodesia to Winston Field's Rhodesia Front. Accepting the *fait accompli* on a dramatic afternoon at the end of March, Butler admitted that 'We accept that none of the territories can be kept in the Federation against its will.' Welensky was furious, storming against those of us in London who had always opposed federation; Kaunda and Nkumbula were jubilant. The hated federation was dead, the British government had been forced to eat its own words, the threats of Welensky and his cohorts had been shown to be empty, the way to an independent Zambia lay wide open. To Kaunda this was not simply a personal triumph; it had been proved that united African action could prevail over those with all the weapons of power – save public opinion – in their hands. Here was a lesson for the whole of white-dominated southern Africa.

It may have been continuing euphoria over this crucial victory which led Kaunda into one of the rare, but momentous errors of judgement to be attributed to him. The following June a conference was held at Victoria Falls to divide the federal estate. It was agreed that the federation should be officially dissolved on the last day of that year, which sealed Kaunda's triumph. Yet in the distribution of federal assets Southern Rhodesia was allowed to take the whole federal air force, which included eighteen Canberra bombers and a dozen Hunter fighters. This appropriation, for which there was no legal, moral or political justification, provided the Southern Rhodesian whites with the power they were later to employ in defying British authority, maintaining their dominance over their African population and constantly threatening Zambia's own security.

It was on the occasion of the March conference that Kenneth took Betty, his wife, to London for the first time. She had already taken a four-month course at the Mindolo Ecumenical Centre in preparation for her new responsibilities, for now that he was a minister Kaunda had moved from Chilenje to a large house in Prospect Hill where he had much entertaining to do. In the future, as the wife of a president, Betty would have to transform herself from the wife of a teacher, farmer, politician, prisoner, into the consort of an international personality. Her time in Britain, visiting various parts of the country and mixing with many new people, was part of the transformation. After a few weeks Kenneth returned to Britain to take his wife with him on visits to America, Sweden and Italy.

The principal reason for the American visit was to receive an honorary degree at Fordham University in New York State. Kenneth used this occasion to pay two remarkable tributes, one to his wife and the other to his mentor, Mahatma Gandhi. Of Betty he said, 'I know it hasn't been easy for her, it has meant great sacrifices on her part, from the comforts of a headmaster's home to one in which even finding food became a problem; long absences from home on my part have been common features of our life . . . I cannot repay her for all this.' He also quoted in agreement Gandhi's view that Britain differed from other colonial powers:

Although the British will harass and embarrass you, beat you up, send you to prison, shoot and kill some of you, if you still have guts, when you come out of these detention camps and prisons, to continue to do what you believe in – and this process may be repeated several times – in the end they say, 'These fellows are determined, give them some little power and let's see how they behave,' they will eventually give you what you want.

Yet, despite these international travels, it was the problems at home which demanded most of Kaunda's attention during 1963 and 1964. Violence increased, in spite of the new government. It reached dangerous proportions on the Copper Belt. An official report attributed it to unemployment, disappointed expectations and political frustration. The first two of these causes were to remain crucial problems for Kaunda for many years. The third not only emphasised the urgency of securing a new constitution, but probably created a political reaction which was to have profound consequences. A new constitution was agreed with the British government, leading to another election at the beginning of 1964. Yet the frustration caused by the artificial electoral arrangements imposed both by the federation and by the British, together with the resultant auctions between the parties, probably disillusioned most of the politically conscious section of the population with the whole multi-party concept. As in many other colonies, the common people of Northern Rhodesia were taught by bitter experience that this form of British 'democracy' could be contrived to produce whatever result those in power determined. The seeds of a deep suspicion of the multi-party concept were sown.

Certainly the menace of unemployment was very real, for by mid-1963 there were 50,000 without work on the Copper Belt alone. As about half of these were youngsters who could not secure a school place, the dangers to the next generation of drugs, violence and aimlessness in the rough mining townships were apparent. This was a legacy from federal and colonial government; it became increasingly obvious that if the country was to be pulled together to meet the major social and economic problems now rising to the surface, a government fully elected by the people would have to be introduced quickly.

Under the new constitution, therefore, elections were scheduled for January 1964. The electoral campaign was nothing like as bitter as that of 1962, if only because UNIP had drawn so far ahead of the ANC in organisation that it was obvious from the start that Kaunda's party would win a large majority. The leader's personal attitude to his opponents was also influential in minimising hostility. On one occasion during the campaign a man fired his gun at Kaunda during a rally in Lusaka. Although he knew that the assailant was a member of the ANC, Kaunda immediately described him as a crank, denied that any party was responsible, and went to protect him from being beaten by the crowd.

In the election itself, in a poll of over 90 per cent, UNIP won its expected majority, gaining fifty-five of the seventy-five seats, the ANC taking ten and Roberts' successor to his federal party the remaining ten. Yet there were disappointments for Kaunda, which were omens of future difficulties. His party was shown to be unable to make serious inroads into the ANC stronghold in the south, Nkumbula's home territory. And Kaunda's passionate pleas to forget race in politics were almost unheeded. Most white votes went to the Roberts party. In this Kaunda was unlucky. Just before the election mutinies occurred throughout east Africa, threatening Nyerere in Tanganyika, overthrowing the government in Zanzibar, and creating fears for the stability of Kenya and Uganda. The reaction of the whites of Northern Rhodesia was predictable; they voted with their skins.

Constitutional progress after the elections was smooth. At a conference in Marlborough House in London in May the final details of an independence constitution were quickly agreed. The most important decision was that the nation would be led by an executive president, who would combine the roles of Prime Minister and Head of State. It was felt that this was essential to provide strength and unity within a government which would be faced with awesome decisions. The arrangement certainly did not reflect any desire for personal power on Kaunda's part. He was urged several times to become Life President of UNIP and the country. He always refused, stating his profound belief in the electoral principle, with its opportunity to remove unpopular leaders. He had been appalled with the megalomaniac behaviour of Hastings Banda at the celebration of Nyasaland's self-government; he did not attend the birth of Malawi's independence.

If progress to independence was smooth, the tasks to be accomplished before it was attained nine months after the elections were colossal. Cabinet ministers and their assistants had to be carefully selected to balance regional, tribal and party factions. They then had to learn their new jobs. A whole new corps of diplomats had to be trained, for it was important that the new nation should be intelligently represented in the crucial capitals of the world. This task was particularly delicate because the new Zambia was not going to be content to accept that confinement within Western society which had been imposed by colonial Britain. Kaunda was convinced that the future of his country lay in the newly emerging non-aligned group initiated at Bandung in 1956 by Nehru, Nkrumah, Soekarno and Tito. This was to be combined with a Pan-African stance, for Kaunda also placed great value on the Organisation of African Unity established in 1963 and the Pan-African Freedom Movement of east, central and South Africa, of which he had been chairman. It was significant that the first Zambian diplomatic missions were based in London, the United Nations, Washington, Moscow, Dar es Salaam, Leopoldville, Accra and Cairo.

Meanwhile, Kenneth spoke at huge rallies throughout the country, and also held monthly press conferences, practising his belief in open government, in keeping the people informed of problems and policies. One particular tendency he had to combat was the hostility shown in some circles, including some in his own party, towards the whites. This feeling was hardly surprising, considering the history of white prejudice. Moreover, the practice of discrimination did not cease with the establishment of African government. Kaunda and his companions were detained in Salisbury airport as they were returning from Banda's self-government celebrations; a member of the new Northern Rhodesian parliament was refused admission to an hotel in Livingstone; a strike by European railwaymen threatened to throttle the country's economy; and many Europeans in key posts left the country.

Yet Kaunda resolutely used all his powers of persuasion against every form of discrimination. At the independence conference in London he

declared, 'We offer the hand of friendship to all men, whether they have
been our friends or opponents,' adding, 'When we look back along the
path which led to this conference room today, we cannot entirely forget –
but we can forgive – the days of our imprisonment.' This attitude of non-
racialism he was determined to apply at home and abroad. Just as he
harboured no resentment against the colonial rulers who had harassed
him, so he insisted that any European prepared to accept the new situation
in Northern Rhodesia was welcome to remain, with rights equal to those
of any other citizen.

Another domestic issue which disturbed the political surface from time
to time were the rumours of discontent with Kaunda's leadership. On
most occasions they were linked to the suggestion that Simon Kapwepwe
was Kenneth's rival. Despite firm denials from Kapwepwe, the rumours
persisted. They were to be revived after independence.

But the most painful problem which faced Kaunda during this pre-
independence period was the tragic question of the Lumpa sect. Fanatical
followers of the prophetess Alice Lenshina had been organising for several
years in Kaunda's home district around Chinsali. They were prohibited
from adopting political allegiance and refused to obey government regulations. There were strong suspicions that the sect was supported and used
by Kaunda's opponents at home and abroad, that Lenshina obtained
money and arms from outside the country.

Kenneth's own agony about having to use force against a sect claiming
to be part of Christianity was compounded by the fact that his own
mother had been close to the sect, his brother one of Lenshina's 'deacons'.
Yet when her followers began to use their stockaded villages as bases
from which to terrorise neighbouring districts, Kaunda was forced to use
the security forces and for three months death and mutilation reigned in
the area. Lenshina surrendered in August, but violence continued. At
least 700 lives were lost, with hundreds of Lumpa followers hiding in the
open, until they were either brought into camps or crossed into the Congo.
Yet even this bitter experience demonstrated the generous spirit of many
Africans of the time. UNIP, which had been the main target of the
attacks, still found enough goodwill to organise relief efforts to succour
the refugees.

Kaunda and his ministers had also to deal with the thorny issue of the
British South Africa Company. At the time this created a great deal of
heat; in retrospect it hardly warranted such significance. Nevertheless, it
provides another instance of Kaunda's refusal to sacrifice principle on the
altar of expediency.

The BSA controlled the mineral rights of Northern Rhodesia. Up to
1963 these had brought the Company over £160 million gross and £82
million net. Their control was due to last until 1986. The royalties were

at that time bringing the Company £6 million net a year. By the time the agreement was due to end it was estimated that it would collect another £130 million.

It was argued that to expropriate the royalties would damage the confidence of international capital in the new state. It was also hinted that the Company would accept £50 million to buy out its rights. Kaunda and his colleagues, however, refused to accept that the Company had any moral right over the minerals of their country and that any legal claims had been granted not by them but by the British government. If, therefore, there was to be any question of compensation, it would have to be sought from Britain. Their firm stand paid dividends. Only a few hours before independence an agreement was reached by which the Zambian government would hand over £2 million to the British government to give to the BSA; Britain was to pay a similar amount.

If there were complex domestic problems to solve, the international climate was even more stormy. Political trends in Southern Rhodesia had moved continually towards even greater reaction. Garfield Todd had been replaced by Whitehead in 1958; Whitehead was defeated by Winston Field and his Rhodesia Front at the end of 1962; Field was then supplanted by Ian Smith who chose a Cabinet of intransigent, unimaginative white supremacy fanatics. Before independence Kaunda was given evidence of their plans to institute an economic blockade of Zambia, which was being left as a result of federation with almost all its essential services and trade dependent on the south.

Nor were conditions to the north, in the Congo, much more promising. Kaunda had actually visited Tshombe in Katanga twice during the critical time when Nkumbula was deciding whether to ally himself with UNIP or the white UFP, for Tshombe was known to be working with Welensky and financing Nkumbula. Now, surprisingly, after a period of absence, Tshombe had been made Prime Minister by President Kasavubu. His appointment was followed by another revolt in which hundreds were killed, whilst disturbing news came of many white Rhodesian mercenaries being recruited into Tshombe's national army. It seemed probable that further troubles could be expected across the northern border.

The one encouraging international event occurred only a few days before independence. The Labour Party won the British general election, although only by a tiny majority. As Kaunda had such warm memories of his earlier days with the Labour Party in Britain and had established personal relationships with several of its leading members, it was natural that he rejoiced. He believed that he could count on much greater support from them in his nation-building and in protecting him from his enemies in the south.

So came the great day of independence, characteristically chosen by

Kaunda as United Nations' Day, 24 October. The Princess Royal represented her niece, the Queen, at the celebrations, and partnered the ex-convict President in opening the State Ball. Governor Hone, who had worked closely and warmly with Kaunda in the last stages of decolonisation, accompanied the new President as the Union Jack was lowered, to be replaced by the green, black, red and orange Zambian flag – green for the land, black for the majority of the people, red for the blood of the martyrs, orange for minerals. The nation gave itself up to rejoicing. Betty and Kenneth Kaunda moved into Government House, the seat of power, a far cry from their first home in Lubwa.

But, although Kenneth has always been happy to join in celebrations, and certainly savoured this, the greatest satisfaction of his life, the festivities were only peripheral in his mind as Northern Rhodesia was transformed overnight into Zambia. He had already coined the slogan, 'UNIP is Work'. He had symbolically discarded the Europeans' collar and tie for the bush-shirt, although sartorially still elegant with its accompanying cravat and pocket handkerchief. It was the opportunity for greater service which was uppermost in Kaunda's mind as independence dawned, the staggering mass of problems to be tackled before Zambia could become a happy, united, secure nation, and Africa a free, democratic, people's continent. It was to these tasks that he turned himself and his chosen colleagues even before the sounds of revelry were stilled.

11

President Nyerere of Tanzania

The day after Tanganyika's independence I had a long talk with Nyerere. He had moved into the ex-Chief Secretary's house next door to Government House. We sat in the garden under scarlet blossoms of flamboyant trees overlooking the Indian Ocean. The Prime Minister was undetermined. He felt he was in a dilemma. Yet, beside his wife Maria and his mother, surrounded by his children and their friends, he was undeterred. It has never been Nyerere's way to worry over problems. His clarity of mind enables him to identify them, then to be confident that thought will provide him with his answer. And he has always been able to relax.

On this occasion he said to me, 'Now we have won independence I don't know what to do with this country.' He added that he was going straight to the United Nations to lead Tanganyika into membership. When he returned he would have decided what policy he was to adopt.

That decision startled the world. Six weeks after independence, on 22 January 1962, Nyerere resigned as Prime Minister. He became a back-bencher in parliament, having nominated Rashidi Kawawa as his successor.

It is virtually unknown for a politician to surrender his office voluntarily. It is certainly unique for a man to lead his country into independence and then almost immediately retire from the leading position. Inevitably, therefore, speculation over the cause of his unprecedented action spread throughout the country and far beyond. It was increased because of Nyerere's characteristic lack of concern over how his decision would be interpreted. He was warned by Turnbull, now Governor-General, to prepare his own people and foreigners. He did not do so. Even Kenyatta in Kenya did not know his reasons. Nor did the Tanganyika High Commission in London. Naturally, it was widely assumed that he had been driven out by the efforts of his critics in the party and trade unions who had openly opposed him, especially on racial policy, during the months preceding independence.

There are two versions of Nyerere's motivation in resigning. The first, which was that usually given by overseas journalists, was that in the first flush of independence, the party was certain to employ harsh, aggressive measures in reaction to its past experience at the hands of non-Africans, and in asserting its new power. Certainly a number of Europeans were deported without any chance to answer the charges of incivility made against them. Asians and British civil servants were attacked in the press. After Nyerere had left the government a law was passed virtually banning strikes, a preventive detention law was introduced allowing the government to imprison anyone without trial and Africanisation was speeded up throughout government service. The atmosphere, at least in Dar es Salaam, became unusually tinged with racial hostility during 1962.

Nyerere escaped being held responsible for all this. Yet, although he was the last person to condone racial prejudice, there is no reason to suppose that he disapproved of the actual legislation. He argued that the tiny minority of industrial workers organised in trade unions had no moral right to use their collective power to widen the already large gap between their disproportionate share of national wealth and the much lower standards of the masses in rural areas. He believed that the unions should come within the national framework which was being established by the party, a belief that he was to put into practice two years later. On preventive detention Nyerere simply considered that in a new country without the benefit of a large, respected police force and security network, with scanty communications and many enemies, it was necessary to sacrifice the liberty of a few innocent people to prevent the sabotage of the whole nation.

There may have been a grain of truth in the supposition that Nyerere had no stomach for the rough measures of the first year of independence, that he tired of the constant struggle against his emotional, narrow-minded critics. Turnbull spoke of his hope that Nyerere 'was being unnecessarily pessimistic' in contemplating resignation. Yet, if there was a grain, it was minute. For Nyerere's vision was far broader and longer than that of one year. He could trust Kawawa to maintain the direction that he and TANU had charted. The government did not confine itself to tightening security and discipline. It announced its intention of abolishing freehold in land, took the chiefs out of the political arena and devised a republican constitution, all measures that Nyerere himself had planned. Moreover, Kawawa never entertained an atom of personal ambition. He always made it clear that he was merely a temporary substitute for the man he called the 'Father of the Nation'.

Nyerere remained President of TANU. He had decided and persuaded his colleagues that his first task must be to provide the party with a new *raison d'être* now that independence had been won, to assert its paramountcy as a nation-building institution, to identify the people with it in facing the problems of their developing society. He retired to the back benches in parliament, but spent most of the next nine months amongst the people throughout the country. Once again, when faced with a major issue,

Nyerere turned back to the common people of Tanganyika, listening to their needs, hopes and ideas.

Yet, although he did devote this period to the party, it is an exaggeration to suggest, as some have, that he reorganised TANU during this nine months. It would have been a physical impossibility for him to have done so in such a huge country and in so short a time. Moreover, during the same period he was acting as president of the party, and also writing some very important political essays which were to have a profound effect on future policy.

By far the most important achievement of this nine months was his composition of the paper 'Ujamaa – The Basis of African Socialism'. When published it was read specifically as one of Nyerere's philosophical treatises. It was not until five years later that its significance to the life of most Tanganyikans was recognised.

The paper begins with a somewhat rambling dissertation on the acquisition of money. It is when Nyerere reaches his view of society, and particularly of traditional African society, that its message rivets the attention. After asserting that : 'In an acquisitive society wealth tends to corrupt those who possess it. It tends to breed in them a desire to live more comfortably than their fellows, to dress better, and in every way to outdo them,' he proceeds to open his perspective to traditional society in Africa.

The core of Nyerere's social philosophy is revealed in these words :

. . . when a society is so organised that it cares about its individuals, then, provided he is willing to work, no individual within that society should worry about what will happen to him tomorrow if he does not hoard wealth today. Society itself should look after him, or his widow, or his orphans. This is exactly what traditional African society succeeded in doing. Both the 'rich' and the 'poor' individual were completely secure in African society. Natural catastrophe brought famine, but it brought famine to everybody – 'poor' or 'rich'. Nobody starved, either of food or of human dignity, because he lacked personal wealth; he could depend on the wealth possessed by the community of which he was a member. That was socialism. That is socialism. There can be no such thing as acquisitive socialism, for that would be another contradiction in terms. Socialism is essentially distributive. Its concern is to see that those who sow reap a fair share of what they sow.

After pointing to the essential relationship in African society between the rights of the individual drawn from membership of his community and the responsibility of contributing through his work, together with the justice of taking only a fair share of the total proceeds, Nyerere then compared African and European socialism. He pointed out that whereas European

socialism had been born out of the struggle against capitalism, and therefore tended to depend on the existence of capitalism for its own justification,
Africans had never known the class struggle because class was unknown to
them. He thereby reached this conclusion:

'Ujamaa', then, or 'familyhood', describes our socialism. It is opposed to
capitalism, which seeks to build a happy society on the basis of the
exploitation of man by man; and it is equally opposed to doctrinaire
socialism which seeks to build its happy society on a philosophy of inevitable conflict between man and man.

We, in Africa, have no more need of being 'converted' to socialism
than we have of being 'taught' democracy. Both are rooted in our own
past . . . Modern African socialism can draw from its traditional heritage
the recognition of 'society' as an extension of the basic family unit. But it
can no longer confine the idea of the social family within the limits of the
tribe, nor, indeed, of the nation . . . Our recognition of the family to
which we all belong must be extended yet further – beyond the tribe, the
community, the nation, or even the continent – to embrace the whole of
mankind.

It is in this paper that we can discern most clearly the development of
Nyerere's philosophical development. He had been educated in a conventional British manner, his schools, college and university all conducted
by the British educational establishment. His years in politics had been
occupied in fighting against the British colonial system. He had therefore
to adopt its tactics, to seek to capture the colonial institutions, to gain power
through local and central government elections. He had to create a conventional political party for this purpose and when he achieved success, to
run a conventional government machine, replete with its traditional British
civil service.

It was inevitable, therefore, that Nyerere had absorbed a large fund of
British mores. He had been taught that the Westminster multi-party
political system represented the highest known stage of democracy; that
independent trade unions were essential to maintain the freedom of the
workers; that the civil service, police and armed forces must be entirely
separated from political influence; that educationalists set their own
standards and curricula. When in Edinburgh he had considered himself a
socialist, but only of the conventional British type, approving nationalisation and the welfare state which Clement Attlee was building.

During the ten years after his return home Nyerere was constantly
brought up against the issue as to whether the British assumptions he had
absorbed were as universal as the British believed. He could see the danger
in any political system which gagged opposition to those in power. He was

never so infuriated with opposition groups that he was tempted to abolish their liberty to express criticism as, for example, Kwame Nkrumah was. Yet the British party system really arose out of the industrial revolution, which, together with the agrarian revolution, separated worker from employer, landless from landowner. Contending parties simply reflected conflicting class interests. In Tanganyika there were no classes and scarcely any dissent from TANU policies. At elections, therefore, the majority of seats were filled by unopposed TANU candidates. The electors in most constituencies never had any choice of candidate. Once the party machine had selected the TANU candidate he automatically became a member of parliament or of the local authority. And Nyerere believed in elections. This was one part of British political practice of which he thoroughly approved. Whatever method was employed, the right of the individual citizen to decide who should represent him in building the society in which he would have to live has always been fundamental to Nyerere. So he began to ponder how to devise a system in which this right would be more validly established than in the party elections which had become farcical.

The trade union issue was simpler. A rural nation like Tanganyika was hardly suitable for a transplant from the trade union movement of a complex industrial society such as Britain. It would simply allow the tiny sector of organised workers to gain an unjust advantage over the mass of peasants and agricultural workers who comprised 95 per cent of Tanganyikans. Nyerere retained affection and respect for British trade unionists like Marjorie Nicholson and Walter Hood of the British TUC, recognising the contribution they made to the practice of worker organisation in colonial Tanganyika; but he found their ideas to be too rooted in British practice to remain relevant after independence. He knew that this practice would have to be changed.

The case of government servants, civil and military, was more complex. It was directly related to the party system. Whilst he realised the danger of government servants being attached to political organisations when political power changed from one party to another, this had a different connotation in Tanganyika from that in Britain. For the foreseeable future there was no prospect of TANU being replaced by another party. The immediate issue was not of a change in the party control of government. It was rather that all government servants had been accustomed to serving the colonial régime. And he had been shown by the British that their servants must remain loyal to colonial government. They had not even been allowed to join his own party. Could such civil servants, police and armed forces now be expected so to change their whole ethos as to enter fully into the tasks of nation-building? Could their expertise be harnessed to the totally new challenges and suppositions essential to the creation of a new society, in many ways wholly contrary to the ethics of a colonial régime?

The educational problem was, in many ways, the most intransigent of all. It has never been entirely resolved. Nyerere himself, and most of his major colleagues, had received their education from some branch of the international educational establishment, heavily influenced, even in America, Europe and Asia, by British assumptions. The basic supposition was that educational values are universal, that the pursuit of knowledge is a valid end in itself, that all educational institutions acknowledge certain common standards. This assumption was reinforced not only by the educational experience of leading TANU officials, but by the training of the multitude of foreign teachers who had to be recruited by Tanganyika in the post-independence drive for educational expansion.

Since the industrial revolution education had provided the main avenue of social advance for the poor throughout the developed world. It offered their only road into the sanctums of the elite. It was natural, therefore, that those who enjoyed its advantages and consequently governed its institutions, should create a closed shop, surround their assumptions with a *cordon sanitaire*.

But could the educational training provided for the young of industrial nations be relevant to those who were to spend the rest of their lives on the land? Who were called to identify and then adopt values contrary to those inculcated by the colonial régime? Who were asked to reject the Puritan ethic of competition, of 'making good' and to preserve their tradition of communal co-operation, inter-personal friendliness and universal responsibility?

The debate on this issue raged throughout Africa, mainly centred on the formation of the new universities. Traditionalists won in almost every case. Thus post-colonial Africa witnessed the creation of a string of universities aping the European model.

Nyerere extended the argument into a new dimension. He allowed the university in Dar es Salaam to develop with almost complete independence. In its first few years it was a constituent part of the University of East Africa, supposedly with its own specialisation, on the principle of federation. This would have made it more difficult to guide its development, but perhaps Nyerere had not entirely shaken off his reverence for Edinburgh, which had given him such a valuable opportunity to contemplate. In any case, he was more interested in the character of his schools, which was not considered a major issue in other African states. He began to question whether the conventional British curriculum was relevant or constructive in the lives of Tanganyika's children which would have so little in common with those of British children. He was also concerned to enable adults to achieve literacy and to provide opportunities for those in public life to consider and discuss the new ethics of national policies. For this latter purpose a college was built across the Dar es Salaam harbour at Kivukoni.

It had a chequered history, for several years closely resembling Oxford's Ruskin College, which was almost as irrelevant to Tanganyika's needs as a conventional university. Not until the 1970s did it begin to realise its potential as a genuine party college where party officials could train themselves for leadership throughout the nation.

These ideas were latent, rather than explicit, in this 1962 paper of Nyerere's. They were all to develop out of it over the next few years. For the concepts in the paper were integral with his action in turning from government to party. His short experience in government had taught him that the social revolution for which independence had been fought could not be conducted by a government remote from the vast majority of citizens, nor by a civil service trained to administer and conserve, rather than to initiate. Even the appointment of political personnel as regional and provincial administrators did not fully serve this purpose, for they had to spend most of their time in local administration rather than inspiring innovation.

If, therefore, Nyerere was to reverse the trends introduced by colonial government and convince his people that their own traditional mores were superior to what the white men had taught, he had to have the services of a different kind of institution. It is true that he romanticised traditional African society, that his description of it did not entirely conform with practice in many parts of his own country, still less in other areas of the continent. Yet if his was not a strictly accurate historical description of African life, it did contain moral, social and political concepts which most Tanganyikans recognised as ideals, even where they had often fallen short of performance. It was this fact which gave Nyerere his intimate relationship with his people, which in its turn provided him with mass support in his efforts to devise the means by which ideals could be translated into practice.

One can therefore date from the presentation of this paper Nyerere's conviction that his party must represent the nation and take precedence over the government as the policy-making body. When this crucial paper is taken in conjunction with those which followed it, its germinal character becomes apparent.

On the anniversary of independence Tanganyika became a republic. Richard Turnbull took his farewell, with genuine affection on both sides. Nyerere re-emerged as the first president. One of his first actions was to propose to the party's annual conference that Tanganyika should become a de jure single-party state. Already the country had only one de facto party, for no other organisation had been able to challenge TANU seriously since elections were first introduced. The first presidential election had again substantiated this fact. Nyerere was challenged by Zuberi Mtemvu, who, along with the trade unionist, Tumbo, had tried to form an opposition party in 1962. They campaigned on the claim that TANU's colour-blind policy unfairly discriminated against the black Africans who had never had a chance of promotion under colonial rule. But whereas Nyerere secured 1,127,978 votes, Mtemvu only received 21,276. So, on the issue of racialism, Nyerere proved that he had the support of the vast majority of the voters. It was equally clear that opposition to TANU remained insignificant.

Nevertheless, the election substantiated one of Nyerere's main fears. The total number of votes cast represented probably less than one in four of eligible voters. To Nyerere this proved two points. First, that people did not feel that there was any point in voting as the outcome of every election was certain. Secondly, that the majority of people in the country had not identified themselves with either party or government, were not therefore involved in the nation's decision-making. His conclusions were that a different form of election must be invented; that the party must seek to penetrate down to the grass roots of the nation to organise a truly democratic system in which everyone participated in deciding the form of society in which they were to live.

Nyerere's proposals were by no means universally welcomed by members of the party. Many of them feared that they were likely to lose their political careers through such an electoral process, which was, of course, exactly Nyerere's purpose. He did not believe that it was good for the country or for his party that members should be able to count on a parliamentary career for life without regular submission to the approval of the electorate.

It was to be eighteen months before the new system was agreed. In the meantime, a commission had been set up under Kawawa's chairmanship to elicit public opinion. Tanganyika also waited until after Kenya, Uganda and Zanzibar had attained independence before putting her scheme into practice. Nyerere hoped, right up to the end of 1963, that an East African Federation might be forged. But the hope was vain. Each of the other three countries insisted on gaining its own sovereignty. As Nyerere had predicted, once national sovereignty had been attained, the chances of federation rapidly faded. Efforts to keep them alive were made and many fair words spoken; but vested interests in each country steadily obstructed action being taken. So Tanganyikans realised that they would have to devise their own system, irrespective of the directions taken by the others.

The first elections under the single-party constitution took place in 1965. They completely fulfilled Nyerere's hopes. After primary elections had been held, two candidates were nominated in each seat. Both were members of TANU, but campaigned according to their service to the community, their interpretation of TANU policies, their proposals for the future, with all reference to tribal, religious or racial considerations forbidden. The validity of this type of election was established by the fact that 86 of the 107 members elected were new to the Assembly, whilst two ministers and six junior ministers were defeated. Of equal gratification to Nyerere was the fact that 76·1 per cent of the electorate voted in the Assembly elections and 77·8 per cent in the election of the president. He, himself, was the only candidate nominated for the presidency. Electors were therefore invited to vote for or against him. Over $2\frac{1}{2}$ million voted to give him another term; just over 90,000 voted against him.

Thus Nyerere was able to start his second period of nation-building with new, younger, more critical members of the Assembly. Racialism had been decisively defeated, a European and three Asians had been elected. Four women also gained seats. In the local government elections of the following year the same pattern emerged. Many of the old guard of TANU had disappeared from public life. The dangers of a self-perpetuating oligarchy had been overcome. Nyerere now had the critical support of a team of fresh, nonconformist minds. He was equipped to take new, imaginative initiatives.

By this time – the mid-sixties – Nyerere had begun to realise that new policies were essential if the form of social development at which he was aiming was to be achieved. He has never been an economist, but has always realised that his political and social objectives can only be achieved through an integration of economic and political policies.

Yet the early economic plans applied by the new state could never have produced the social justice which was Nyerere's central objective. The economic assumptions of those who guided the government's policies were still drawn largely from colonial sources, even when their objectives differed from those of their former rulers.

Tanganyika had been left with a conventional colonial economy, though on the scale of a very poor country. Although there were far fewer settlers than in neighbouring Kenya, their estates supplied half the total value of agricultural exports. In addition, in a handful of specially fertile areas, African peasants had been encouraged to produce cash crops, mainly coffee and cotton. The basis of the economy was to produce for export in order to secure resources for industrialisation and social services. What little industrialisation existed was also almost entirely owned and operated by foreigners.

Two major consequences followed from this situation. First, the economic fate of Tanganyika depended almost entirely on world market prices. If the price of coffee, sisal or cotton fell – and Tanganyikans had no power over such movements – national housekeeping would be upset. Secondly, the whole process created small pockets of prosperity in which some people lived at standards of life bearing no comparison to those of the vast majority. The Western educational system, based on the concept of proven worth through individual competition – irrespective of the lottery of opportunity – supplied most of those accorded such material privilege.

Nyerere objected both to his country's dependence on external economic forces and to the elitist conception. Yet he and his economic advisers took some years to liberate themselves from colonial preconceptions. They had inherited a three-year development plan which owed most of its measures to a World Bank report published in the year before independence. Inevitably, given the frontiers within which the Bank operated, this plan never questioned the existing economic structure. It was based on a capital expenditure almost entirely devoted to improving the country's infrastructure, roads, railways, irrigation, water supplies and schools. This would facilitate an expansion in exports, a gradual growth in the domestic market economy and eventually the introduction of light industry, owned, financed and managed by foreigners.

Nyerere and his party had been too busy organising politically to gain independence to make any serious analysis of the economic structure of the country or to plan an economic strategy. Yet neither Nyerere nor his colleagues accepted the legacy of this conventional plan without question. From well before independence Nyerere had been preaching the importance of self-help. Immediately after independence the government introduced a 'Peoples' Plan' designed to encourage the growth of village development committees which would stimulate people to initiate self-help projects. At this stage, however, they could consist of little more than minor improvements to local facilities. Nyerere continually exhorted the people he met in his 1962 journeys to take their own initiative in improving their lot.

Yet, until the president and his party had worked out their own economic strategy, they had to accept the legacy which they had been bequeathed. When they turned to examine the colonial and World Bank concept of development they were dissatisfied. Yet their criticism took a conventional form. They were not content to accept the slow process of accumulating capital by increasing agricultural production, gradually generating increased domestic incomes and then channelling investment into industrialisation. Because the government was the major source of investment, as in every ex-colony, they assumed that it was the government's responsibility to promote industrial development in order to increase the standard of living at a much faster pace than that envisaged by pre-independence planners. As many of those who had been active in the independence struggle expected living standards to rise rapidly as a result of independence, this policy seemed essential to satisfy popular expectations.

Nyerere was sceptical. He had seen the mass of his people in the countryside asking for little more than small increases in food supplies for their families, a clinic where disease could be treated or pain assuaged, a chance for some of their children to gain literacy. He feared that the conventional policies of development, approved by orthodox communists and capitalists alike, would bypass the simple needs of these people. He had seen in other countries that development usually took place almost entirely in towns and cities, with the country people left almost untouched. And he had seen the vast migrations from countryside to town by people looking for better-paid work and higher living standards. He feared that the same would happen in Tanganyika. Already he saw the streets of Dar es Salaam crowded with unemployed loafers. According to the African tradition of hospitality they never went without shelter and some food, for they could always share whatever other members of their family possessed. But he realised that this trend was both obstructing urban development and depriving the rural areas of their able-bodied young men and women. He tried to meet the immediate danger by using police to deport unemployed from Dar es Salaam back to their villages, but realised that this could only be a temporary palliative. He had to seek the roots of the social forces which induced young people to leave their homes and migrate to towns, even when they knew that no employment awaited them.

At first Nyerere hoped that he had found an answer in his Village Settlement Agency. This was to co-ordinate development and especially help self-reliant schemes in the villages. A great deal of money was made available and considerable loans granted to farmers. Yet at this early stage (1963) no Tanganyikan managers were available. The programmes were run by expatriates, inefficiently managed and quickly encountered repayment difficulties. By 1966 it was found necessary to halt the expansion of the plans, consolidate those schemes which were still viable and close down the rest. Nyerere had discovered, like many before him, that the provision of capital does not ensure improved farming. In those areas specially selected for this experiment little enthusiasm had been shown for an acceptance of the new responsibilities, whilst heavy debts had been incurred. Meanwhile, greater enthusiasm had been evident in voluntary schemes of village co-operation, but they had been starved of funds. Nyerere decided to concentrate on these in the future, laying a heavier emphasis on self-help and less on government finance.

By this time it was evident in various directions that the social aims Nyerere had set the nation were not being achieved. The theory of the single-party state presupposed that the whole nation accepted the social philosophy of TANU, that methods of putting it into practice would be debated at all levels within the party, and that then the elected representatives of the people would provide the policies to achieve it. All evidence proved that the vast majority of the nation accepted the philosophy; but it seemed equally clear that the policies were not succeeding.

In fact, most of the evidence suggested that Tanganyikans were following the conventional post-independence pattern of social life. The efforts of the trade unions brought a quick increase in wages and cash earnings. Inevitably, as most paid employment was controlled by private, largely foreign, companies, this resulted in a reduction in the number of workers. This only increased the unions' demands and strengthened their insistence on Africanisation of management. The emphasis on industrialisation produced a growth in manufacturing four times as large as that of agricultural production. The civil service expanded rapidly, including a large number of Africans. In the areas favourable to cash crops land was being accumulated in fewer hands, accompanied by the growth of a landless class. In town and country a new African elite was rising; those earning over 200 shillings a month multiplied by almost six between 1960 and 1968, passing the 10,000 mark. The gap between this new elite and the mass of peasants widened rapidly.

Nyerere observed these developments with growing concern. This was not the kind of society which he had conceived during the fight for independence. Yet he was still dependent on the experts for the nation's economic policy. He might dream of a new form of society, based on different values, but he had not yet discovered the practical means of building it. Whilst he taught ideals to his people, wrote philosophical essays and debated with the younger generation, he still left economic planning to the technocrats.

It was an international team of economic experts who prepared Tanganyika's own first national development plan. They were drawn from France, Britain, the United States, Israel, West Germany and the United Nations. Each of them, therefore, came from a society generally antagonistic to a centrally directed economy.

It is not surprising, therefore, that the plan was based on conventional suppositions. It considered Tanganyika as a whole, without regard for the problems of different regions or sections of society. The average income was to be increased, Tanganyikans were to be trained to replace skilled expatriates and the expectancy of life was to be raised. In order to secure the resources to achieve these goals, large foreign loans would have to be negotiated by both the public and the private sectors of the economy and foreign investment encouraged.

This plan was accepted by Nyerere, his cabinet, the party and the Assembly. It is evident, therefore, that at this stage they all retained the conventional view of development. Industrialisation was to take them out of under-development. It was to be largely financed from abroad and sited in the more prosperous areas of their country where spending power was highest. Secondary and higher education must take precedence over primary schools so as to provide the skilled personnel and the teachers necessary to replace expatriates. Rural living standards would eventually benefit from the general growth of the national economy.

It is interesting to speculate on how Nyerere would have reacted if this plan had gained even a moderate success. It seems probable that, given the social philosophy he had already espoused, he would have tried to reverse its results. If so, he would certainly have faced a difficult task, for it was bound to encourage the growth of the elite, accompanied by considerable regional contrasts in wealth.

In the event, less than two years after it had been introduced in 1965, the plan had clearly failed. Only about half the required foreign loans had been obtained, industrial production was expanding rapidly, but not as fast as wages or prices, employment in agriculture declined as the young migrated to the towns, the rural–urban gap was widening and elitism was ever more evident in urban life.

Although he had not realised what consequences this economic plan was likely to produce, Nyerere was constantly watching the social climate. He himself set a rigorously austere example, living on a salary of only £3,000 a year, surely the lowest paid head of state in the world. And when an occasion of crisis arose he would lead the way by cutting ten per cent off it.

He was concerned at the attitude of many members of the Assembly and civil servants. To him it seemed that they had absorbed a philosophy based on money. The Assembly expected the finance minister to provide money to expand the economies of their constituencies. The civil servants expected to be given loans to buy cars. Nyerere felt that thoughts of money had come to dominate national life, at least among the leadership groups. When he changed the loan system so that civil servants could borrow money to build a house instead of buying a car, he found that they then began to sell or rent the houses they built.

Characteristically, he wrote an essay on his fears. He wrote about the need for frugality, drawing lessons from his visit to China. Then he asked, 'How could anyone expect this enthusiasm and hard work to be forthcoming if the masses see that a few individuals in the society get very rich and live in great comfort, while the majority continue apparently for ever in abject poverty?'

But, although it helped to clarify his thoughts and perhaps to purge his personal anger, Nyerere knew that he would have to do something more drastic if he was to reverse the direction in which the new nation was moving. In 1966 he was infuriated by university students who marched to State House to protest against being included in the scheme for national service. In order to train the young to develop a sense of responsibility to society, it was decided to introduce a limited form of national service. Under this scheme a certain number of young men and women were to spend two years in the service. There would be some degree of military training, though for most of the time the youngsters would be doing the job for which they had been trained, but in uniform and for only forty per cent of the normal wage. The university students protested that they should not be included. To Nyerere they were precisely the first who should be recruited. All of them were on government scholarships, they were living a privileged life and they would receive wages far above the average. He felt that they ought to be setting an example in showing that privilege entailed responsibility. He was so angry at their protest that he dismissed them all from the university, sent them back to their villages, and only allowed them to return when they had proved that they had fulfilled their responsibility to their village communities.

This was a small but significant incident illustrating Nyerere's increasing frustration that his words were not influencing his people's attitudes, however much they might declare their adherence to them. He had spoken, written, shared people's work with them; but still people in the party, government, civil service and university continued to claim the privileges of elitism.

With this evidence constantly before him, Nyerere began to make notes on the things which a socialist cannot do if he is to be true to his philosophy. In 1966 Simon Kapwepwe, Kaunda's friend and colleague in Zambia, gave him a book. Its title was *False Start in Africa*, its author René Dumont, the famous French agronomist who had spent most of his life in advising Third World governments on agrarian reform. Dumont believes that Africa's greatest mistake since independence has been to try and imitate Europe, both in the life-style of her elites and in her economic policies. He has consistently argued that agriculture should take priority, but an agriculture growing gradually from the experience of the peasant. This involves evolving from the hoe to the bullock-driven plough, with improved methods of sowing and planting, and more rational use of the land.

It was, however, Dumont's condemnation of the destructive effect of the elite on society that impressed Nyerere most strongly. The analysis of post-independence developments in ex-French Africa and the dangers entailed catalysed all the ideas which had been gathering in his own mind. Later he was to invite Dumont to his country to examine its agricultural progress and recommend improvements. But now he realised the need for a new statement of policy which would reverse the dangerous trends which had appeared.

These were the origins of the famous Arusha Declaration. At the beginning of 1967 Nyerere went on a safari to more than half the country's regions. His journey ended in the northern town of Arusha, on the slopes of Mount Kilimanjaro. Here he met district commissioners and the party's executive. He put his proposals to them. They contained nothing that he had not either said or written previously, but they were brought together in such a manner that they committed the party this time to put them into effect. Some members of the party were shocked. They were unwilling to admit that the principles for which the party had always stood must be applied by them in personal life. There was much argument and a few amendments. But the document was accepted and published. It had an immediate and profound effect on the consciousness of the nation. It can be said that from 5 February 1967, the country possessed a written philosophy to which every action, measure or policy in public and private life could be referred.

Nyerere has constantly insisted that the Arusha Declaration must be regarded as a guideline to action, rather than a policy document. If it is read in conjunction with the speeches and essays with which he expanded and interpreted it in the following year, a clear outline of his ideas and feelings on personal and social behaviour can be gained.

There is no necessity to reproduce the Declaration or the subsequent addenda here. But the main themes can be seen in their context as emerging from his experiences over the five years of independence, or having more fundamentally guided him throughout his life.

The document opens with a statement of the party's creed. This begins with a commitment to build a socialist state and then proceeds to define the principles of socialism. These can be said to stem from the assertion 'That all human beings are equal'. It then proceeds to enunciate the human rights of every individual, the claim of society over the nation's natural wealth and the duty of the state to control this wealth so as to prevent its unfair distribution. It is also the government's responsibility to attack the evils of society, such as poverty and discrimination, to encourage social organisation such as co-operatives, and to pursue African unity and world peace.

The second section defines the policy of socialism. It includes an absence of exploitation, control of the means of production and exchange by peasants and workers, a strong insistence on democracy, with the government chosen by the people, and the assertion that socialism is a philosophy, a way of life, governing actions and attitudes, that a socialist society can only be built by those who believe in and practise its principles.

The third part of the Declaration emphasises Nyerere's detestation of the obsession with money which he had observed creeping into all the national institutions. Eight times the word 'money' is spelt with capital letters, so that no one can escape from recognising it as the chief evil dragon to be fought. Throughout it is contrasted with the real objectives of development, food, education, health. The dangers of foreign financial assistance to the nation's independence are then stressed. This is followed by a significant admission that there had been too much emphasis on industrialisation, which required that foreign capitalists should be encouraged to come to the country. Finally, the priority role of the peasant is asserted, with agriculture given first place in development. Hard work, intelligence, self-reliance, good policies and good leadership are the requisites of success in this approach to the construction of a socialist state.

The next short section deals with party membership. It reminds the party that it was supposed to be composed of peasants and workers, that all members were expected to adhere to party beliefs and socialist policies. Although during the struggle for independence the aim had been to secure as many members as possible, the time had now come to ensure that every new member genuinely accepted both the faith and the regulations of the party. In other words, Nyerere had begun to realise that he and his party could only lead the people towards socialist ideals if it was composed of members who practised what they preached.

It was Part Five of the Declaration which provoked the most passionate argument and that aroused tremendous enthusiasm amongst the rank and file. It followed naturally from the tightening of qualifications for membership. It was not sufficient to insist that new members should be committed to socialist principles; it was much more important that the nation which was being asked to obey those principles should witness leaders setting an example. In what has come to be known as 'The Leadership Code', this behavioural example was spelt out in clear detail. All party and government leaders were to be peasants or workers, having no association with capitalism or feudalism. They were not to be allowed to hold company shares or directorships in any private company. They were to be forbidden to receive more than one salary, or to own houses for rent.

This code of conduct clearly reflects the frustration felt by Nyerere as he had witnessed many of his colleagues in national life preaching socialist principles whilst using their positions to build their own privileged life-styles. It represents his contemplation of the principle which he himself has described as 'What socialists cannot do'.

The central issue at Arusha was not whether the major part of the document could be approved. The general lines of national policy, which involved a decided change of direction towards government control over the most important sections of the economy, a switch from emphasis on industry to priority for agriculture, and self-reliance rather than seeking foreign finance, were approved with little opposition. The real question was whether the socialist principles which had been enunciated should apply to members of the party leadership. Nyerere had already thought this out and come to the firm conclusion that they must do so. But there was consternation when the proposal was put to the party executive. One of Nyerere's ministers told me shortly afterwards that a large section of the party leadership genuinely believed that those who did most to serve the community were entitled to the highest rewards. They had retained that measure of colonial ethics which taught that qualifications and service should be reflected in greater material possessions. When Nyerere suggested to them that they were privileged to be able to serve society, that those who had obtained qualifications had been given exceptional opportunities denied the mass of the people, and that therefore their service was a duty, their privileged position a responsibility entailing setting an example of austerity, many felt their security threatened.

Nyerere was fortunate at this time – and on many other occasions – to have beside him members of the party who thought as he did, who had the integrity and the self-confidence to support him even over measures which were opposed to their own material self-interest. With their help he won the argument. Henceforth, the party's and the nation's leaders had to live within this austere code or leave public life. One of the first examples given was by Maria, Nyerere's wife. She immediately gave her small poultry farm to a co-operative. Julius sold his house in Magomeni.

On his return from Arusha Nyerere acted promptly. He first made a long speech explaining the significance of the Declaration and calling on the country to rely on the efforts of its own citizens, to make a vast national effort to prove that the people themselves could build the nation without having to depend on foreign assistance. Then he immediately announced plans to nationalise the banks, insurance companies, trading firms, the sisal mills and estates. The government was also to take a controlling interest in firms making beer, cigarettes, shoes, metalware and cement. Thus, within a week of the Declaration being published, the President and his government had showed the people that they were serious in their new policies, that words were to be translated into action.

Over the next few months Nyerere supplemented the Arusha Declaration in his usual manner. He participated in seminars, made speeches, wrote essays, interpreting and expanding the guidelines which the Declaration had laid down. The most important paper was that on 'Education for Self-Reliance'. In it he examined the educational legacy which had been left to the country, pointed out that it did not satisfy the needs of the nation-building policy they all accepted, and called for an educational revolution. The paper stimulated widespread discussion between teachers and educationalists on the content and forms of instruction offered to the children of the country. Out of this discussion arose the introduction of school farms, agricultural lessons, workshops and increased technical training.

The second crucial paper bore the title 'Socialism and Rural Development'. It built on the foundations of his 'Ujamaa' paper of five years previously, adding more precise proposals for action. In it he suggested that peasant farmers should combine to form a village in a location suitable for farming, establish communal plots on which they could work together, share the proceeds and then form a communal farm. He stressed that this would have to be a gradual process, taken in stages, that it would not guarantee wealth, but could bring everyone a little bit extra.

In the second half of 1967 the enthusiasts for the Arusha Declaration began to demonstrate their support for it by organising marches. There was no practical point in this form of demonstration, but it roused the country and created a great spirit of brotherhood. Maybe the determination was aroused in defiance of those who had chosen to leave public life rather than surrender their wealth. Bibi Titi, for instance, who had done sterling work in recruiting and organising the women's movement, resigned in order to keep her income from rented property. What was more remarkable was that so few took this option. Nyerere himself took part in one of the marches. He walked 138 miles in eight days, revelling in the comradeship and the exercise, keeping everyone in good humour with his repartee. They ended the march in Mwanza in time for the party's annual conference. Soon afterwards, however, the rains arrived; Nyerere said it was time to stop the marches and return to the farms.

I talked with Julius, soon after the Arusha Declaration had been published, in the most unlikely location of Kubbeh Palace in Cairo, one of ex-King Farouk's domains. He was there for a mini-summit attended by a group of African leaders. As we sat on a balcony overlooking the massive estate, Julius was obviously in an exuberant mood over the effects of the Declaration. He felt that for the first time he had steered his nation on to a track which could lead to the kind of society about which he dreamed. Above all, he felt that his people now had something idealistic to work towards, with leaders whom they would recognise as sincere because of the form which their personal lives had to take.

Nor was he nervous about the problems of nationalisation. He told me that Asian citizens were giving tremendous help, especially in managing the banks, that he had been promised more managerial help from Western Europe and Canada. He pointed out that his object in nationalising industry, trade and finance had been to secure a base from which to move forward to self-reliance. I was particularly impressed by his conversion to the priority of agriculture over industry. He said that he had found that the main effect of expanding industry had been to increase expatriate profits, instancing the soaring price of sisal during the Korean war which, apparently, had brought no benefit to his country. He had found it increasingly difficult to answer his people when they asked why they should practise austerity at a time when so many of the profits they produced were being sent abroad. But my most lasting impression of this discussion was the tremendous spirits Julius was enjoying, every problem raised being greeted with deep belly-laughs; I had not known him so in tune with life since he realised that he had won the battle for independence. At last he could discern on the horizon the vision for which independence had been achieved.

Arusha set the country on the socio-economic road it has followed ever since. The second national plan, published in 1969, reflected the change in strategy. Financial provision was to be sought mainly from domestic resources. Agriculture was to be given priority. Industry was to grow only slowly, largely dependent on agricultural production. Priorities were identified and specific crops nominated for special encouragement.

The ujamaa programme inevitably moved slowly, but it was always intended that it advance by trial and error, in place of the rush for growth which had characterised the earlier period. It took a great deal of organisation to persuade millions of people to group themselves in villages, to provide the local and central government support and facilities, to gain experience in management. Moreover, the country suffered from severe drought over a number of years and in places famine relief had to be mobilised. The price of sisal, the most important export crop, fluctuated wildly, making planning a hazardous, if not impossible, task. Food shortages constantly menaced the nation, aggravated by the severe droughts of the early 1970s. The sudden leap in oil prices in 1973–4 weakened the country's ability to supplement its own production from abroad, although its refusal to incur large foreign debts had left it more credit-worthy than most Third World states.

Nevertheless, the guidelines set in 1967 were followed and ujamaa villages were established throughout the country. There was some resistance from the farmers of wealthier areas and from certain sections unaccustomed to settled life or agriculture, like the Masai. Corruption, nepotism and greed almost disappeared from public life, although again after some resistance from wealthier public servants. The government extended its nationalisation programme, participating in the oil industry, taking control of the wholesaling business, commercial buildings and rented property.

Yet his fellow-countrymen were still not moving fast enough for Nyerere's impatient mind. By 1973 it was estimated that only about 1,000 ujamaa villages had been established, inhabited by about two million people. As nearly 90 per cent of the national population of some fourteen million lived in rural areas, it was clear that the movement towards ujamaa was proceeding very slowly. According to Nyerere many party leaders who should have been organising the development of these villages were simply doing nothing.

Nyerere therefore publicly insisted that the whole country should be living in ujamaa villages by the end of 1976. This was a drastic assertion. In some ways it contradicted his previous attitude, for he had always argued that it is only possible to persuade people to follow principles, never to compel them to do so. It was clear that Nyerere was impatient again, that he was not prepared to await slow evolution. His demand certainly speeded up the process, for officials in every district vied with each other to establish new villages. This undoubtedly led to rough treatment in certain areas. Some officials, far from scrutiny by national leaders, often tend to interpret instructions as licence to achieve the end by any means. Some houses were burnt, rough coercion was used, a number of peasants even fled across the border into Zambia. These methods were certainly not those of which Nyerere would have approved, but he was prepared to take the risk that they would be used in a few cases as the price of moving towards the full ujamaa model. He was far too realistic to expect that he would gain 100 per cent success by the end of 1976; but it would be a triumph to achieve 80–90 per cent, particularly if that included the wealthier areas of Sukumaland and of the Chagga.

Yet it would be quite false to suppose that Nyerere was expecting or urging that this programme of ujamaa development should be conducted simply by the leadership. In 1971 he had added a new dimension to the Arusha guidelines. He published a document entitled *Mwongozo* which urged still further popular control, still less dependence on or reverence for leaders. Two extracts from it make its message clear :

There must be a deliberate effort to build equality between the leaders and those they lead. For a Tanzanian leader it must be forbidden to be arrogant, extravagant, contemptuous, and oppressive . . . Similarly, the party has the responsibility to fight the vindictiveness of some of its agents. Such actions do not promote socialism but drive a wedge between the party and the government on the one side, and the people on the other.

The duty of the party is not to urge the people to implement plans which have been decided upon by a few experts or leaders. The duty of our party is to ensure that the leaders and experts implement the plans that have been agreed upon by the people themselves. When the people's decision requires information which is only available to the leaders and experts, it will be the duty of the leaders and experts tó make such information available to the people.

As always, Nyerere was observing with critical eyes the actions and attitudes of those who had risen, for the time being at least, into positions of influence and power in his party, government and country. He was using all his powers of persuasion, exhortation and insight to expose the dangers of power consciousness, to enthuse the ordinary citizens to exert their authority and recognise their responsibilities. He was convinced that the new nation could only build the kind of society he visualised, and which was universally given lip-service, when the energies of the whole population were released. The publication of these additional guidelines, distributed in the form of a small booklet, immediately aroused workers, students and some peasants to attack authoritarian and unnecessarily bureaucratic attitudes amongst party or government officials. The climax was reached with the acceptance that the leadership code must apply to all party members, not just its leaders.

It should not be thought, however, that Nyerere was able to spend this post-independence decade simply in preaching or composing epistles. An executive president has to deal with a constant stream of routine government work, and Nyerere has always been as great a reader as a writer. Even more important, he had to face a number of internal crises, to participate in pan-African, Commonwealth and international issues, make many journeys abroad, and to be constantly watchful over the unremitting threats from the white south. After 1971 his border with Amin's unpredictable Uganda was never safe, whilst frequent streams of refugees from central Africa and Mozambique had to be found shelter.

The most traumatic year for Nyerere was 1964. At the beginning of the year a revolution took place in nearby Zanzibar. Only a few weeks after the island had gained independence the Arab-dominated government, elected on a minority vote, was overthrown by a small group of Afro-Shirazi Party supporters, under the leadership of the mysterious John Okello. The Afro-Shirazi Party had close links with TANU. Indeed, Nyerere had warned the British minister, Duncan Sandys, of imminent dangers if the minority government was allowed to take the islands into independence.

Zanzibar's revolution was bound to have some effects on the mainland. Nyerere immediately sent a section of his police force over to the island to help to maintain order.

It was at this time, too, that Nyerere had decided that 'Africanisation', as opposed to 'localisation', had lasted long enough. He issued a circular declaring that in future merit must become the criterion for appointments and promotions, that all citizens should be considered equally, irrespective of their racial origins. The hostility of many trade unionists to this attitude has already been mentioned.

One set of trade unionists, however, discovered themselves in a unique position. The army found that all its senior officers were still Britishers. Its lower ranks were also profoundly dissatisfied with their rates of pay. The soldiers might not have the orthodox benefits of trade union organisation; but they lived and worked together and possessed the most effective bargaining weapon – their guns.

On the night of 19 January 1964, troops stationed in Colito barracks just outside Dar es Salaam mutinied and invaded the city. No one has ever thoroughly explained the causes or objectives of the mutiny, but it seems likeliest that it can be equated with a trade union strike. The soldiers wanted African officers and higher pay. So they reacted as discontented soldiers are apt to do, they used their organisation and the knowledge that they carried guns to demonstrate against the civilian authorities whom they believed to be frustrating their desires. Their action was certainly more explicable because, in the British tradition, they had been insulated from political ideas. They were therefore separated from the political discussions and arguments centred on the need for austerity and abolition of racial consciousness in nation-building. It is also significant that the mutiny was not an isolated occurrence in Tanganyika; similar mutinies broke out almost simultaneously in Kenya and Uganda.

This incident shook Nyerere's self-confidence probably more profoundly than any other event in his life. It was not that he was worried about his own life, nor that an army revolt particularly surprised him, for they had occurred elsewhere in the continent. What disturbed him most deeply was his realisation that in that crisis he could only safeguard his state by asking for the intervention of British forces. This contravened every belief he had fought for, affronted every instinct, and gave him a deep sense of shame he could not assuage for many months.

When Nyerere was awakened in the early hours of the morning and warned that the soldiers had entered the city his reaction was to wait and talk with them. It took all the desperate persuasions of his wife, Rashidi Kawawa and his aides to get him to leave the State House whilst the mutineers were already in the drive. What would have happened if he had maintained his determination to remain is simply speculation; yet he has never been fully convinced that he could not have deployed arguments which would have satisfied the mutineers.

Two days later Nyerere re-appeared in public, driving to every part of the city with his wife. Seventeen soldiers and civilians had been killed in the disorders resulting from the mutiny. The following day he held a press conference and in the evening delivered a Dag Hammarsköld memorial lecture as previously arranged.

But the mutiny was not yet ended. The soldiers were becoming recalcitrant in negotiations with the government. Obote in Uganda and Kenyatta in Kenya asked the British for help. Although he felt deeply that the whole affair had been a disgrace to his nation and was desperately reluctant to seek outside help, by the next day there seemed no alternative. There had been no suggestion that originally the army had sought to overthrow the government; but by now it was strongly suspected that certain trade unionists were using the situation to link up with the disaffected soldiers and destroy Nyerere's régime. On 24 January the President eventually was convinced that the government was threatened and powerless to repel the threat. He asked the British government for assistance. The following morning sixty British marine commandos were flown from an aircraft carrier and ended the mutiny within an hour. Tanganyikans had been shown how fragile was the security of their state when a few soldiers out of an army composed of only two thousand men could menace the existence of their government. Nyerere declared, 'The whole week has been one of most grievous shame for our nation.' The following month he added, 'It's a double shame – shame at being let down by our own men, and shame at having to call in the British.'

The army was disbanded. Nyerere apologised to his people for having to call in the British. He summoned a special meeting of the OAU to Dar es Salaam to explain his actions and asked for African troops to replace the British. The Nigerians responded, sending forces to train a new army. This time it was built as a Peoples' Defence Force, staffed by members of the party and its Youth League. After the initial work of the Nigerians had been completed, Israel, West Germany, Canada and China all assisted in organising an integrated defence force. But the most important new feature was introduced by Nyerere himself. He realised that, as with the civil service, there could be no 'neutral' public servants in the process of nation-building. Unless all sections were working towards the same objective, and fully conscious of national ethics and objectives, there would always be dangers of self-seeking, apathy or deliberate sabotage. So he introduced political education into the security forces, encouraging their members to form their own party branches. The consequence is that the army, police, national service and the small air force have been integrated into the national effort, working alongside all other sectors of the community. There has never been another threat of mutiny.

Within a few weeks of the mutiny Nyerere was involved in trying to prevent the situation in Zanzibar from disrupting the whole of east Africa. Western states had been slow to recognise the new régime (established by Abeid Karume) in the islands; the communists, led by the East Germans, had seized the opportunity to assist Karume and thus create a base for their influence. Nyerere feared that this might lead to subversion along the east African coast, not just by the communists, but by intervention from the West. It should be remembered that almost as soon as the Congo began to suffer from her post-independence difficulties in 1960, the Cold War was imported there, with continual conflict between the West and the communists for several years.

Nyerere grasped this nettle by agreeing with Karume that their two countries should participate in a union, in which they would be connected in much the same way as Great Britain and Northern Ireland. The united republic would be known as 'Tanzania'. This agreement, which entailed Nyerere taking some responsibility for various actions on the islands over which he had virtually no control, brought him frequent criticism. He felt that this was very unfair, especially when it came from other east African public figures, for, as he said, none of the others in the region were prepared to help in a policy from which they stood to gain as much as Tanganyika.

The union also brought the communist–capitalist conflict to his doorstep, much to his annoyance. The West Germans, with whom he had friendly relations, protested that the presence of an East German consulate in Zanzibar could not be tolerated by them. Nyerere, irritated by this intrusion of European conflicts into African affairs, refused to be coerced. As a consequence, relations with West Germany became cold for a period and Tanzania lost the technical assistance which the West German government had promised.

Those who assume that national leaders and governments always follow the path of expediency, usually known by the euphemism, 'national interest', should also study Nyerere's relations with Harold Wilson, Britain's Labour Prime Minister from 1964 to 1970. It might have been expected that the two men would have been natural allies and friends. During the seminal period when Nyerere was formulating his political philosophy, studying political organisation, and seeking allies in his fight against colonial rule, Wilson was a member of the Labour Party's National Executive. During this time the Labour Party was affording Nyerere every facility he requested, helping his fledgling party and constantly harrying Conservative governments over their policies in Tanganyika. Nyerere openly adopted a socialist philosophy after independence and was trying to put it into practice in building his new nation. One would have supposed that the advent of a Labour government in Britain in 1964 would have opened a new chapter in warm friendship between the two leaders and their governments.

Events proved quite the reverse, entailing a break in diplomatic relations. Two issues, one superficial but significant, the other fundamental, caused the breach between the two men. To Nyerere pomposity was 'the very reverse of democratic', as he asserted in a letter to party and government members when instructing them to reduce useless ceremony in the country. But Wilson, like all his colleagues, had been reared in the concept of 'Britannia rules the waves'. Even after most of the colonies had gained independence they were not regarded as equals. (Wilson's successor, Edward Heath, received an even ruder awakening on this point at his first Commonwealth Conference in Singapore in 1971.) Commonwealth Conferences were still held in London, with the British Prime Minister in the chair. Wilson enjoyed this role, but rather as a latter-day emperor than as a chairman of equal friends.

The clash of temperaments between the two men was witnessed when it was proposed that a Commonwealth peace mission be appointed to try and persuade both sides to make peace in Vietnam. Wilson assumed that he would be the mission's chairman. When Nyerere quietly pointed out that it would be inappropriate to have a British chairman as the British government was openly committed to the American side, Wilson lost his temper. Banging his fist on the table he shouted that if he was not fit to be chairman of the mission, then he was not fit to be British Prime Minister. Contrast between two men's conception of socialist attitudes can never have been more sharply exposed.

The second issue was much more fundamental. It was raised over British policy in Rhodesia. Nyerere, like most African leaders, believed that the British government should have been prepared to use force to suppress the revolt of Ian Smith when he declared his country independent in 1965 against all international authority. He considered that Wilson had betrayed Britain's responsibility to the Africans in that country by assuring Smith before UDI that force would not be used. This was contrasted with De Gaulle's actions against French settlers in Algeria and the US–British airlift from Stanleyville.

However, the real clash of principles came when UDI was discussed at a Commonwealth Conference. All Nyerere insisted on was that the British government should pledge itself not to grant Rhodesia independence until majority rule had been established. As Britain had always maintained this principle before giving non-Europeans independence in her colonies, it seemed an unexceptional request to make.

Wilson, however, believed that he could rid himself of his Rhodesian embarrassment by negotiating with Smith, who he knew would never contemplate a settlement on the basis of majority rule. So he prevaricated over the principle of NIBMAR, to Nyerere's intense anger.

Apart from the hostility between the two men engendered by these issues, they provide further evidence that Nyerere based his foreign policy on deeply held principles, whatever the material consequences might be. The NIBMAR principle was fundamental to his concept of a common responsibility to all Africans. Although he probably did not fully agree with its wisdom, the OAU determined that if Britain did not settle the Rhodesian issue, it would call on all its members to break off diplomatic relations with the United Kingdom. When the time-limit expired, Nyerere obeyed the resolution and put the instruction into effect. He knew that by so doing he was sacrificing a British loan of £7·5 million. But he considered that, whether he approved the policy or not, if the OAU was ever to gain authority its members must obey its instructions. He was one of only a handful of African leaders who put OAU policy into practice on this occasion.

It is perhaps in his relations with the Chinese people that Nyerere has been most deeply affected. He began to make friends with the Chinese at a time when the West was ostracising them and the Russians becoming hostile. His friendship therefore increased suspicions in the West that he was coming under communist influence. The Americans, who had at first been very friendly towards him, had been offended when two of her diplomats were accused of spying in Tanzania. They were therefore all the more ready to point the finger of communism at him when he visited China and in 1965 received Chou en Lai as his guest.

Nyerere did not worry. It was not communism which attracted him in China, but the discipline of the workers and the self-reliance of the people. His reply to his critics was, first, that to arrive at a genuinely non-aligned position after years of European colonial rule he had to move towards the East to rid his country of its exclusively Western posture; and, secondly, that there were 700 million Chinese in the world, in which case it was nonsense to ignore them.

Chou en Lai made a lot of mistakes on his first visit to Africa in 1963. In particular, his comment that 'Africa is ripe for revolution', antagonised his hosts, who would themselves be the victims of any revolution. Nyerere agreed with him that revolution was needed in the continent, but he identified it as a social and economic revolution.

When Chou made his second visit in 1965 he had learned from his earlier mistakes. It was during his time in Tanzania, at a state banquet in his honour, that Nyerere emphasised what he had learned from his own experience in China earlier that year, and also gave a friendly warning. He said first, 'There is, however, another lesson which we can learn from the Chinese revolution. It is that courage, enthusiasm, and endurance are not enough. There must also be discipline, and the intelligent application of policies to the needs and circumstances of the country and the time . . . The singlemindedness with which the Chinese people are concentrating on development was the thing which most impressed me during my visit to your great country. The conscious and deliberate frugality with which your people and your government efficiently and joyfully conduct their affairs was a big lesson for me, and through me for my people.' Then came the warning. 'But from no quarter shall we accept direction, or neo-colonialism, and at no time shall we lower our guard against the subversion of our government or our people. Neither our principles, our country, nor our freedom to determine our own future are for sale.'

It was Mao himself who assured Nyerere on this point. He told him that if ever there were any suspicion of Chinese interference in the internal politics of Tanzania, Nyerere had only to inform him and he would immediately recall the culprit, however high an office he might hold. When Chinese workers arrived in Tanzania to build the Friendship textile mill and then the great railway from Dar es Salaam to Zambia, Nyerere watched them with fascination. He pondered how he could instil the zest for hard work and disciplined co-operation into his own people. But there was never any hint of interference from them in the affairs of the country.

Nyerere's greatest concern over events outside Tanzania itself has always been the situation in southern Africa. At the same banquet for Chou en Lai he concluded by saying, 'Tanzania is not yet wholly free, because Africa is not wholly free. We cannot concentrate all our energies on the economic battle until that situation is remedied. We are still hoping, and still working, to see that freedom gained by peaceful means. But we know that whatever happens, freedom for the whole of Africa must be won. And Africa is determined to win it.'

He has always believed that a people must win their freedom for themselves. Yet it is possible to help them. Dar es Salaam became the centre of nationalist movements in exile, and it was there that Eduardo Mondlane, the leader of FRELIMO, the guerrilla movement operating in Mozambique, was killed by a parcel bomb. Nyerere had a high regard for Mondlane; he also influenced FRELIMO by encouraging it to apply his principle of rural, co-operative development in the areas it liberated. Mondlane's assassination was only one of many pieces of evidence that Tanzanian security itself was endangered by the stand the president took over white domination in southern Africa. There was never any doubt that South Africans, Rhodesians and Portuguese would have liked to destroy his régime, if necessary by assassinating him. Their planes continually overflew his country and he had no means of preventing them.

Yet he remained a man of peace. He realised that force might be the only alternative to continued helotry if the southern whites remained intransigent. Yet he believed that a peaceful transfer of power from minorities to majorities could prevent the bloodbath which had followed independence in the Congo. He and Kaunda continually sought the opportunity to convince white leaders of this, marked by the conciliatory Lusaka Manifesto of 1969 and the important negotiations in Lusaka in 1974, which will be described in more detail in the last chapter. Yet about the final issue he had no reservation; no one in Africa was free until the whole continent had been liberated from minority rule; and whether it had to come through force or could be sought by negotiation, total freedom for Africa remained his guiding star.

12

President Kaunda of Zambia

Kenneth Kaunda became President of the Republic of Zambia nearly three years after Nyerere led Tanganyika into independence. Kaunda and Nyerere had worked closely together for several years in the organisation known as PAFMECSA, in opposing the white domination of southern Africa and in seeking to remove colonialism from their continent. Since their first meeting in Dar es Salaam in 1958 they had felt an empathy. Amongst all Africa's leaders these were the two whose outlook, ideas and philosophy marched along the closest paths. Whatever the future might hold for the two men and their respective countries, it could be assumed that the two presidents would extend their mutual respect and friendship into alliance.

Yet although their paths were adjacent, they were separate. For the condition of their two countries revealed greater contrasts than similarities. Whereas Tanganyika was composed of a society in which more than nine out of ten citizens depended on the land for their living, Zambia already possessed a complex economy; it was certain to become ever more complicated in the future. Not only did her copper mines dominate national economic life, but the wealth they produced attracted many other smaller industries. She shared with Rhodesia the huge Kariba hydro-electricity dam and plant, her railways were linked to the south and west, her foreign trade was enormous compared with that of Tanganyika, her towns much larger, her economy far more dependent on international influences. When she became independent Zambia became a new front line in the black–white struggle. To some extent she acted as a buffer for Tanganyika, for her frontiers bordered Rhodesia, Angola, Namibia and Botswana, as well as Mozambique. Kaunda inherited a country wealthier than Nyerere's, but much more vulnerable.

The challenge of these multiple problems did not daunt Kaunda or his colleagues. They had been tempered in the fires of battle against the federation and British governments led by Churchill, Eden, Macmillan and Home. They were no longer political innocents, but warriors who had tested their steel against the most sophisticated leaders of Europe and southern Africa. Yet it still remained to be seen whether the experience of fighting anti-colonial battles would prove adequate training for the new tasks of nation-building and cutting into the international poker game.

Kaunda set the tone from the moment that the new nation attained its sovereignty. At the Independence Stadium, filled with rejoicing Zambians, the Princess Royal handed to him the instruments of independence on behalf of the Queen. In his speech, the new president did not confine himself to the platitudes usual to such occasions. He declared to the royal princess, the retiring governor, the foreign dignatories and to his own people, 'Government spending on schools and teachers' houses was only a little over one and a half million pounds last year. In 1965 we intend to spend six million pounds. It is also intended that there should be very substantial increases in government investment in defence, housing, agriculture, health, roads and the provision of electric power. Altogether we expect government spending on construction alone to pass a figure of twenty-seven and a half million pounds compared with eleven and a quarter million pounds in 1964.' Already, with the new state only a few minutes old, Kaunda was calling his people to work, to demonstrate that the neglect of the colonial period could be transformed by applying the wealth produced by hard work into a new life for the people. Later in the same speech he was to say, '. . . I am aware of the many forces at work, some of them will be tribal, religious and indeed political, to say nothing of those other forces that limit progress when we try to fight the hunger, poverty, ignorance and disease that is so prevalent in our midst. I might mention the most dangerous one and this is unwillingness to work hard. Perhaps it is fitting that at this point I should thank all the people of Zambia for their wonderful response to my call to the nation for hard work. I am most encouraged but I should emphasise that this is only the beginning.'

The determination to master the problems which faced the new nation was visible from the whole appearance of the leadership. During the latter years of the anti-colonial struggle Kaunda had become aware of the importance of symbolism to a leader anxious to inspire his followers. He forswore the eating of meat, the drinking of alcohol, coffee, tea. After visiting Ghana in 1958 he took to wearing a kind of toga in the style of the Ghanaian kente cloth.

With first self-government and then independence the symbolic image had to change. Most African leaders adopted the uniform of their former colonial masters, the suit, collar and tie, often adding evening dress for formal occasions. There was a form of symbolism here; the common people were being shown that black men now had the power formerly exercised by the white colonialist, that blacks could run the country as the whites had done, that they now possessed the badges of 'respectability' in their suits, cars and houses.

But Kaunda, like Nyerere, had no desire to be seen as simply a black successor to the whites. He aimed to lead a revolution in social habits and activities. He therefore adopted the bush-shirt as his normal dress, symbolising the end of the era of 'respectability', of the superiority of clerical over manual work, the priority which every kind of labour should be given in the task of nation-building. Kapwepwe, his principal lieutenant, also discarded the toga he had worn during the anti-colonial period and wore a Chinese-style, collarless tunic suit, somewhat similar to those which Nyerere made popular in Tanzania.

This type of social example has been extremely important in postcolonial societies. They have probably been amongst the most influential factors in determining whether such societies developed a classless unified attack on poverty or became divided between a privileged elite and the ordinary people, many of whom found no change in their lives. But it must not be thought that Kaunda's lead was followed by all his colleagues. There was much more money available in copper-rich Zambia than in agricultural Tanganyika. This offered many more opportunities for the growth of an elite, and some of the new African leaders were attracted into it.

The crucial factor on which the future of Zambia would depend was Kaunda's temperament, because he was bound to be the focus of the national effort. In post-colonial Africa the character of the head of state has been vital. Every new nation has been under extreme pressures, some so excessive that no human being could have supported them. Yet as each country was taken into independence under the leadership of a charismatic leader, that single man was held responsible for the fate of the people. There have been over forty coups or revolutions since the colonial powers began to withdraw, an indication of the weight of pressure, the unsuitability of success in anti-colonial struggles as a qualification for nation-building, the interference of external forces or inability to identify with the people. How would Kaunda fare?

In many ways he faced the most daunting problems of all African leaders. He was bound to meet constant domestic dangers from his economic and tribal difficulties, whilst he would always remain vulnerable to unremitting external hostilities. He had shown himself capable of unceasing labour in the anti-colonial battles, at times working eighteen or twenty hours a day. He immediately demonstrated that he carried this commitment into his presidential office, rising before dawn and continuing his duties well into the night. Yet he had very little knowledge of state administration. It should not be forgotten that African ministers had less than two years' experience before independence, that most of the electorate had never voted before 1962. In the nationalist movement Kaunda had proved that he had organising ability of a very high order, that he was a shrewd tactician and a persuasive speaker. Yet perhaps his main appeal to his people had been a proven sincerity and a profound emotional inspiration. How would these qualities meet the complex challenges of national leadership, executive action and international pressures? Would his deeply emotional nature collapse under the weight of hostility and chicanery? How would his insistence on basing action on principle survive the Machiavellian nature of domestic and international politics?

It seemed to Kaunda and his colleagues that the first problem to be tackled was that of education. The new state began its life with no more than 100 graduates and only about 1,200 Zambians who had completed secondary education. Not only did this necessitate heavy dependence on expatriates in all skilled sectors of national life, but it made it impossible to provide the new embassies, high commissions, central and local government offices and departments of state with well-trained Zambians. If the country was ever to become independent in its most sensitive areas of decision-making or in its conduct of social and economic affairs, it needed a crash programme to train its own citizens.

Within a few weeks of independence a transitional development plan was published. This was to extend over eighteen months whilst a complete national plan could be prepared. In order to secure a quick supply of trained young people the first emphasis was placed on higher education. Within the eighteen months of this plan the number of children at secondary school was doubled; by the time the first full development plan had run its course in 1970 there were over five times as many children in secondary schools as in the year of independence. Meanwhile the nation's first university had opened its gates in 1966; by 1970, 1,200 undergraduates were studying there.

These educational achievements were a source of great pride to Kaunda. They also helped considerably to fulfil the ever-growing demands for qualified Zambians in the various branches of government service. Yet the President himself did not have the time to monitor the development closely. He had to accept that the sudden expansion of secondary education could only be achieved by employing many more foreign teachers. What he had not anticipated was that this would inevitably increase the influence of alien culture. The teachers had been trained in the conventions of their own societies. These were always contrary to the philosophy which the President himself was persuading his people to accept. Yet Kaunda was surprised and disappointed some years after independence to find that many young people treated his philosophy with cynicism, making no effort to practice it.

The same lesson applied to the university. I had many discussions with Kaunda before independence about the character which the university should be given if it was to play a crucial role in his plans for building a socially just nation. He agreed that it must not follow the Oxbridge-Sorbonne model which had become almost universal in new African universities. He accepted that it ought to concentrate on providing the nation with Zambians trained to take responsible jobs in the most critical sectors of national life, that the government should provide it with manpower projections and use its control over scholarships to ensure that this objective was achieved.

But the conventional academics soon gained control over the new institution. Nor were these only the Europeans recruited to the staff and administration; they also included Africans influenced by European academic traditions amongst administrators, staff and students. Before long the mass, low qualification entrance provisions were changed, original research, whether relevant or not, was encouraged, whilst the political science department was filled with aspiring young politicians or diplomats. Instead of concentrating on agriculture, mining and administration, as Kaunda had agreed it should, the university was well on the way to becoming another elitist institution.

Kaunda himself, of course, never had the time to keep sufficiently in touch with university developments to ensure that it grew in the way he intended, as an important element in his programme of national development. But there may be another factor which influenced him against interfering. He had not been to a university himself, although he was very proud of his honorary degree from Fordham. He may well have held the academics in too high regard. It is interesting that Nyerere, having taken two degrees, also allowed his university to develop along broadly conventional academic lines; but as soon as the students exposed their elitist regard for themselves he stamped sharply on their pretensions.

This respect for the expert dominated Kaunda's early years as president. He had much more complex problems to face than Nyerere, and had to meet them under far greater external pressures. Yet he brought to his presidency an expectation that learned men would produce policies for him that was never shared by Nyerere.

The first major challenge to his social objectives illustrates this point. He was bound to encounter difficulties with the copper-miners. The social proximity of the 35,000 workers in the mines, together with their families and those who provided services for them, made the community into the most coherent in the country. They had established what was probably the strongest black-led trade union in the continent. It had played a vital, although sometimes disruptive, part in the struggles against the Federation. The publicity which colour discrimination in the mines received brought international support for the union. Its members could hold the country to ransom because of the crucial role their production played in the national economy.

Independence brought an end to racial discrimination in the mines, but it did not erase the sense of injustice. The lack of qualified Africans for skilled jobs ensured the preservation of de facto racial differentials. So strikes continued after independence. Eventually one of them became so severe that it closed down production.

In this crisis Kaunda displayed his reliance on the learned. He appointed a commission and brought in Roland Brown, Nyerere's Attorney-General, as chairman. The Brown Commission, after chiding the companies for preserving discrimination and the miners for striking during a national crisis, awarded the workers a 22 per cent wage increase. This might appease the miners, but it made nonsense of Kaunda's pleas to close the urban–rural gap. Because no strict terms of reference had been imposed on the wise men, their solution ran directly across the grain of declared national policy.

The same pattern emerged from Zambia's first efforts at economic planning. At this stage the President regarded his role in economic affairs as largely that of a chairman. He and his party had laid down the main guidelines for the kind of national development they sought. It was now the task of the ministers involved in the economic field, their civil servants and any outside experts they might recruit to compose policies capable of achieving the stated objectives. Kaunda presided over the deliberations on their efforts, but could not personally participate in policy-construction. In any case, he just did not have time. He was continually occupied in balancing the various elements in his party through the stream of appointments he had to make; and in working night and day to establish the security of his nation, at this time gravely menaced from the manoeuvres of Ian Smith in Rhodesia.

It was not until some years later that Kaunda realised how his ministers, civil servants and experts had based their policies on suppositions which could not create the kind of society of which he dreamed. It is only fair to point out that the legacy which Zambians inherited was hardly conducive to the creation of an egalitarian man-centred Utopia, that external pressures often demanded measures inconsistent with an emphasis on rural development, and that the minimal progress made under federal and colonial rule made quick growth virtually imperative. For, inevitably, during the campaigns against federation and colonial government, the people had been led to believe that self-rule would bring instant material improvements. In a country like Zambia, with a considerable urban population and the example of European life-styles clearly visible, it tended to be the townspeople who clamoured loudest for immediate benefits.

Nevertheless, Kaunda was to find that much of this early growth programme, which he and his colleagues had approved when it was placed before them by the experts, produced contrary results to those he desired.

The transitional plan, for instance, not only greatly accelerated the educational development of the country, but introduced a massive government construction programme. Although it was obvious that many new buildings were urgently needed, for houses, schools, hospitals, factories and the like, the main purpose was to find employment for the large army of urban unemployed. Yet the fact was that as soon as it was known that increased employment was being offered in the towns, migration from rural to urban areas accelerated. So unemployment grew, accompanied by all the social evils of poor housing, lack of public services, crime and prostitution, whilst the agricultural areas were denuded of able-bodied young people needed on the land.

A similar approach was followed in the first national plan which covered the period 1966–70. When it was drawn up and submitted to the government Kaunda was still immersed in party and international problems. It was not until its effects began to be apparent, after two years of its operation, that he realised the direction his society was taking. By the time he began to try and take remedial measures, the pace at which materialism was already travelling greatly multiplied the magnitude of his task.

As with most development plans, the advisers to the Zambians began with an attempt to increase national production. The argument behind this approach was obvious, for not only had the country actually lost income through the federation, but its own annual rate of growth had been a mere 2 per cent a head from the mid-fifties. Indeed, once it became clear that the federation would be dissolved, the economy stagnated until just before independence. Although the average per capita income at the time of independence was much above the average for the continent, it only amounted to about £63 a year. The planners felt that their first task was to increase this figure.

They succeeded. By 1970 it had almost trebled, although allowance must be made in such a figure for the increase in copper prices. But was 'more' necessarily 'better'? This depended on who was passing judgement or on one's philosophy. The peasant, who had seen little if any improvement in his standard of living and an increasing differential between his family and those in urban employment, would give a contrary answer to the miner or factory worker. For whereas such workers had seen their wages increase by between 30 and 50 per cent, there had hardly been any rise for peasants or other rural dwellers. The average miner was paid about ten times as much as the peasant farmer. Moreover, industry was growing rapidly as the collapse of federation and the declaration of independence in Rhodesia made Zambia a more attractive investment proposition, with the planners encouraging the trend. Social injustice was increasing since independence and the rate of increase was accelerating.

Kaunda had always made it plain that independence was sought in order to right the injustices in Zambian society, not simply to replace white with black rulers, nor even to expand that abstract concept, 'the gross national product'. On one occasion he declared, 'I do not want, even in economic terms, the government of Zambia to think of our people as if they were mere pawns in a game.' Yet now he found that the policies his government had approved were aggravating the social evils he had laid at the doors of the federation and the colonial rulers, increasing the privileges of those who lived near the railway line which had been the focus of colonial development, giving preference to the towns over the countryside. He also saw that as this materialistic nature of society consolidated and deepened, so some of his colleagues were falling victims to it. They had begun to use their offices for personal gain, to adopt European life-styles, whilst rumours of corruption began to spread.

What could he, as president, do to turn the tide? Like Nyerere he was impressed by René Dumont's book and invited the professor to visit Zambia to report on the agricultural situation. Dumont paid him a rare and generous tribute. He wrote, 'I have encountered, in my whole life, only one Head of State who truly seeks to live as a Christian: he is an African, a black, President Kaunda.'

Yet was it enough 'to live as a Christian'? Kaunda had no illusions that simply by setting a personal example he could persuade his fellow-countrymen to turn from the materialism which was beginning to dominate society throughout the urban areas. He began to write and speak more about the philosophy he offered to the nation, which he now christened 'Humanism'. He made an example of certain individuals in public life accused of corruption, including ministers, by dismissing them. He started to refer in speeches to the need for leaders to set an example, to live simply, to serve the community, to spurn opportunities for personal gain.

During the first few years of independence the President had to rely largely on exhortation to influence policies in the various branches of national life. At Cabinet meetings and in discussion with his ministers he tried to create a framework of development which would benefit the whole people, with most emphasis on helping the poor and weak. He issued a constant stream of memoranda, had his speeches printed and distributed, and wrote pamphlets. This strategy was inevitable because his onerous commitments did not allow detailed supervision, but it did not work. He lacked the assistance of a tightly knit group of like-minded colleagues on whom he could unfailingly rely, which had been such a source of strength to Nyerere. With far more complex tasks to face, Zambia had even fewer trained or experienced staff to carry them out. And Kaunda, like Nyerere, discovered that the legacy of conventional methods extended beyond independence, and equally failed to produce the objectives sought.

In the second half of 1968 and again in 1970 I had occasion to examine developments in Zambia since independence with Kaunda. We started from the premise of the President's Humanistic principles. Significantly, he had first outlined these just two months after the publication of Nyerere's Arusha Declaration. The outline has been followed ever since by inter-pretative and expansionist speeches and pamphlets.

Although his party constitution laid down as its first objective 'To achieve African democratic socialism for Zambia', Kaunda chose to give his philosophy the name of 'Humanism' rather than 'Socialism'. It has been suggested that this was because he did not want to appear to be imitating Nyerere or that so many African states professed to be socialist that the name had lost its meaning. Actually, the President considered that 'Humanism' expressed his philosophic concept better than any other word. The reason is apparent in the passage which he himself has always con-sidered focal to the concept he is trying to teach his fellow-countrymen and fundamental to his own convictions:

This high valuation of MAN and respect for human dignity which is a legacy of our tradition should not be lost in the new Africa. However 'modern' and 'advanced' in a Western sense this young nation of Zambia may become, we are fiercely determined that this humanism will not be obscured. African society has always been Man-centred. Indeed, this is as it should be otherwise why is a house built? Not to give Man shelter and security? Why make a chair at all? Why build a factory? Why do you want a State ranch? For what else would there be need to grow food? Why is the fishing industry there? We can go on asking these questions. The simple and yet difficult answer is 'MAN'. Simple in the sense that it is clear all human activity centres around MAN. Difficult, too, because Man has not yet understood his own im-portance. And yet we can say with justification and without any sense of false pride that the African way of life with its many problems has less setbacks towards the achievement of an ideal society. We in Zambia intend to do everything in our power to keep our society Man-centred. For it is in that what might be described as African civilisation is embodied and indeed if modern Africa has anything to contribute to this troubled world, it is in this direction that it should.

It will be seen that there is one fundamental concept in this passage, but that its application in detail is much less precise than in the Arusha Declara-tion or the interpretations of it made by Nyerere. Yet, if the policy details remained vague in Kaunda's statement of his humanist philosophy, we had certain guidelines from which to test the direction which his country had taken since independence. In addition to his favourite passage quoted above, he had written in the preamble, '. . . if the distribution of wealth is not done properly, it might lead to the creation of classes in society and the much-valued humanist approach would have suffered a final blow'. In other words, Kaunda's 'Man' included all Zambian citizens. He was concerned to ensure that no division between 'haves' and 'have-nots' developed in Zambian society. The fact that this division did exist, was usually attributed to colonial rule; it was the responsibility of Zambia's leaders to destroy the division and bring society together as one community.

Kaunda himself recognised that many leaders were not accepting this responsibility when he wrote in the same booklet, 'One has strong fears that although leaders preached the importance of man before independence and have continued to do so after it, this and its true meaning has not begun to permeate the rank and file of the Party, Civil Service, the Police, our Army and the general public to any appreciable extent.' The problem was to analyse the trends since independence in order to discover how far the objectives of Humanism were being achieved and what could be done to guide Zambians to work harder towards their achievement.

The record, as we found it, showed positive and negative accounts. Giant steps had been taken to increase national production and therefore provide a larger total supply of goods. Whereas in the pre-independence decade the domestic product had risen by an annual average of only 5·8 per cent, after independence this rate had been almost doubled. Thus average income had multiplied by two and a half.

Successes had also been recorded in providing employment. In 1964 there were 269,000 wage workers in the country; in 1970 this had grown to 390,000. In education the early crash programme had borne fruit to the extent that primary places had been almost trebled, secondary almost quadrupled and over a thousand undergraduates were at the new university. In health, the number of hospital beds had been doubled, the supply of doctors and nurses was increasing rapidly, and some endemic diseases wiped out.

This was the positive side. Taken as a whole, Zambians had more money, more paid employment, better education and health facilities. Yet, by the humanist test, the negative outweighed the positive side. Although the average income was much higher, it was more unequally distributed. The earnings of peasant farmers had increased by 3 per cent, those of miners by 35 per cent and other wage earners by over 50 per cent. Although new employment had been provided, the number of unemployed had risen, because of the influx into the towns. The urban population was growing at 8·7 per cent annually. Industry was expanding far faster than agriculture and three times as much was being spent from the development plan on urban provinces than in the rural areas. Increases in productivity had never kept pace with wage rises, with an inevitable steep rise in prices, which bore heaviest on the poor in town and country. Perhaps most alarming of all, the population was found to be increasing at a rate of 2·7 per cent a year. There was no doubt that Zambia could sustain a much higher population than the four million it reached about 1970; but a sudden increase in population at this stage posed intractable social and economic problems. The number of inhabitants under fifteen years old had grown to 46 per cent of the total population. This brought an intolerable strain on to the provision of social services, greatly increasing the burden on the working-age section of the nation. And just when all resources needed to be mobilised for productive investment, a rapidly increasing proportion had to be devoted to social provision.

Zambia was both fortunate and unfortunate to be in a position to bear these costs for a time because of her copper production. She was fortunate in that she escaped economic disaster; unfortunate in that this wealth led many leaders and people to assume that their country was rich, whereas, in fact, it remained basically poor. In any case, the fluctuations of world copper prices added another instability to Kaunda's problems. During the first few years of independence the price remained fairly high; early in the 1970s it collapsed. Planning for the future could not be safely based on a stable copper price. Yet all the planners assumed that they could do so.

How did Kaunda face this analysis of the directions his nation was taking? Two elements in Kaunda's character should be understood. First he is profoundly religious; secondly, he sees himself in a long-term perspective, as an agent for changes which will eventually bring man in society to a state of perfection, but which he will probably not live to see. He has never lost the Christian faith which he was taught by his parents, but believes that he has broadened it. He once wrote to his children : 'But religious faith has played a central role in my life, and even at the price of being considered old-fashioned or naïve I must declare the fact.'

The preamble of his first booklet on Humanism begins with these words :

The art of colonisation, if it is to succeed, means a coloniser sees to it that the victim is not only colonised politically, but also economically and culturally. This being the case, the act of political independence forms but the first part of the process of decolonisation. This process is a very long one.

Perhaps it is not possible to complete it in one generation, for it does not only require careful thought and planning, but also a lot of material, human and other-wise, to bring it about.

Thus when he was shown failures or problems, Kaunda was sustained by that faith in a personal God which had given him the strength to survive prison and detention. Yet he has never been a pious, monkish personality, remote from the deeds of the world. He is provoked to anger by the appearance of injustice, but exudes humour, tolerance and understanding when faced with the difficulties raised by human frailty. He has always remained a keen football fan and, from his recent addiction to golf, will talk about his 'birdies' and 'eagles'.

I remember one occasion when he was told that an important secret had been leaked because a woman journalist was believed to have secured it from her minister lover. Kaunda laughed loud and long. 'If there were more women ministers,' he responded, 'you male journalists could do a better job.'

Thus the proof that Zambians were taking many paths leading away from his objectives was considered by the President to indicate no more than temporary aberrations. He set himself to correct them, but was unshaken in his conviction that the eventual goals would be achieved.

Kaunda's reaction to the picture was more decisive than previously. He again drew his ministers' attention to the false directions which some of their departments were taking, sending them personal memoranda, raising the issues in Cabinet and directing his speeches specifically to the weaknesses which had become apparent. But, like Nyerere, he was proceeding by trial and error; it was from this period that he recognised that he must move from his chairmanship role and initiate action himself.

He had learnt that most experts tended to think in conventional economic and social terms, that the less conventional usually cancelled out each other's proposals. He had found that too many of his ministers were apt to ape the attitudes of their white predecessors assuming it to be their right to form a new elite. He was often dismayed by the inefficiency, bureaucracy and conservatism of civil servants, particularly when he was told that government expenditure had risen by 20 per cent a year from 1964 to 1968, four-fifths on civil service salaries.

Kaunda had also learnt another lesson similar to that which experience taught Nyerere. Even methods considered socialist or progressive, if used without adequate planning, imaginative forethought, or efficiency, can bring disaster. In his first Humanism booklet he had quoted from a speech made to the National Council of his party in April 1965. The passage he commended to his readers again related a modern concept to the traditions of his people. It read:

If the Co-operative movement in Zambia is meant to be a way of life and not just a way of solving our unemployment problems, then it is desirable that all of us should give it serious thought. In trying to philosophise on co-operative activities as they affect us, we should recall that from the cradle to the grave most Zambian people of old lived in the co-operative way. This had been accepted as a way of life without the philosophising of pundits, and there is no earthly reason why we should not be proud of it, for it was enjoyed by our ancestors.

Kaunda and his colleagues took the co-operative principle at its face value, believing that co-operative farms would increase agricultural production without creating a class of wealthy landowners. As in Tanganyika, they found that they were wrong. Too much easy capital, generous loans, and constant state help, produced an attitude of mind quite contrary to what had been hoped. Because the plentiful supply of capital was public money farmers habitually considered that loans did not need to be repaid, that they could be lax over interest payments, that hard work on the farms was unnecessary. A large number of them eventually had to be wound up. Kaunda learnt that, however sound the principle, its application to practice needed constant supervision and strict enforcement of contractual terms.

It was during this period of re-examination that Kaunda moved from his chairman's role into the centre of executive action. The change was marked by a number of innovations introduced over a period of about two years. He took firmer control of the party, built up his own State House staff, expanded political education and began to cultivate the grass roots of the nation, down to the village level. Above all, armed with this greater authority and personal advice, he initiated an economic revolution designed to shake out the seeds of personal aggrandisement and elitism which he had observed growing in his society.

The economic revolution was heralded by a speech at the national shrine of Mulungushi where many of his most potent pre-independence declarations had been made. In April 1968, he announced that the government was to take control over more than a score of foreign-owned companies in the commercial and industrial fields. It is significant of Kaunda's new mood that he did not consult his Cabinet before making this announcement. An Industrial Development Corporation was to be established so that Zambians, who owned almost nothing in such economic activities, should possess some stake in their own economy.

At this time Kaunda did not feel strong enough or sufficiently well prepared to take over the most important wealth producers in his country – the copper companies. Nevertheless, in neighbouring Congo, President Mobutu had just nationalised the mines owned by Union Minière; if he was successful, this would become another card for Kaunda to play. In the meantime, his 1968 economic revolution stiffened the country's resolve to become master of its own economic fate. The measures represented a direct appeal by the President to his people, over the heads of those who were prepared to allow the economy to remain in foreign hands so long as they benefited from it. Kaunda had begun to lead from the front.

The nationalisation measures themselves did not solve the central economic issue. Wages continued to rise, productivity lagged behind, inflation extended the widening gap between the well-paid and the poor.

Imports, many of them luxury consumer goods, continued to flood into the country, and everything remained dependent on the maintenance of the copper price.

It was clear that for both economic and political reasons the momentum initiated by the nationalisation tactic would have to be sustained. The first necessity was to curb the wave of spending which was causing misuse of precious foreign exchange, could denude foreign reserves any time the copper price fell, was diverting resources from priority needs, handicapping the growth of Zambia's own infant industries and deepening the chasm between the elite and the masses. Yet to take the tough measures essential to halt this process would inevitably entail courting serious resentment amongst the privileged, especially within the ranks of the comparatively affluent miners.

Kaunda showed consummate political shrewdness in facing this dilemma. The Copper Belt formed the heart of the Bemba community. It was they who had borne most of the brunt of the anti-federal and anti-colonial struggle. Many of them had died, been injured, imprisoned or detained during the disorders which had, among other consequences, forced Macleod to revise his constitutional proposals. Before and after independence they had been the most unruly, often allowing their hot-heads to take actions which gravely embarrassed Kaunda, facing him with situations in which he had to accept the lesser of two evils.

Many of the Bemba looked on Simon Kapwepwe as their leader, con-trasting his reputation for 'toughness' with Kaunda's conciliatory approach. Kapwepwe was already showing signs of becoming the 'rogue elephant' of the party and government; he had ousted Reuben Kamanga, who came from the Eastern Province, as Vice-President of the party and therefore of the country. A militant section of the Bemba clearly had ambitions for their nominee and were prepared to play tribal politics to achieve them.

Kaunda made the decisive stroke of making Kapwepwe Minister of Finance with the responsibility of introducing a retrenching, unpopular budget. Kapwepwe had to announce higher taxes and increased duties on luxury imports. He then had to face the wrath of his own Bemba miners as they saw their cost of living rise. Of course the government as a whole became unpopular amongst privileged Zambians, but the involvement of Kapwepwe as the minister principally responsible avoided the austerity measures being used by the Bemba to inject divisions into the government, insinuating that their hero was opposed to the policy. Kapwepwe himself was unhappy. There is no evidence to suggest that at this time he was, disloyal to Kaunda; but he knew that he was now expected by an im-portant section of his community to represent their interests against the President's national policies.

Six months later, in August 1969, crisis appeared. Kaunda was still taking the initiative. In a four-hour speech on 11 August he extended the economic revolution he had started the previous year. This time he took the bull of economic power by the horns and announced that his government would take over 51 per cent of the copper companies. Again he spoke from his own tent, without consulting any of his lieutenants. To avoid any dangerous demonstrations he allowed no discussion of his speech from his party's national council, but closed the meeting as soon as he had finished, and warned the army to be vigilant against any disorders.

Two weeks later Kapwepwe resigned as Vice-President, alleging that the Bemba were being persecuted. The only possible connection between this allegation and the nationalisation of the mines was that the government might now have more control over the miners. Such a convoluted argument could hardly be put forward by those who claimed to be 'militants'.

Kaunda asked his boyhood friend to return to help his country in a time of crisis. As no move had been made by the Bemba to support his resignation or promote him as their leader against Kaunda, Kapwepwe compiled, promising his President that he would remain in office for at least another year. But Kaunda had already foreseen the dangers. He took away the Vice-President's departmental responsibilities, dissolved the party's central committee, assumed the office of secretary-general, prohibited all public meetings and set up a commission to devise a new party constitution which would raise safeguards against further tribal factionalism within the party.

Kaunda had shown resolution when threatened by schism in his party and government, by a drift towards elitism in the nation. But he gambled in taking a majority interest in the copper companies. The news of nationalisation caused copper shares to plummet, hostility from the City of London financiers, and reluctance by foreign capitalists to invest in Zambia. Scant preparation had been made to manage or govern the companies when the government acquired majority control. Yet the national economy still depended so heavily on copper production that a conflict between the government and the companies could have destroyed it for many years.

Yet Kaunda won his gamble. Not only did he gain heightened respect from his people, enthusiastic over the sight of their President defying international capital in order to ensure national control over their most precious resource, but the companies collaborated in negotiating new arrangements. The negotiations were conducted for the government by Andrew Sardanis, a Cypriot businessman who had been so keen a supporter of UNIP that he stood as one of their candidates in 1962 and had now become chairman of the Industrial Development Corporation.

The collaboration of the copper companies and the business experience of Sardanis enabled Kaunda to succeed in what for him at the time was a crucial gamble. If he had had more time to study the negotiations or a more sceptical negotiator with socialist experience of bargaining, the President might have been saved future trouble. For the contentment of the companies was due to the generous bargain they secured for themselves. Not only did they issue a set of interest-bearing bonds to the government, but they retained a management contract and extremely favourable terms for writing off capital and repatriating profits. Government revenues from the companies actually fell catastrophically following nationalisation. Part of this was due to a fall in the price of copper, but a substantial part of the loss was caused by the terms of the agreement. Kaunda had again to learn from experience. He quickly proved that he could do so. In 1973 he paid off the bonds so as to open the door for a newly negotiated agreement. He recognised that a new basis would have to be provided if his country was not to lose a great deal of its wealth and his development plans be sabotaged by the operations of these multi-national corporations.

Nevertheless, the announcement of copper nationalisation served its immediate purpose. It kept the country conscious that the President and his colleagues were making profound changes in the form of society they had inherited from the colonial rulers; and it kept the initiative in Kaunda's own hands now that he realised that it must be he personally who would have to direct the revolution. When he reshuffled his Cabinet in October 1970 and replaced Kapwepwe with Mainza Chona as Vice-President, the danger of a challenge to his leadership was removed. For Chona had no power base, being a Tonga, and, in any case, had no personal ambition to confront the President.

It was at the 1970 meeting of the party's national council that Kaunda tackled the vexed question of the personal life of Zambia's leaders. He issued a Code of Leadership which followed broadly the lines laid down by Nyerere in the Arusha Declaration. It was to include all UNIP leaders, senior civil servants and senior officials of para-statal organisations. Whilst its form was closely akin to that of Arusha, the challenge it made was far more complex. For Nyerere had only a tiny elite to face, and in a country where opportunities for making money were extremely scarce. Kaunda, on the other hand, had already seen the emergence of a privileged group of considerable size in which the new Zambian elite mixed with the established Europeans and adopted their habits. The declaration of the Leadership Code caused apprehension amongst them; still more significantly it was met with scepticism, with disbelief that it would be put into practice.

It was during this period that Kaunda also became convinced that he must base his main strength in the task of nation-building amongst the people outside the towns, in the rural areas. He believed that they were more open to his ideas of morality and that if he was to build a nation which fulfilled the ambitions of the majority, the peasants who formed that majority must be enabled to participate. So he instructed the party and the government to establish village and ward productivity committees, where the local people could express their needs as well as understand government policies. These committees were to take a full part in policy-making, especially in the formation of the new national plan due to come into effect at the start of 1972. As he had already insisted that certain ministers be allocated to the provinces and reside there, a process of decentralisation of decision-making and activity was being forged. It was to take some considerable time for its operations to be accepted, for his colleagues to inject genuine enthusiasm into this attempt to diffuse power outside Lusaka and other towns.

The new and personal initiatives taken by the President from 1968 onwards naturally entailed a change in his working arrangements. No man could have composed such comprehensive speeches, been aware of what was happening in the country, or have collected the facts on which new policies are based as a solitary individual. During the first years of independence Kaunda had accepted the role of a chairman supplied by ministers, civil servants and party officials with the data of their various responsibilities. When he found that this was insufficient he realised that he needed an expert staff at State House, outside the general milieu of party and government, responsible to him alone. This was particularly essential because, as we shall see later, he himself was constantly occupied in combating factionalism within party and government and dealing with desperately dangerous international problems.

Gradually he built up such a staff, although with many disappointments and tribulations. One of his greatest weaknesses in conducting public affairs, although an endearing personal trait, was his loyalty to personal friends and associates, even after he had reason to suspect their devotion to him, his policies or to the national interest. He made a number of mistakes in the selection of confidants and employees, especially amongst the Europeans he chose. On the other hand, some of his staff, European and African, offered him unstinting devotion. Their names are not to be publicised, but everyone close to the President now knows who is in each category.

There was another handicap in the creation of this presidential staff. Kaunda once facetiously complained to me that 'intellectuals are always wanting to know more'. He was referring to the impending loss of his economic adviser, Dr Justin Zulu, who was leaving him to spend some time at the International Monetary Fund in order 'to gain more experience'. It is inevitable that highly trained Africans should be drawn into international organisations and activities. Yet this has certainly been a drain on the resources needed at home, especially as, in addition, quotas of trained personnel have had to be found for the various United Nations', OAU and Non-Aligned agencies.

Nevertheless, despite these handicaps, a reading of the President's speeches, pamphlets and booklets reveals how well he had been informed of the most important trends at home and abroad. And, although since 1968 he has had to take much greater personal initiatives, he has used both his knowledge and his ideas to put the issues to his party, government and people. Indeed, his main objective has been to see that the people recognise the real issues and participate in deciding how to deal with them.

It might appear that the problems faced by Kaunda in his first decade of nation-building ran in a parallel direction to those of Nyerere. To a degree, this is true, but two important factors rendered Kaunda's task far more difficult, complex and dangerous. As we have seen, Nyerere's greatest strength was the absence from Tanganyika of the ethnic rivalries which had created such a maelstrom in the political life of countries like Kenya, Nigeria and the Congo. Although Zambia was never to suffer the tragic fate of these extreme examples, neither could it show the political homogeneity that produced such harmony in Tanganyika. Consequently, Kaunda was never as free as Nyerere to choose his leaders according to their abilities, to meet problems with rational policies irrespective of factional susceptibilities, or to use his party as a national unit, confident that it would carry out its main function of political education strictly according to accepted policies.

Secondly, although Tanganyika was vulnerable to attacks on its borders consequent on Nyerere's support for FRELIMO in Mozambique, it was never as exposed as Zambia. On independence Zambia moved into the role of Africa's front line against the whole of the white-dominated south – South Africa, Rhodesia, South-West Africa (Namibia) and the Portuguese territories. As Zambia had been born from the womb of Northern Rhodesia, herself a member of the white southern African family, its inheritance took the guise of a consanguineous feud. It was born almost entirely dependent on the south for its survival. From the start, therefore, Kaunda had to fight his enemies with one hand, whilst accepting sustenance from them with the other.

The ethnic problems were particularly bitter for Kaunda. He himself had been brought up amongst the Bemba in the north, but he belonged to no Zambian tribe, his parents having been sent as missionaries from Malawi. Tribalism, like racialism, is absolutely anathema to him. He becomes passionately angry at its appearance, or reduced to tears at the tragedy of its subversion of his attempts to build a united nation. Yet he had to spend much of his time in the decade following independence in dealing with its very lively presence in every aspect of Zambia's national life.

There are many tribal groups, or ethnic communities, in the country, but four dominate the political scene, tending to secure allies from the lesser communities in their region. In the north the Bemba, together with other Bemba-speaking communities, are strongly entrenched. In the west the Lozi dominate what used to be Barotseland, which had a separate treaty with Britain and frequently showed signs of holding secessionist ambitions. The south is led by the Tonga, where Harry Nkumbula and his Congress drew their main strength. In the east the Ngoni-speakers are more loosely grouped, but tend to act politically as a unit.

Because of the inter-communal rivalries between these four communities, Kaunda had to be continually shuffling his ministers, diplomats and party officials, both to keep a balance and to prevent any one of them from gaining a power dangerous to the equilibrium. Yet he could not prevent conspiracies amongst them. Between 1967 and 1970 they threatened to erode the state on a Congolese pattern. The Bemba arranged an alliance with the Tonga which enabled them to drive leading Lozi ministers like Arthur Wina and Munu Sipalo from public life. It was this alliance also which replaced Kamanga with Kapwepwe as Vice-President. Early in 1968 Kaunda became so hopeless with what he had described as 'a spate of hate' emanating from 'tribalism, the wasting disease of Africa', that he walked out of a party national council meeting, vowing to resign as President. He actually started packing in State House, resolved to return to his farm and quit politics. Kapwepwe, and a Cabinet deputation, spent all night persuading him to change his mind.

The damage caused by this constant tribal conflict had many consequences, all of them damaging. It diverted the President, the party and the government from their vital tasks. It influenced appointments. It offered opportunities to Zambia's enemies to subvert the régime from within. It prevented the party from growing into a truly national unit and thus concentrating on economic development as TANU had been able to do. It dislocated national policy by lifting factional demands above the nation's interest. It also prevented Kaunda from following the strict principles in which he believed. He took his courage in his hands by dismissing ministers suspected of corruption; but when the youth wing invaded the courts, he lost his valuable Chief Justice, James Skinner, because he did not feel that he could afford to discipline them.

Perhaps the most unfortunate result of this disease was the barrier it presented to the establishment of a single-party state. All Kaunda's experience with the conservative civil service, with internal subversion, with wasted efforts in politiking, with the divisive effects of party strife and with the needs of economic policy pointed in the same direction that Nyerere had taken. Yet Kaunda believed in 'liberal democracy'. He knew that his policies needed a single-party state, but felt that he should not legislate for it, that it should come naturally through inter-party elections. Yet the strife within UNIP made this impossible. All the evidence pointed to the virtual certainty that Nkumbula's Congress would quickly wither away after independence. It did not do so because UNIP's schisms kept it alive. In the 1968 elections, when Kaunda expected such a complete victory that would convince him that the time was ripe to declare UNIP as the only party supported by a significant number of citizens, the Congress won over twenty seats. They were handed to them by factionalism within UNIP. Again, in 1971, when twelve by-elections were held, Congress maintained its position, despite the fact that some of its leading members had joined UNIP. Eventually, Kaunda was forced to introduce the one-party state as much in order to bring factionalism between members and ex-members of UNIP to an end as because of the ineptitude of Congress and the other opposition parties which had grown out of UNIP's dissensions. When he did reach this unpalatable decision, Kaunda ensured that a commission toured the country for several months to consult the people on their wishes.

The contrast between Nyerere's loss of Kambona and Kaunda's of Kapwepwe illustrates the difference between the political situations of the two countries. Kambona deserted Nyerere because of character defects, the pressure of events and, perhaps, because he was not content to live under the terms of Arusha. There was no hint of tribalism in his defection. As we have seen, Kapwepwe at least allowed himself to be used for particularist tribal ambitions. Once he had found himself in that position, he could not escape. He left party and government in 1971 on account of the new party constitution whose main objective was to outlaw tribalism from the party. He even went so far as to complain that this discriminated against the Bemba. Once on this slippery slope he could not halt his descent. He formed an opposition party, entirely contrary to all that he had previously stood for, allowed it to provoke disorder, and continued to try and undermine the UNIP he had helped to create. The banning of his party and eventually Kapwepwe's own detention was only decreed by Kaunda after the President had exercised extreme patience. But it was the logical result of flirting with tribal politics.

In the end, with a new party constitution which made tribalism impotent as a political factor, and a single-party state, Kaunda seemed to have mastered this dangerous disease. Yet he knew himself that he still had to shape his party into a genuine national unit, capable of leading and inspiring the nation to face the many challenges that still remained. It is significant that at the moment that UNIP became the only legal Zambian party, Kaunda revived his Leadership Code, this time insisting that leaders were to be given only five years to meet the obligations they had incurred before having to live according to its rules. To a considerable degree the future character of Zambian society and of the presidency will depend on the vigour with which this imperative is enforced by the end of 1977.

These domestic problems might appear too onerous to be borne by any one man; they were minute compared with the unceasing pressure of external events. Zambia, as Northern Rhodesia, had been forced into the Central African Federation against the will of her African population. Her resources were used to promote the interests of that federation, the benefits accruing mainly to Southern Rhodesia. When she gained independence Zambia thus depended for her life-lines on Southern Rhodesia, the Portuguese territories and South Africa – all her natural enemies. As a landlocked state she had to import her oil from the Mozambique coast on Rhodesian railways through Rhodesia. The coal which fuelled her copper smelters came from Rhodesia, her electricity from the Kariba hydro-electricity plant, whose power house was on the Rhodesian shore of the Zambesi. Her copper had to be exported along Rhodesian railways or through Portuguese Angola. Her airlines, railways and electricity grid were operated as common services with the Rhodesians. In the first full year of independence she received 31 per cent of her imports from Rhodesia.

This situation boded ill for peaceful development. The prospects were rendered monstrously worse by the declaration of unilateral independence by Ian Smith's régime less than thirteen months after Zambia's own independence day. Smith's declaration was illegal. It defied British authority, for Rhodesia remained a British colony until the Westminster parliament should grant her independence. This action was, therefore, a rebellion by the Rhodesian white minority against the British Crown.

All Africa waited to see whether the British government would act against the rebellion as it had done against African revolts against colonial rule. They also recalled De Gaulle's decisive action against his white rebels in Algeria and the British–American air drop into Stanleyville the previous year to rescue white hostages. Kaunda, with his long emotional attachment to the Labour Party, was confident that Harold Wilson would quickly suppress the rebellion. Some of his colleagues were more sceptical and not averse to spreading quiet rumours that the President was so friendly with the Labour Party that he would risk Zambia's national security to save its face.

The British government took no decisive action. Wilson had already guaranteed that he would not use force before UDI was announced. Instead, the British decided to impose economic sanctions. The United Nations supported them, first asking and later demanding that member states apply the sanctions policy. But, as no action was contemplated against South Africa and Portugal, who had no intention of acting against their Rhodesian allies, and as the sanctions themselves were limited at first, there seemed no reason to believe that they would destroy Smith's defiance.

The issue as to whether or not Zambia should impose sanctions against Rhodesia faced Kaunda with a similar dilemma as Nyerere encountered over breaking diplomatic relations with Britain as resolved by the OAU. He did not believe that economic sanctions could defeat Smith. Yet he was a loyal supporter of the United Nations. He saw clearly that the imposition of sanctions by Zambia would bring her much more hardship than any other country would suffer. He knew, too, that he had many supporters of Smith amongst the white section of his population. He therefore faced not only a dislocation of his economic development plans, but a bitter harvest in soured race relations just as he was trying to build a non-racial society in which people trusted each other irrespective of race.

He also realised that to support sanctions was to offer a hostage to his opponents who would accuse him of sacrificing the interests of his country. Despite all these risks, the President put loyalty to his nation's membership of the United Nations first. He was supported by a majority of his ministers. Within two years Zambia's imports from Rhodesia fell from 34 to 11 per cent. The economy suffered badly, and was only saved from collapse by an air lift to Dar es Salaam and then by the 'hell run' of trucks along the Great North Road taking copper out of the country to Tanzania and bringing fuel back. It seems incredible that the infant nation was allowed to bear the brunt of this effort made in order to pursue a British policy about which it had not been consulted and in which it did not believe. Britain even refused to build an oil pipeline from Dar es Salaam to the Copper Belt to prevent the operation of oil sanctions from starving Zambia's mines of essential fuel. It was eventually built by the Italians.

Kaunda's personal trust in the British Labour Party was best illustrated by his encounter with Harold Wilson in January 1966. Wilson had made the gesture of flying to Lusaka after he had assured a Commonwealth Conference in Lagos that his policies would quickly defeat Smith's pretensions. He soon overcame Kaunda's initial coolness by confiding in him his intention to hold a general election in Britain in March. Armed with his expected greatly increased majority, Wilson assured Zambia's President that he would be able to deal with Smith. He led Kaunda to believe that he would be prepared to use force if necessary. Kaunda was completely duped. He assured his Cabinet that 'Harold' could be trusted and persuaded them to refrain from attacking British ministers for the duration of the British election. During election night he sat with Nyerere and Obote of Uganda, cheering every Labour victory announced by the radio.

Labour won a large majority. Hardly had he returned to Downing Street than Wilson set about probing the Smith régime to seek possibilities for negotiations. Four weeks later he announced that 'talks about talks' had been held. Kaunda was deeply pained and livid with anger. He found it hard to believe that his Labour friends had betrayed him. Years later he was still discussing it with an attitude of disbelief. More immediately he had to face a Cabinet which, led by Kapwepwe, accused him of having been hoodwinked by Wilson. Students broke the windows of the British High Commission and tore down the Union Jack.

Kaunda had learnt by bitter experience why Britain had acquired the epithet 'Perfidious Albion'. He was deeply disillusioned. He had thought that there was a fundamental difference between the foreign policy outlook of the Tories and that of the Labour Party. He believed that the two sets of men differed in principle. He had no illusions when he was fighting the Tories over federation, but he never expected to find that Labour leaders also placed narrow, short-term self-interest before principle or loyalty to friends. He revealed this disillusion in his references to the British government and its members in his speeches. He was no longer surprised when Wilson threatened to cut off British aid if he carried out his threat to leave the Commonwealth. Yet the final twist of irony came in 1968 when he had to visit London in order to purchase missiles considered essential for the protection of Lusaka from bombing from the south. When really faced with the issue of his country's survival he had no hesitation in pocketing his pride.

From 1966 onward the Rhodesian situation made it necessary for Kaunda to harbour an increasing number of banned nationalist movements. This sometimes caused security dangers, for exiled movements are frequently infiltrated by spies. Often, too, more than one nationalist organisation from the same country had offices in Lusaka. Their rivalry constantly threatened order. Moreover, some of them tended to interfere in Zambian politics, their causes being specially taken up by one or other of the factions in UNIP. Their very presence in Lusaka endangered the safety of Zambia. Both the Rhodesians and the South Africans frequently threatened to pursue freedom fighters across the borders, which could be made an alibi for invading the country. As it was, raids from across the Zambezi and over the Portuguese borders were frequent, whilst regular overflying of Zambian military installations took place.

After the British betrayal Kaunda and Nyerere gradually came to the conclusion that the only possibility of a principled solution to the Rhodesian issue would have to be found inside Africa. Wilson had followed up his deluding of Kaunda by making desperate attempts to persuade Smith to agree to a settlement. On the *Tiger* and the *Fearless* the British Prime Minister negotiated with the rebel leader, on both occasions believing that he had persuaded Smith to reach an agreement. Each constitution proposed by the Wilson government, and the subsequent one suggested in 1972 by Heath's Conservative administration, would have left the whites in power for an indefinite period. The future of African representation, therefore, would have remained at the mercy of the white minority. As the white leaders, supported by the majority of their community, were determined that power should never be handed over to the Africans, this would have entrenched white power for the foreseeable future. On each occasion Wilson was saved from the final betrayal by Smith's mulish perversity. After appearing to agree to the negotiated settlements on the warships, he and his colleagues rejected them on his return to Salisbury. (In 1972 a commission under Lord Pearce found that the majority of Africans were opposed to the Conservative proposals, which were therefore left in abeyance.)

Kaunda and Nyerere watched with contempt. Both men stood by the standard of 'No Independence Before Majority African Rule', NIBMAR, as it was christened, which had been agreed at the 1966 Commonwealth Conference, but from which Wilson was trying to escape.

In 1969 the two decided that the time had come for them to take their own initiative, if only to set a framework within which the future could be moulded. They published what came to be known as the 'Lusaka Manifesto', which clearly outlined the alternatives of peaceful or violent change in southern Africa. The two presidents stated their definite preference for the peaceful path, but insisted that changes towards democracy must come, that if peaceful reform were refused the Africans of the southern countries would have no choice but to use violence.

It was to be five years before this initiative bore fruit. In the interim guerrilla warfare had intensified in Rhodesia, Angola and Mozambique. In April 1974, however, as the Portuguese army tired of wasting its strength and sacrificing its men in the three anti-colonial wars, in Guinea-Bissau, Angola and Mozambique, it overthrew the Caetano régime which had succeeded that of Salazar in Lisbon. The new Portuguese rulers wanted to bring the long era of Portugal's colonial government in Africa to an end as soon as possible. This entailed handing over power to the nationalist movements which had been fighting for over a decade.

Kaunda immediately recognised that a new situation had been created in southern Africa. With the nationalists in office, Rhodesia would no longer be able to break the sanctions' net through Beira and Lourenço Marques. Namibia would be vulnerable to raids from Angola. The South Africans would see the grip of black Africa closing in. He believed that

Mr Vorster, the South African Prime Minister, would recognise the dangers that confronted him and be anxious to negotiate.

Kaunda realised quite clearly that white southern Africa could only be pressurised one state at a time. He had recognised this fact when he increased his imports from South Africa in order to apply sanctions to Rhodesia. He had refused to capitulate to blackmail when Vorster threatened to expose correspondence between them, publishing the letters himself and proving that he had never proposed a meeting with the South Africans. Similarly, when Smith closed his border with Zambia at the beginning of 1973 he had called the Rhodesian's bluff by refusing to re-open it, causing Smith to rely even more heavily on South Africa.

Now he believed that the South Africans would like to get rid of the embarrassment of supporting an illegal and costly régime. In particular, he concentrated on the presence of South African para-military police on the Rhodesian–Zambian border. If he could persuade Vorster that he was paying too high a price, currently and in the future, for supporting Smith's régime, the white Rhodesians would be caught in a net. He quietly took soundings of the new situation which had arisen from the Lisbon coup. He sent private emissaries to talk to Vorster. At his tenth anniversary of independence celebrations in Lusaka in October 1974 he gathered Nyerere, Seretse Khama from Botswana, Mobutu from Zaire (influential in Angola), and Samora Machel, president of FRELIMO, around him for a mini-summit. They decided to attempt to put the Lusaka Manifesto into action.

First the South Africans began to make conciliatory speeches, both at the United Nations and through the mouth of Vorster. Then Kaunda made a speech at his university when receiving an honorary degree. He spelt out again the lesson of the Manifesto, declaring that there must be changes, but they should come peacefully, that the security of whites in southern Africa depended on them, that black Africa would help to encourage settlements.

Suddenly the entire atmosphere changed. Vorster pressurised Smith, who released the nationalist leaders, Nkomo and Sithole. Conferences were held in Lusaka, with the released nationalists and Smith's representatives participating. Communication was established between Lusaka and Pretoria. Machel, in many ways the key man who could bring pressure to bear on Salisbury through his control of Mozambique and on the Rhodesian nationalists by his hold over their arms and bases, co-operated fully with Kaunda and Nyerere. The log-jam was broken in Rhodesia by African leaders, after all Britain's unsuccessful temporising. The gap between the demands of Rhodesia's nationalists for democratic government and Smith's continued obstinate insistence on continued 'responsible' – i.e. white – rule continued to yawn. Yet his entrenched position had been breached. But Kaunda was taking fearful risks. With the Rhodesian nationalists still deeply divided, Smith stubbornly refusing to contemplate majority rule, and Vorster constrained by his own white electorate, violent confrontation throughout southern Africa still appeared inevitable. Kaunda would then face bitter criticism from his own opponents for his attempt at pacific policies.

Kaunda had other triumphs on the international stage. He became chairman of the Non-Aligned Conference after its meeting in Lusaka in 1970. He took this task very seriously, believing that the Third World should carve out its own policies through such organisations as the Non-Aligned Conference and UNCTAD.

Immediately after the Lusaka non-aligned meeting, Kaunda took an OAU delegation to Europe and America to warn against the dangers of supplying arms to South Africa. The issue had again been raised because of the Conservative victory in the British general election and its pledge to drop the ban on arms imposed by the Labour government on the basis of United Nations' policy. Kaunda met Edward Heath in London, quickly discovering that Britain's new Prime Minister had little grasp of the issues involved and was still so emotionally insecure that he would lose his temper under criticism. Earlier in the same week Heath had had a row with Nyerere over the South African question, but Nyerere remained cool and unruffled; he had a much longer experience of international affairs than Heath. Kaunda possessed a different temperament. After a late-night dinner in Downing Street attended only by the two leaders, the Zambian High Commissioner and Lord Carrington, Kaunda returned to his hotel deeply disturbed. Apparently the British Prime Minister had completely lost his temper, unable to pose any argument other than the assertion 'Britain must be free to determine her own policies' which he could not understand was never under question. The following morning the British High Commissioner was sitting outside Kaunda's suite, waiting to try and ensure that the President 'had not misunderstood'. The President had indeed understood, and was shocked that a British Prime Minister could act so irrationally.

Mr Heath carried this emotional instability under criticism from Africans to the Singapore Commonwealth Conference three months later. Kaunda had prepared a Declaration of Commonwealth Principles in December 1970. At this stage he had more faith in the value of the Commonwealth than Nyerere. He had threatened to resign from the organisation when Wilson appeared likely to betray the Rhodesian Africans. Then he changed tack, asserting that the Commonwealth now belonged to all its members, not particularly to Britain, and that therefore it was Britain which should be expelled if she betrayed its principles. The idea was born that the time had come to define these principles, before the association degenerated into an amorphous collection of member states with nothing in common.

Kaunda circulated his draft declaration to Nyerere, Obote and Gowon in Africa, to Indira Gandhi in India, to Pierre Trudeau in Canada and to the secretary-general, Arnold Smith. The idea was to alert those likely to be sympathetic, but to avoid a wide public discussion before the conference as it might destroy the whole concept.

When Heath arrived in Singapore, however, he was still obsessed with the suspicion that the Africans were trying to undermine his right to decide his own policies, especially over supplying arms to South Africa. He scanned Kaunda's document minutely, convinced that it formed part of the plot against him. Much of the conference, in and out of the conference hall, was taken up by arguments over the details of the declaration, simply lest they inhibit British sovereignty, which had never been at issue. Nevertheless, with minor amendments the declaration was approved and stands as an historic witness to Kaunda's international vision.

As President, Kaunda took his international responsibilities as seriously as his domestic duties. He believed that African leaders had something new to offer to world society and was determined to play his full part through the United Nations, the Non-Aligned Conference and the OAU. He travelled widely, from Santiago to Peking. He pressed his views on Willi Brandt, De Gaulle, Pompidou and the Italians, although President Nixon displayed his ignorance of the African significance by avoiding meeting him in 1970.

It was in his relations with the Chinese that Kaunda's most intriguing development took place. He had been convinced from before independence that if he was to escape from the stranglehold of the white south a railway must be built from Zambia to Dar es Salaam to give him an alternative outlet to the sea. Everything that happened after Rhodesia's UDI confirmed this conviction. He made strenuous efforts to persuade the West to build it, but was met by disinterest, by the irrelevant argument that it could not pay for itself. The central purpose of the railway was political, not commercial.

When the Chinese showed interest in helping Tanzania and Zambia to build their railway, however, Kaunda was deeply suspicious. He had been fed by Western assertions that communists only helped other countries in order to subvert existing régimes. This seemed to have been substantiated by Chou en Lai's declaration that Africa was ripe for revolution. Kaunda was ever conscious of the dangers in the Copper Belt and feared that the Chinese might encourage the Bemba dissidents to indulge in further subversion. He was equally conscious that most of the freedom fighters could only find training in communist countries and that this might add to the security danger.

Nevertheless, as the West remained stubborn whilst Nyerere appeared blithely confident that the Chinese were offering help without ulterior motives, Kaunda finally agreed to the Chinese proposals. He was encouraged by a personal visit to China in 1967 when he saw for himself that the Chinese were engaged in a social revolution with many similarities to what he was trying to promote in his own country. He has never regretted the decision. Since the construction began in 1970 there has been no reason to criticise Chinese behaviour in either Zambia or Tanzania. Thousands of his own people have been trained in various branches of mechanics and have observed the excellent example set by Chinese technicians in working hard and co-operatively. Now that the rail link has been opened Zambia has escaped from dependence on the south and has discovered new opportunities to develop hitherto neglected areas of her country.

By the mid-seventies, therefore, Kaunda had consolidated his unique, though solitary, position in his own country and had established an international role in his own right. On the occasion of his tenth anniversary celebrations in October 1974 he published a second booklet on Humanism and its application. It illustrates how far he had travelled since the publication of Part One in 1967.

This time he stated unequivocally that 'Humanism seeks to create an egalitarian society – that is, a society in which there is equal opportunity for self-development for all.' He then admitted that 'in spite of various important reforms, something basic seems to have gone wrong. Irrespective of socially significant changes, Zambia today is in a state of acute unease.' He suggested that the enemies of Humanism, those inside and outside the country whose interests could be damaged by the philosophy, were fighting hard to prevent its acceptance. He then reiterated his conviction that Zambia was now becoming a people's democracy in which all citizens could participate not only through their elected representatives, but also by direct involvement in decision-making.

There was still some confusion about how private enterprise could exist in a society committed against exploitation, profit-making and capitalism. On the one hand he asserted that 'One of the principal threats to the democratic working of our Republic stems from the rapid growth of a new class of property owners . . .,' and, again, 'These trends signal the rapid emergence of a powerful Zambian elite whose thoughts and actions are couched in terms of the very rapine system which Humanism in Zambia was meant to combat.' On the other, 'There is room for the time being for private enterprise on the basis of small family business.' This was to be controlled to the extent that 'no individual will be allowed to run a business concern that earns him a gross profit margin which goes beyond K500,000 per annum'. After that a public body would step in.

What was clear from this new formulation of Kaunda's philosophy was that he had become conscious of the major dangers threatening the construction of the kind of society which he believed to be moral. He might be more vague in the means he visualised employing to meet these threats, and still be relying heavily on appeals to people's morality, to their acceptance of God's will. Yet his experiences over the first decade of his presidency had taught him a great deal – and he was still learning. To identify the evils is half-way to removing them. He made it clear that he was leading a crusade: 'Saying we are Humanists is not enough. Behaving like Humanists is what must be done. Humanism is our guiding light.'

13

Two Africans

The goatherd and the missionary's son both trod the path from mud hut to State House. To neither of them did the social achievement possess an iota of significance. Indeed, Nyerere was always apologetic, making a constant nuisance of himself to his security guards by trying to admit the public to the grounds. Both sensibly realised that family life was virtually impossible in such surroundings. They built homes away from the pomp and ceremony which inevitably surround the official residence of a Head of State. As Betty Kaunda wrote, 'It is not all roses living in State House. In the first place it is a house and not a home. In fact it is more like an hotel than a home.'

Both men were fortunate in that their wives placed as little store by their elevated social status as they did themselves. In both households the achievement of attaining the presidency is ignored; it is the achievement of independence which is valued. Indeed, there is sometimes nostalgia for the simpler days of the fight for freedom. To quote Mrs Kaunda again:

We have come a long way from the Shambalakale days, and life is in many ways more varied and interesting for me now, as well as more secure. But when I think back to those and other times, even when things were difficult and the future uncertain, I remember that I was often very happy. There was the excitement of plans and friends and of being part of a great movement together, with a goal always in view. And there were the children and the simple pleasures of keeping house and garden, the waiting to see my husband again soon, no matter how tired he was, or of hearing from him by letter. The postman coming in the morning, the noise of children, friends calling, the smell of cooking, the sun in the dusty evening – all these things were part of happiness . . .

What factor took the two men along their parallel paths, from obscurity to the halls of international fame where their words, in a language not their mother tongue, are read or heard by millions? Why were these two dubbed out of all their contemporaries?

The answers of the two show a subtle difference, yet an essential common element. Nyerere believes that his astonishing life story stems from a series of accidental events or choices which, by random combination, has determined his particular fate. He cites the fortune of going to school, of being so bored that he accompanied his friend to the religious instruction classes where the fathers convinced him intellectually in their teaching of the superiority of Christianity over tribal gods. His religious belief has accompanied him ever since, but it has never become dogmatic. When he was in Edinburgh he used to find peace by simply sitting on his own in a church. He even considered for a time that he might become a priest. Belief in God and a future after death have given him optimism and strength. Yet it was only offered to him accidentally. He considers that this chance pattern describes his whole life.

By contrast, Kaunda was taught the concepts of Christianity by his parents from birth. They have never left him, although he believes that he has transcended the narrow precepts held by his parents. He wrote to his children:

I believe in a Supreme Being whose love is the great driving force working itself out in those three worlds which interpenetrate each other at any moment of time, the worlds of Nature, History and Eternity. For me, God is more a Presence than a philosophical concept. I am aware, even in solitude, that I am not alone; that my cries for help or comfort or strength are heard. Above all, my belief in God gives me a feeling of unlimited responsibility. What a terrifying thing that is! I am guardian rather than owner of such powers and talents as I possess, answerable for my use or abuse of them to the One who has loaned them to me and will one day require a full reckoning. This sense of responsibility seems to be a great burden but at least it frees me from worrying too much about popularity or fame.

Thus, although both men have been motivated by a profound sense of responsibility, their perspectives start from slightly different angles. Kaunda comes close to perceiving that he has been divinely ordered to take up the cross of social responsibility – that he will be required to give 'a full reckoning' as to how he has used the gifts which have been bestowed on him. He considers that he has a direct relationship with God to whom he must account for his stewardship. Over the past few years this concept of God had broadened. No longer is He simply the God portrayed by his parents. To his children he said, 'I have travelled the globe, in the Far East, Asia, Europe and the Americas let alone Africa, and felt the impact of other cultures and religions. This rich experience has led me to question, re-assess and add to my youthful beliefs.' He explained that he does not repudiate his parents' teachings, but has added to them wider dimensions.

'Because I happen to be one of those odd people who feels equally at home in a cathedral, synagogue, temple or mosque, I recognise the power inherent in all the major faiths and urgently desire to see that power harnessed for the welfare and good of humanity.' So Kaunda's God, to whom he is responsible, and who has given him the opportunity and duty to serve his people, has become an ecumenical God. But that God is focal to the motivation and explanation of his road from the Lubwa mission hut to State House.

Nyerere would probably not totally reject this personal relationship, but his emphasis is somewhat different. His commitment to service is as profound and complete as that of Kaunda. From his boyhood his guiding motive has been to serve people. When he was at school, then as a teacher at Tabora and later as a student at Makerere, his determination to serve his people grew and deepened. But during this period 'his people' meant to him his tribal community, the Zanaki. It was only in subsequent years, particularly whilst he was in Edinburgh, that he began to realise that 'his people' embraced all Tanganyikans. Where this sense of service originated is a matter of speculation, even to Nyerere himself. Perhaps it came from the example of his father, as a chief, and of his father's chiefly friends. It must have different origins from those which first motivated Kaunda, for Nyerere was brought up in a very different environment from that of the missionary's son.

Nyerere's religious outlook is also somewhat different from that of Kaunda. Perhaps because Kaunda was emotionally involved with Christianity from the start of his life that faith has always been central to his political principles and philosophy. Nyerere, however, was converted intellectually to Christianity by the Fathers' arguments. So, although his political principles have always been entirely consistent with his religious beliefs, they have developed more independently from religion than those of Kaunda.

Nyerere, indeed, has at times been severely critical of the churches. In 1970 he addressed a congress of the Maryknoll Sisters outside New York, an order much of whose work in Tanzania he admired. His address was subsequently widely distributed throughout the church. In it he criticised the Church for being too often on the side of the established order, however unjust it might be. He baldly asserted that 'What all this amounts to is a call to the Church to recognise the need for social revolution, and to play a leading role in it.' Later in the address he spelt out the way in which he viewed the Church's responsibilities:

For the purpose of the Church is man – his human dignity, and his right to develop himself in freedom. To the service of man's develop- ment, any or all of the institutions of any particular society must be sacrificed if this should be necessary. For all human institutions, including the Church, are established in order to serve man. And it is the institution of the Church, through its members, which should be leading the attack on any organisation, or any economic, social, or political structure which oppresses men, and which denies to them the right and power to live as the sons of a loving God. In the poor countries the Church has this same role to play. It has to be consistently and actively on the side of the poor and unprivileged. It has to lead men towards godliness by joining with them in the attack against injustices and deprivation from which they suffer.

There are echoes here of Kaunda's insistence on man as the centre of all social action. Kaunda too could criticise the Church or, more usually, churchgoers. He had no time for parrot-like religious teaching of children which he considered an insult to their intelligence. He warned against those who simply attend church on Sundays and forget about its precepts for the rest of the week. Yet Kaunda's Humanism has been firmly planted within the religious ethic. He never separates himself from it to look at religion from an objective viewpoint as Nyerere is seen to do in the address quoted above. To Kaunda political activity is inspired by spiritual values, its main objective to assist men to reach as close as possible to divine perfection. Nyerere regards man's freedom as a fundamental value in itself, even if it is also an element in the life of a son of God. Thus the Church should assist secular organisations working for its achievement. To Kaunda philosophical concepts are justified by reference to the spiritual values emanating from God. To Nyerere, God is personal, mankind's values are absolute, and it is the responsibility of all God's churches to help attain them.

It is interesting to observe that both men have been profoundly influenced by the life and work of Gandhi. Kaunda took the opportunity of a visit to India in 1958 to see the places associated with the Indian prophet and to study his work.

In particular, one aspect of Gandhi's teachings which has influenc̆d both men is his emphasis on the value of people's traditional culture. He tried to insulate the Indian people against the materialist philosophy of the West and its accompanying technology. Over the period following independence, both Nyerere and Kaunda had gradually realised that if they were to avoid their societies stratifying into classes and to bridge the existing gap between their urban elites and their rural masses, they would have to preserve and foster the traditional communal spirit of their people. Moreover, the character of the societies they sought to establish was inimical to the values of the West, although many of their educated people had begun to imitate the ways of their former masters. They found, too, that their appeals to their people needed an alternative cultural basis if they were to wean them from imitation of the life-styles which had been followed by colonial administrators or by those Western communities in which some of the younger generation had been educated.

Later Nyerere was to recognise the relevance of Mao Tse-tung's work and teachings to African development. Kaunda took longer to accept this. He had, perhaps, been more deeply conditioned by Western assumptions than Nyerere, whose mind was always the more iconoclastic. Eventually, however, and especially after he had seen the attitude of the Chinese workers on the railway and had visited China himself, Kaunda came to the same conclusion as Nyerere. China was a developing country, and, in her commune system, could offer lessons to Africans. Their situations were certainly not identical, nor could be the answers. But both presidents recognised that the ethic of China and the kind of Africa they sought were more closely associated than those of either the West or of the Soviet bloc.

The difference of emphasis which we have seen in the spiritual or religious content of their philosophies can be seen even more clearly in their policy statements. Nyerere has been prolific in his speeches and writings, detailing both his ultimate objectives and the methods he is trying to apply to achieve them. Kaunda, although not so consistently detailed in expression, has also made long speeches and published statements of his political perspectives. The most important revelation of these is contained in his 1974 booklet, *Humanism in Zambia, Part Two*.

There are two significant aspects of each man's ideas. First, their development over the years since independence; secondly, the different emphases which they show on their views of man and his society.

The development of Nyerere's ideas is the simpler. From being a passionate nationalist with vague socialist tendencies at the time of independence, Nyerere has grown into a fully fledged socialist. In many ways he has become the most radical socialist leader in the world. The development of his ideas and of his policies has been influenced by a combination of practical experience as leader of his newly independent state, his observation of his people's needs, and his own contemplative study. The Arusha Declaration, although a party document, represented the stage of thought he had reached by 1967. He had identified those dangers which might weaken the construction of a new nation based on social justice, and especially the influences which could take the leaders along false paths. He had recognised the need to vest the major productive sectors of the economy in the state, which he considered was the best representative institution of the people. Yet he himself insisted that at this stage he could only offer general guidelines, that much thought, discussion and experience were still needed before specific policies could be determined.

By 1973, six years later, Nyerere was still asserting that, 'although Tanzania is engaged in building a socialist society, it certainly is not one at present'. In his report of the first decade of independence he had pointed out that in 1968 'there were still some 400 private importers, 400 private wholesalers, and about 3,600 private sub-wholesalers, operating on the mainland of Tanzania – and this was after the nationalisation of the major import/export firms.' The point was that the government was continually having to deal with problems of this kind, so that the socialist objectives which had been set in Arusha in 1967 and the party's guidelines of four years later could only be achieved through an evolutionary process which would take many years. Indeed, the guidelines demanded an even more gradual evolution than Arusha, for they called for an understanding of the real meanings of democratic socialism by management and ordinary people, for public discussion of issues, followed by public decision-making.

Nyerere was engaged in social engineering. He believed in persuading people to create certain institutions and then leaving them to experiment within them. For instance, the ujamaa village should never be considered as simply drawn from a stereotyped model. Nyerere declared in his ten-year report that 'among these 2,700 ujamaa villages there can be found almost every stage of development . . . For we have no blueprint which tells us all the answers to questions about how such villages should be run and should operate . . . By our present method we shall learn as we go along, and learn from each other.'

Nor did Nyerere believe that he was constructing a universal or even a pan-African model. He told the Sudanese on one occasion, 'My first assumption is that any discussion about the appropriate economic and social organisation must, for the time being at least, be conducted within each nation-state, and the decision must be made exclusively by the people of that nation. Thus, it is the people of Tanzania as a whole, or The Sudan as a whole, who will decide the path for their country.' He added that as there was some degree of autonomy in both the Southern provinces of The Sudan and in Zanzibar, smaller units would also have the right of choice, rather than the whole nation.

Yet, by 1973, Nyerere had become unequivocally committed to fundamental socialist principles. Many details and practices had still to be thought out, but the lines of guidance had become firmer. They are delineated in this passage from the same address to the Sudanese :

The vital point is that the basis of socialist organisation is the meeting of people's needs, not the making of profit. The decision to devote the nation's resources to the production of one thing rather than another is made in the light of what is needed, not what is most profitable. Furthermore, such decisions are made by the people through their responsible institutions – their own government, their own industrial corporations, their own commercial institutions. They are not made by a small group of capitalists, either local or foreign – and the question of foreign domination through economic ownership is thus excluded. Further the workers of the nation can receive – directly or indirectly – the full fruits of their industry; there is no group of private owners which constantly appropriates a large proportion of the wealth produced.

Such a clear, unequivocal statement of Tanzania's objectives could not have been made in 1961; it would have appeared then as demagogy. In any case, Nyerere had neither the experience of the barriers to be crossed in building a nation based on social justice, nor the insight into the implications of his socialist faith. He had come a long way in those intervening dozen years. As was his custom, he was stating the principles, confident that once they were accepted the details would be filled in.

Kaunda moved even further during the first decade of his presidency. Although he had close contact with and affection for the British Labour Party during the independence struggle, he had not had the time to study the socio-economic implications of seeking to build his new nation on socially just foundations which Nyerere had been accorded. While Nyerere was working out his political philosophy in Edinburgh, reading the ideas of others who had addressed their minds to the same issues, and observing Clem Attlee's Labour Party in government and opposition, Kaunda was already in the midst of the political battle. He had not only to organise the activities of an infant Congress, but to travel vast distances to recruit members or collect funds, at the same time attending to the minutiae of party organisation and seeking a living for his growing family. During the following years he had to fight against the federation and colonial rule, and the bitter fratricidal battle within the nationalist movement against his former friend and leader, Harry Nkumbula. There had been little time for study or contemplation; what there was was mainly occupied in religious or moralistic reading, later accompanied by a study of Gandhi's works.

When Kaunda became President he would probably have described himself loosely as a socialist; but his definition of this philosophy would have been confined to a desire for social justice and moral behaviour amongst his people.

His problems from the start were immensely tougher than those faced by Nyerere. If Tanganyika at independence was a mixture of minor capitalism, some plantation feudalism and mass subsistence, Zambia was dominated by the capitalist sector, with its plantations and subsistence playing minor roles. Kaunda had to handle a treble rather than a dual economy. He had a strongly entrenched white community, a clamant African working class and the mass of subsistence peasants. To set course towards anything resembling social justice in such circumstances entailed overcoming huge hazards.

It was inevitable, therefore, that Kaunda had to content himself with constantly reiterating principles, with exhorting his colleagues and people, giving time for his concepts to be accepted, and being reconciled to a continuing gap between precept and practice. There has never been the possibility that any form of socialist principles can be quickly applied in the materialist jungle he inherited from federation and colonialism.

Nevertheless, Kaunda's ideas have developed fast and, in one way, to an even more ambitious pitch than those of Nyerere. He has never been a social engineer in the manner of Nyerere. Without the party cohesion, tribal harmony and economic autonomy of Tanzania, he could never have played that role if he had wished.

Kaunda's method has been rather to set out principled objectives to his party and nation, preaching sermons rather than providing close political analysis. At times, however, as we have seen, he has taken decisive political action, assisted only by a tiny group of close personal confidants. His political skill has been shown in his ability to appeal directly to the instincts of the people and then to secure the support of his party colleagues in carrying out measures on which they were not consulted.

The central dilemma which Kaunda faced in equating his principles with the economic realities of his country was illustrated in three extracts from his 1968 Mulungushi speech. First, he declared, 'It is important to remember that as humanists we cannot allow Zambians to develop into capitalists at all and here is where a serious problem arises. In the final analysis all this boils down to one major point. Our society through its institutions – its man-made institutions – must fight with all it has at its disposal against the exploitation of man by man in whatever field.' Yet, although he was announcing major state intervention in commerce and industry, he was still acknowledging that Zambia would remain a mixed economy. 'The very fact that we have declared ourselves in favour of a mixed economy is more than an indication that there is a place for individual initiative...'

Then came the apparent contradiction. 'We cannot declare ourselves in favour of private enterprise and forbid Zambians from participating in the private sector.'

This was a different language with different objectives from Nyerere's Arusha Declaration. Kaunda was not blind to the apparent contradiction and his consequent dilemma. He knew that he could not immediately transform the private enterprise system of Northern Rhodesia, with all its cultural influence on his people, into a Zambian socialism, necessitating a cultural and ethical reformation of his people. What he was trying to do at this stage was to limit the power of the private sector, replace foreigners with Zambians in major parts of that sector, and so provide a better opportunity for himself, his party and government to control it. It was obviously a dangerous ploy. For if he succeeded, he would have introduced many of his own people to capitalist practices. Even though he believed that he could limit the size of their enterprise, he was nevertheless giving them a taste of precisely those influences which he wanted to extirpate from his country. He might reduce foreign capitalist influence, but at the expense of corrupting a section of his own people, whom he hoped to convert to contrary values.

By the middle of 1975 Kaunda recognised that the impact of the economic situation on his country was rapidly destroying many of his basic objectives. Copper prices had plummeted; government revenues and foreign reserves inevitably followed the same trend; the increased oil prices, together with the extra transport costs caused by the continued closure of the Rhodesian border and dislocation of the Benguela railway due to chaos in Angola, increased bills to a staggering level; import expenditure continued to skyrocket; above all, the rich and the middle class continued to live in complacent affluence.

At the party's National Council meeting in Mulungushi Hall in Lusaka at the end of June, the President gave delegates a seven-hour speech, followed by a long television broadcast to the nation. He announced that freehold land titles would immediately be transformed into 100 year leases; that subsidies to para-statal organisations would be drastically reduced; that the unemployed would be sent back to their home districts to increase farming manpower under the supervision of student-teachers from agricultural colleges; that urban landowners would be nationalised in five years; that the *Times of Zambia*, owned by Lonrho, would be taken over by the party. He insisted that his people recognise that the country was basically poor despite its copper wealth, which in any case was a wasting asset. He warned the wealthy that Humanism would not tolerate their excess in the striking phrase, 'The decoration on the front of the Mercedes has almost become our national emblem instead of the pick and hoe displayed on our coat of arms.' He warned the country's leaders who were flouting the Leadership Code by refusing to declare their assets and liabilities that they would be fined a month's salary. In short, the President was seen to be applying the principles of Humanism to a social and economic situation which had increasingly been exposing the contrast between Zambia's few wealthy and many poor. Another long step had been taken towards a fully socialist society.

Kaunda faced a parallel situation in the countryside. He recognised that he must find the means of improving rural living standards if he was to have any chance of creating social justice. Yet, like Nyerere, he wanted to preserve the best of traditional culture because the values he was preaching approximated to those accepted in the villages. He admitted that the ideals of mutual aid and inclusiveness were not always achieved in village life, but they were accepted as ideals at which to aim. Kaunda was striving to persuade all Zambians to accept them as a way of life, preferring superior quality to material quantity. In traditional society mutual aid was a practical necessity for survival. Kaunda had to face the possibility that it might prove impossible to preserve when it became no longer essential. Just as he faced the dilemma of trying to reconcile urban economic growth with his prohibition of capitalism, so he had to discover whether it was possible to improve subsistence communities without introducing the exploitation of man by man. And as the conventional manner of promoting growth in the agricultural sector had been to concentrate on those areas close to the railway line, he had also to discover whether rural development was possible without aggravating the existing regional contrasts in rural living standards.

By 1974 Kaunda had reached a much more forthright definition of his objectives. Although many traces of the 1968 Mulungushi speech remained, he was now roundly declaring that:

Zambia is just now emerging from the stage of a capitalist economy and is moving to a State-controlled one and from there we are determined to move to a socialist or common ownership economy. How long it takes us to socialise all the means of production depends on the determined efforts that we as a people make to implement meaningfully the conscious decision we have taken to move towards the attainment of a Humanist society. It should be pointed out that as Humanists we know and believe that socialising the economy is only a means to a noble end. It is not an end in itself at all.

Later Kaunda expanded this analytical concept of the stage of Zambian development and the direction it was taking:

Humanists also believe that before the means of production and distribution are placed firmly in the hands of the people, that is, before complete participatory democracy in our economic life is established, the State has a key role to play in the development of the nation. In other words, before Man reaches spiritual and moral maturity insofar as his economic responsibilities towards his fellow-men are concerned, State control through State participation is essential.

Kaunda had now firmly nailed his colours to the mast of complete socialisation, later to lead to democratic control of all economic activities by the people themselves. He still found it necessary to insist that private businesses would only be allowed up to a certain profit margin, after which they would be taken into the public sector. But his objective was now clarified. State control necessary in the current transition stage of Zambian development would eventually wither as common ownership became universal in 'a society controlled completely by the working people of Zambia'.

If Kaunda had clarified his mind on the issue of Zambia's development path by 1974, why was he still terming his Utopia a 'Humanist society' instead of a 'socialist society'? Here we return again to the strong element of religious content in Kaunda's political philosophy compared with Nyerere's approach.

Kaunda's explanations of the relation between Humanism and socialism sound echoes of early communist reasoning:

. . . one cannot be a Humanist without being a socialist. It is virtually impossible. This is so because socialism is, to a Humanist, the stage of human development attained just before that of the final one which is Humanism. On the other hand, one can be a socialist without being a Humanist.

He then proceeds to outline the classic stages of human development as analysed by Marxist historians, with Humanism taking the place of communism :

While a Humanist has, like a communist, one other stage – Humanism – some of our fellow-men could, and indeed do, believe in socialism as an end in itself . . . to a Humanist, socialism is a way of organising society in such a way as to remove, in the final analysis, all forms of exploitation of man by man. The major instrument applied to achieve this objective is to take away all major means of production and distribution from private hands – unbridled capitalism – and put them under the control of the State.

This is the first stage of development towards the creation of a socialist economy. The final stage comes when the people themselves have, as a matter of principle and/or belief, begun to control the economy, thereby creating a state in which wealth is commonly owned by all the people, on the basis of one doing unto others as he would have them do unto him. At this stage the people have wrested economic power from the capitalist exploiters and they themselves *own* all the means of production and distribution. The end of all this is *Humanism*.

To Kaunda, therefore, Humanism is the stage of man's development which follows that of socialism. But if that is so, what is the difference between Humanism and communism? Kaunda also spells out the answer to this question:

> While a communist believes in what is generally called scientific socialism, a Humanist believes that it is impossible for Man to live by bread alone. It is believed that a true communist believes *not* in the Super-being and after-life. His religion is his ideology. On the other hand, a Humanist believes in the Presence of a Super-being – the source of all life.

A final quotation from Kaunda's guide to Humanism will illustrate the crucial role of religious or spiritual sense which pervades every aspect of his concept and separates it from communism. He is concerned about the part played by the state in the development of society. Indeed, he begins the booklet by relating how a friend who also believed in non-violence had asked him before independence whether, once he had led his country out of colonial rule, he would participate in government or keep out, as Gandhi had done because of the violence inherent in all states. Kaunda is obviously concerned about this personal issue. He therefore addresses himself to the role of the state in what he sees as the development towards Humanism:

> The State exists for Man. But Man needs the State only until he moves from the present state of *imperfection* of his *body* and *soul*, or his *physical* and *spiritual* being, to one of perfection and therefore moves further to a clearer understanding of God. He needs the State because he is still unable to comprehend the true meaning of the teaching 'love the Lord thy God with all thy heart, and with all thy soul, and with all thy mind and with all thy strength' and 'love thy neighbour as thyself'. Before this goal is reached, Man needs a structure of authority to create a framework of order and justice for him. [And later] When time comes in this very long march towards perfection when Man would have learnt to love his neighbour as himself, and as a result did unto others as he would have them do unto him, then at this point in time there would be no need for police forces and prison services because crime would have been wiped out. Man would be living by love . . . The need for the oppressive machinery of the State would be removed.

The State, no longer useful to Man, would be buried in the past together with Man's imperfections that had made it necessary.

Again there are faint traces of the early communists' belief in the 'withering away of the state', but they occur in a totally different context. These sentiments will be characterised by modern sophisticates as sentimental idealism. It is apposite to point out first, that the rejection of idealism has not notably improved the lot of the human race; and secondly, that emotional idealism is meaningful to millions of Third World inhabitants seeking a future less brutal and more hopeful than that provided by the rational machine-centred Euro-American society of the past two centuries.

To Kaunda Humanism is both a philosophy and a way of life. His object is to persuade his fellow-countrymen to accept his philosophical principles so completely that they provide a guide to every aspect of life. In this he and Nyerere are at one. The only differences are that Nyerere describes his ideal society as 'socialist' whereas Kaunda uses the term 'Humanist'; and that Nyerere places more emphasis on the construction of social institutions to encourage people to live in social harmony, whilst Kaunda stresses individual, personal conversion to spiritual principles. Both agree that man can be master of his own environment, which should be used to serve the needs of the total community. Both also agree that in order to transform society from its present materialist obsessions, the role of money in development must be limited, that a lower growth-rate than is potentially possible should be accepted. In this way, they believe, it should be possible to avoid the incentive of wealth from gaining hold over the few to whom its opportunities are offered in the developmental process, rather building prosperity more gradually from the grass roots of society.

Each man, too, has drawn from both his experience of traditional African society and from his understanding of Christian teachings in building his social philosophy. Each considers that man can attain his fullest material and spiritual development by participating in, contributing to, a harmonious community. They both believe that their own traditional societies offered models of how this can be achieved, where the mutual co-operation of the extended family, clan and tribe emphasised mutuality instead of competition. They are equally convinced that this outlook is consonant with the concepts of Christianity and of other religions, that spiritual awareness is essential to man's welfare and is destroyed by any form of discrimination, economic, political or social. Both agree that whilst the mutual aid society was and is witnessed in traditional village life, the poverty usually experienced there is an obstruction to man's development which should be removed for spiritual and moral as well as for material reasons.

The close friendship between the two presidents, the parallel paths of their careers and philosophies, have tended to merge their personalities in the eyes of the public. It is true that politically and philosophically they are very close; yet there are distinct differences in their temperaments and, as we have seen, in philosophic emphases. Nor is either simply the man the public visualises. Nyerere, from the days when he used to appear before the Trusteeship Council at the United Nations, has always seemed the calm, self-confident, rational figure of a man with immense good humour, always totally under self-control. He usually is, and these characteristics are mainly responsible for his persuasiveness and his success as a social engineer.

But Nyerere can become angry, he can be impatient and, above all, vulnerable to a sense of shame. He was intensely angry when the university students marched to State House to protest against their inclusion in national service. Everyone who heard him reply to the students outside State House recognised that he was seething, furious that privileged young men and women could openly assert a claim to contract out of their responsibilities to the nation.

He became impatient when he saw how little was being done by party and government leaders to implement the Arusha Declaration. When he declared the deadline of December 1976 for the whole rural population to be living in ujamaa villages he was exhibiting an impatience that denied one principle which had until then guided his actions. He had always maintained that people can be persuaded, but never forced, to accept ideas. He had applied this principle to all his policies and it was for this reason that he is universally considered in his country to be the 'Mwalimu', the teacher, persuader, the wise father-figure, or modern counterpart of the chief. It was also from this principle that Nyerere drew his decision to recognise Biafra during the Nigerian civil war. He argued that, although he was deeply opposed to the principle or practice of secession, which had riven the Congo so tragically, the Ibo had proved by their armed resistance that they had not been persuaded of the advantages of remaining in the Nigerian federation. On these grounds he therefore objected to the attempt to force them back into the federation against their proven will.

Nevertheless, Nyerere's impatience to see results from accepted policies led him to *tell* his fellow-countrymen that they must live in villages within a time-limit. Inevitably this led to some roughness amongst officials competing to secure the best totals in the shortest time, especially when army units were used to coerce unwilling people. This went right across the grain of Nyerere's convictions; but it had been caused by his impatience to see the conservatism of some of his people removed from barring social progress for the majority. Perhaps he wanted more evidence of social development before he felt he could retire or had to face the imminence of death.

Nyerere's emotional vulnerability was shown most clearly at the time of the mutiny in 1964. He experienced deep pain and a profound sense of shame, both that people in his country could act in this way, and in having to ask for the use of British forces against his own countrymen. The trauma of this whole situation affected him deeply and personally. He tried to purge himself by apologising to the Organisation of African Unity, as though he felt individually responsible for the actions of all Tanganyikans, as if the good name of his country and of Africa were personified in him. Later he took setbacks to his hopes more philosophically, although he never again had to face such a crisis in his own country. He did feel at various times that some African leaders were betraying the high standards they had set themselves. After a particularly stormy and divisive meeting of the OAU he again felt this sense of pained shame; but contented himself with declaring 'There is a devil in Africa'.

Kaunda has always been more overtly emotional than Nyerere. It has not been uncommon for him to break down during the course of a speech, when his own words have appeared to stir the depths of a compassion for the sufferings caused by injustices which lies at the base of his consciousness. It has been his passion rather than his reason which has aroused his people and inspired them to follow him. He too can feel extreme anger, yet it always seems to be mixed with disgust. No doubt this arises from his profound sense of morality, which could at times be described as dogmatic.

Kaunda's most traumatic experience came over the incident of his resignation in 1968. The inter-tribal factionalism within the party brought out this profound disgust that men, especially men inside his own idealistic party, could feel such hate against each other. His mixture of disgust and anger reached such heat that he left the meeting of the party's national council and returned to State House. Here he actually began packing, determined to return to his farm and leave public life permanently. It took a deputation most of the night to persuade him to change his mind, and only then on the promise that inter-factional feuding would cease immediately.

There have been occasions when this anger has led to unconsidered actions. For instance, it boiled over as a result of the 1968 election. Once again tribal factionalism within the party weakened its unity, with the result that most of the seats in Barotseland were lost. Kaunda had set his heart on demonstrating that the mass of the people in the country now wanted a single-party state. He hoped to achieve a similar position to that enjoyed by Nyerere, with an opposition so weak and unsupported that UNIP became the only serious political unit in Zambia. This would enable him to keep his promise to introduce a single-party state only through the electoral will of the people. Strife within his party had led to the disappointment of his hopes. After the election he turned furiously on the opposition members who had defeated his candidates and any civil servants who had assisted them. He publicly threatened them, but, once his immediate anger subsided, allowed his threats to evaporate.

Nevertheless, despite this powerful emotional influence, Kaunda has shown himself to have a most astute political instinct. In the circumstances of Zambia, compared with those of Tanzania, he has never had the same opportunity as Nyerere to plan far ahead. He has had to react to political dangers, rather than forestall them. His tactic in meeting the tribal conflicts within his party and government, for instance, was to move ministers and diplomats rapidly from post to post, so as to prevent the formation of any cabal. It succeeded in its major objective, though at the price of administrative and political inefficiency.

Perhaps his greatest astuteness, however, was demonstrated over the defection of Simon Kapwepwe. This was a painful problem for him to face, for Kapwepwe had been his friend from boyhood days, the two of them working in harness to liberate the country and to build a new nation. There was no way in which he could avoid it, however, for Kapwepwe had become progressively more estranged from his policies and objectives. When he left the party, creating an opposition organisation of his own, the President was forced to react.

Most of his colleagues argued vehemently that Kapwepwe should be immediately arrested, his party banned and its supporters detained. This was an emotional reaction and it is interesting to note that Kaunda, despite the dominance of emotion in his personality, showed his maturity by resisting it. He advised patience, confident from his knowledge of his former friend that he would eventually act in such a manner as to provide valid grounds for his arrest. Even when outbreaks of violence brought the decision to arrest many of its members, Kapwepwe remained at liberty. Kaunda was determined to avoid making him into a martyr, in the meantime aiming to divide the Bemba and so neutralise them as a political force. Eventually Kapwepwe himself was detained and his party banned, but by this time neither the leader nor the organisation had retained much respect amongst the public. As Kaunda had foreseen, they had offered no alternative policy to that of the ruling party they had deserted, whilst many of their actions forfeited public sympathy by appearing to undermine the security of the nation.

It is instructive to note Kaunda's own justification of his original action in detaining members of Kapwepwe's party in 1971 :

. . . Government has followed the activities of the UPP and all opposition elements for twenty-four hours a day. Following a close study of
the objectives of these groups, it has become imperative that, while
the Constitution of the Republic of Zambia guarantees every person
individual liberty, while it guarantees self-expression, which includes
the right to organise politically or otherwise without interference,
drastic action be taken in the national interest . . . These people and
their followers have been among the greatest source of insecurity and
instability in the party, government and the nation. I have now decided
to take measures to guarantee the security of each and every law-
abiding citizen in the Republic.

This issue of national security gradually became Kaunda's primary
concern. Considering the exposed position of Zambia to south, east and
west, together with the known desire of various external interests to
destroy his régime, such concern was not surprising. It alone, however,
explains many of the arbitrary actions which were taken, sometimes,
though not always, with Kaunda's connivance. Certainly he assented to
some measures which he disliked and which, in other circumstances,
he would have considered constituted an infringement of liberty. But
he has come to feel that his first responsibility is to ensure that the state
is secure, even if that entails taking actions which unfairly penalise
individuals.

Although Kaunda came to the conclusion that he had to take severe,
illiberal measures when the security of the state was at stake, he had to
learn the lesson by bitter experience. Indeed, this illumines the most
interesting similarity between Kaunda and Nyerere – their trust in people.

Both men are open-hearted. They have a natural sympathy towards
their companions, assuming that other men and women share the same
principles which they hold themselves. They therefore trust them until
disloyalty is proved to the hilt. This has led both into dangerous, at times
tragic, situations.

Both men revealed their trust, kindness and patience in dealing with
their two respective major defectors. Nyerere paid himself for Oscar
Kambona to have medical treatment in Holland when his erratic behaviour seemed to show that he needed a doctor's care. In spite of
vigorous argument from his colleagues that Kambona should be dismissed on evidence of disloyalty, Nyerere still believed that all he needed
was assurance. He went to the utmost limits to convince him that he was
still needed, to offer him the opportunity to continue his work with party
and country. Kaunda similarly persuaded Kapwepwe to resume his office
of Vice-President after he had resigned. It took a long series of disloyal
actions on Kapwepwe's part before the President could bring himself to

accept that his former friend had actually turned against him and the party they had built together.

This warm-hearted attitude towards friends and colleagues arose naturally from Kaunda's and Nyerere's personalities; but it also led them into situations which could have been, and sometimes were, dangerous or tragic or both.

One does not need to accept as accurate much of Roy Christie's book, *For The President's Eyes Only*, to recognise the danger of Kaunda's trust being abused in ways which could threaten the security of the state. There were certainly occasions in the earlier years of independence when the President's faith in a number of advisers risked security information being given to the Rhodesians, the South Africans, or the Portuguese. Nor would it have been too difficult for an organisation like the CIA to have interfered in Zambian politics, as it had in neighbouring Congo, whilst it was later established that certain East German and Russian diplomats had attempted to undermine the régime. This was not all due to the President's over-trustful nature, but it certainly was one element in offering opportunities for espionage. It was only when his trust had been abused several times with indisputable evidence, that Kaunda realised the dangers which might arise. Then his deep concern for the safety of his state asserted itself and security was tightened. This did not in any way diminish his friendly personality, but it made him more wary, forcing him to exercise greater discrimination. Even then, however, he could not resist inviting some people who were known to have abused his confidence to State House.

Nyerere's experience was much more tragic. It was hardly unexpected that the Union with Zanzibar brought him difficulties. He tried to deploy a humanitarian influence to modify some of the excesses on the islands, though he realised that liberal processes always suffer in revolutionary situations. But he recognised that his influence would have to be used sparingly if it was to maintain any strength. Inevitably certain actions by Tanganyikan authorities were taken in Nyerere's absence or ignorance which he would have dealt with differently, but many people had some degree of authority both on the mainland and on the islands. The governments were not dictatorships, so it was never simply the wills of Nyerere and Karume which prevailed.

One action, however, was Nyerere's responsibility and it exposed the danger which could arise from his trusting nature. Certain prisoners were detained on the mainland, accused of plotting Karume's downfall in Zanzibar. They included Othman Shariff, who had been a representative at the United Nations and was a friend of Nyerere. The President refused for some time to send the prisoners to the island, for he feared the rough justice they might receive there. Eventually, however, believing that the

Union could be jeopardised if he continued to shelter people considered traitors in Zanzibar, he agreed to return them. This was on the strict understanding that they would be given a fair trial. He trusted Karume to ensure that this promise was kept. The prisoners, including Shariff, were murdered. Nyerere was deeply pained by this experience. He did not make the same mistake again. When the trial of conspirators connected with Karume's assassination took place, those on the mainland who were alleged to be implicated were not returned. Othman Shariff was my friend as well as Nyerere's; he had been a student at Glasgow when I was on the university staff there and had been my host in Zanzibar. I know that Nyerere acted in good faith and will always remain profoundly distressed over his mistake.

It may be partially from the effects of such tough, disillusioning experiences that Nyerere's attitude towards discipline has changed perceptibly during the past ten years. He has increasingly realised that much of his hope for the future of his nation depends on his people learning the cohesion of discipline. This recognition has been demonstrated in his attitude to the students who revolted against national service, from his Leadership Code, later applied to all party members, from his insistence on a time-limit for villageisation. He was greatly impressed by the example of Chinese workers on the railway, who caused him to ponder how he could instil the same devotion in Tanzanians.

Community cohesion, based on individual and collective discipline, is crucial to development in all new nations. In any society the conventional example of disciplinary attitudes is found in the armed forces. It is interesting to note that whereas Nyerere has increasingly held up military training as a means towards a greater sense of discipline, Kaunda has not followed him along this path. To Kaunda armed forces are a necessary evil. He has retained his pacifist convictions. To Kaunda they represent a principle of life, in much the same manner as they did to Gandhi. Although the circumstances in which he finds himself make it impossible to put the principle into practice immediately, he would like to believe that Zambia, Africa and the world will eventually be persuaded to live without military forces.

Nyerere used to think in the same way. As I have related, he told me before independence that he hoped that Africa would show the world how to live without armies. Not only has he found from experience with the white south and with Amin's Uganda that this is not yet possible; it is doubtful whether he considers it totally desirable, at least in the foreseeable future. He has begun to talk about military training as a valuable aid to instilling discipline and has introduced it into national service. Some Tanganyikans fear that he is confusing discipline with the mindless obedience taught to soldiers. His oldest sons went to China to do military training and he expected that his younger sons would follow their elders' example. Kaunda's eldest son also went into the army, although his father had hoped that he would become a doctor. Yet Kaunda regarded this as simply a choice of profession. He did not think of it as a specially appropriate form of training for life. His only concern was that his children should fit themselves in their various ways to serve society, which he felt his oldest son was doing by entering the army in the same way as his second son took a medical training.

It is on the international stage that the two presidents have worked most closely together. Their objectives are identical, so that they always complement each other. They both firmly believe in democratic rights which give each individual an equal share in choosing those who will represent him in the shaping of his society. Each is entirely wedded to non-racialism, the exclusion of race as a factor in any social situation, neither having a vestige of colour prejudice in his character. Both agree that the first step in gaining freedom for Africa must be the completion of the process by which citizens of every African country gain full democratic rights. The next step, which each is already taking in his own country, is to release Africa from her thrall to external economic forces. After that may come the release of the individual in society from the constraints of natural tyrannies, hunger, poverty, disease, illiteracy.

The two men have collaborated since before either of their countries gained independence. In the organisation PAFMECSA they strove to associate the countries of east, central and south Africa in the effort to win democratic independence throughout the region and to forge a collaboration which would enable them to face the problems of independence with the strength of unity. Nyerere, who had to deal with these issues whilst Kaunda was still immersed in his battle for independence, clashed with Nkrumah over the strategy for African unity. He never agreed with Nkrumah that such unity could be achieved initially on a continental basis. He considered it more realistic to approach it from a foundation of regional unities. So he placed great store by the effort to create an east African federation. He has been disappointed. Continued Western domination in Kenya, the consequent stratification of Kenyan society, and the coup in Uganda which replaced Obote by an aberrant Amin, have virtually destroyed all hope of a federation amongst the three east African states. It could be that the next regional effort will be made between Tanzania, Zambia, Mozambique, possibly also including Botswana. These four régimes at least have common social objectives.

Meanwhile the struggle with the white south has been pursued through a variety of tactics. Nyerere was able to provide open assistance to FRELIMO, the freedom fighters in neighbouring Mozambique. Kaunda had to be more circumspect. There was always the danger that the military might of South Africa could be used to invade his country or to bomb it. The excuse for such aggression would be that South African forces were pursuing guerrillas over the border to their camps in Zambia. South African ministers frequently made this threat in public. So Kaunda could not be as overt in his support of the freedom fighters as Nyerere, but he gave them constant assistance.

On the other hand, both Nyerere and Kaunda recognised that if they could achieve their aims with a minimum of bloodshed, their own people as well as those in the south would be spared incalculable agonies. In the Lusaka Manifesto issued in 1969 they posed a straight alternative. Change towards full democracy in southern Africa was inevitable. It could come either from peaceful reform or from violent attacks on the minority white régimes. Tanzania and Zambia would assist in peaceful change if sincere efforts were made to use this method. If not, they would help those who fought for the freedom of their countries. The white régimes, which currently held the power, must choose between the two alternatives.

It was over five years after the publication of the Lusaka Manifesto before the opportunity arose for the possibility of peaceful reforms to be explored. During that time the guerrilla movements had gained experience, recruits, training and arms. Although tested on a number of occasions by aggressive threats from both Rhodesia and South Africa, Kaunda had stood firm and Nyerere had constantly supported him. When Ian Smith closed his border with Zambia, vainly imagining that he could cripple the copper industry and force Kaunda to restrain the freedom fighters from penetrating Rhodesia, the President immediately burst the bubble. It was Rhodesia, not Zambia, which felt the major economic effects. The Zambians were so successful in diverting their trade that when Smith wanted to rescind his sanction and re-open the border, Kaunda was able to tell him that it would remain closed until Rhodesian Africans were given democratic rights. When Vorster, the South African Prime Minister, tried to undermine Kaunda by a blustering attempt to smear him in African eyes with the allegation that he had negotiated with the South African government, the President coolly published the correspondence to prove that he had always rejected South African advances to him.

It was the success of FRELIMO which so dramatically changed the balance of power in southern Africa as to make negotiation practical. Together with their fellow freedom fighters in Guinea Bissau and Angola, they so drained the military spirit of the Portuguese army that it revolted against the Caetano régime in Lisbon and took over control of the government in April 1974. One of the first promises made by the new military régime was that the Portuguese African territories would be granted their independence.

By now Kaunda had become an experienced international statesman.

He had led the OAU delegation of 1970 which tried to persuade Western governments to refuse to supply South Africa with arms. He had been chairman of the Non-Aligned Conference. In Singapore, in 1971, he had had the experience of persuading the Commonwealth Heads of State to accept his Declaration of Principles. He had kept his state afloat for ten years under constant pressures from Rhodesia, South Africa and the Portuguese, showing his ability to compromise on the altar of Zambian survival by buying maize from Rhodesia in order to prevent his people starving and buying goods from South Africa to sustain his economy.

So Kaunda treated the new situation with the skill of an experienced diplomat. He had a careful assessment of the consequences of the Portuguese coup compiled from sources in London and elsewhere. He used his most trusted personal assistant to take soundings in South Africa. He thrashed out the whole situation with Nyerere, Seretse Khama from Botswana, Mobutu from Zaire and Samora Machel, leader of FRELIMO, President-elect of Mozambique. Machel was particularly crucial because, once Mozambique gained independence, he would control the ports of Beira and Lourenço Marques, together with the Cabora Bassa hydro-electric dam, all vital to the Rhodesian and South African economies. Moreover, because the Rhodesian freedom fighters had been acting alongside FRELIMO, he would have the greatest influence on them, as they would continue to depend on him for logistic support and arms.

When he had completed these careful processes, Kaunda made his key speech. He chose the occasion on which he was presented with an honorary degree by the University of Zambia, during the celebration of the tenth anniversary of Zambia's independence. His speech was largely based on the Lusaka Manifesto, again offering the two alternatives of peaceful or violent change. It included conciliatory words for the South Africans whose Prime Minister had himself spoken of the necessity for peaceful change only three days earlier.

Kaunda's initiative, supported by Nyerere, Khama and Machel, was designed to deploy South Africa's fear of a violent future in order to break Ian Smith's intransigence in Rhodesia. It was brought to Vorster's attention that, now that Mozambique and Angola were to have black governments, Rhodesia and Namibia had become hostages for his peaceful intentions. The withdrawals of South African para-military police from the Rhodesian borders with Zambia and Mozambique could be used by him to put pressure on the Smith régime. A conciliatory attitude towards the United Nations and the indigenous Africans could avoid Namibia becoming a state hostile to South Africa.

Kaunda's strategy succeeded in so far as the dual pressures on Smith forced him to release the main Rhodesian African leaders, Nkomo and Sithole, to send his representatives to a conference in Lusaka and to re-open talks with African nationalists. The future remained cloudy, because Vorster found, like British governments before him, that Smith always became more evasive in Salisbury than outside his own country, whilst his position amongst his white supporters depended on his maintenance of white supremacy at all costs.

The climax of this strategy so far as Kaunda was concerned came with his remarkable meeting with Mr Vorster at Victoria Falls in August 1975. The dual pressures on Smith by Vorster and the African National Council by the black leaders had led to a conference being arranged. It was held in a railway carriage half way across the Falls' bridge, exactly on the frontier between Zambia and Rhodesia. The South Africans were not confident that Smith would keep his promise to enter into serious negotiations with Rhodesia's African leaders. Kaunda, Nyerere and their associates were concerned lest factional rivalries between sections of the ANC might prevent the African negotiators from considering an evolutionary approach to majority rule. So Vorster and Kaunda both decided to attend the talks themselves. Not only did they meet in the railway carriage during the negotiations; they went away into Livingstone together and held private discussions. The fact that the apostle of apartheid and one of its most bitter critics could thus discuss the southern African situation face to face presented the most astounding facet of this remarkable scene. Kaunda, supported by Nyerere, Khama and Machel, was demonstrating to the hilt his commitment to peaceful negotiations rather than warfare. Although Smith reiterated his determination to retain white rule throughout his lifetime, whilst Muzorewa, Nkomo and Sithole allowed their differences to widen dangerously, the Victoria Falls encounter ensured that the southern African picture would never appear the same again. Kaunda's determined stand for peace might endanger his domestic security as well as be used against him internationally by critics like Amin. The fact that, despite these dangers, he steadfastly pursued this policy demonstrated that his life-long commitment to peaceful solutions was still a priority for him.

Yet Kaunda and Nyerere, with their close associates, had shown that they could surpass British governments, with all their Foreign Office experience, when it came to shrewdness in deploying their diplomatic pressures over Rhodesia. The reason was simple. They understood the realities of southern Africa to an extent which British politicians had never taken the trouble to comprehend. Whilst British leaders of both parties kept one eye on their own electorates and another on the feelings of those they still regarded as 'kith and kin', both Kaunda and Nyerere were aware that their own fellow-countrymen felt kinship for Rhodesian Africans, but also that many white South Africans were members of a kind of African tribe, with southern Africa as their only home. The prospects for them as black rule moved inexorably southward were politely drawn to the attention of Mr Vorster. The civil war in Angola, however, opened a new perspective. Cuban soldiers and Russian arms brought the MPLA into confrontation with South African troops across Namibia's frontiers. Kaunda was at first apprehensive of the effect in Zambia and of potential rivalry between Russians and Chinese. For the first time he and Nyerere differed over international policies, Nyerere supporting the MPLA whoever its helpers. Both, however, appreciated each other's viewpoint. Both, too, realised that the final battle for southern Africa was now joined, involving not only Angola, but Namibia, Rhodesia, and, finally, apartheid South Africa.

On many other international matters the two presidents have worked in harness, whether at the United Nations, in Commonwealth conferences or through the OAU. One of the most painful to both of them was the breach with Nigeria. Both felt that the Ibo could not be forced back into the federation, yet both also abhorred secession which they realised could lead to chaotic Balkanisation of their continent. The outcome of the war perhaps suggested that they had made a mistake, at least insofar as African unity and diplomacy were concerned. They were lucky, and it was fortunate for the continent's future, that General Gowon had a sympathetic, understanding character. I know from personal experience that, even during the civil war, he recognised the sincerity of Kaunda and Nyerere in recognising Biafra. To everyone's credit the breach was quickly healed shortly after the war's end. It would have been tragic if estrangement had continued between Africa's giant and the two most progressive régimes in the continent.

Another distressing event was the overthrow of Obote by Amin in Uganda. Neither president ever felt happy about military coups which, to them, represented a usurpation of the people's participation in government by the power of guns. Both were deeply distressed over the overthrow of Ben Bella in Algeria and Nkrumah in Ghana. Yet they knew that they had to face reality and learn to co-operate with military régimes if any form of African united action was to be preserved.

In the case of Uganda, however, the problem was not just that of a military coup. Obote had been one of the 'Mulungushi Club', those presidents who met from time to time at Mulungushi in Zambia, where a set of lodges was built for their occupation and where policies were discussed and co-ordinated. He, Nyerere and Kaunda had much in common, usually taking the same line at international conferences. In fact, they were doing so at the Commonwealth conference in Singapore on the issue of supplying South Africa with arms immediately before the coup took place. Edward Heath, then Britain's Prime Minister, made no effort to conceal his glee when the news of the coup was announced, as Obote had been giving him such an embarrassing time over the issue.

So losing Obote was the loss of a friend for Kaunda and Nyerere. But there were more serious consequences which deeply concerned both men. It was not long before Amin began to decimate those communities from which his main rivals were drawn. Then he turned on the Asians, at first threatening to expel all of them, even those who had taken Ugandan citizenship. Nyerere made his feelings on this racial issue perfectly plain and public. Speaking in August 1972 he said :

General Amin has recently said to Britain, 'Take your citizens.' But in this quarrel between two countries a lot of people are liable to get badly hurt – people, not animals. But Amin says, 'They are your citizens.' Now he is saying 'All Asians must go – including the Uganda citizens.' How can you argue this ? If you argue – as you can correctly argue in logic – that he has a right to demand that all British passport holders should leave Uganda because they hold British passports, how can you argue the second thing also ?

What does it mean, to say to a large group of people, 'From today – or tomorrow, or next week – you citizens are no longer citizens?' It means that they are people in the world who have no state, nor country; no place where they have a right to live.

Kaunda agreed unreservedly. Both presidents were unafraid to describe Amin as 'a racialist'. Nyerere was to suffer directly from Amin's erratic behaviour. His country was invaded by Ugandan forces. At the time he was near Dodoma making mud bricks with villagers. He went on doing so. He did not rush back to the capital, realising that his military men could handle the crisis without his instructions. He continued his constructive work, confident in the nation behind him.

There have been other distressing events in black Africa during the period in which Nyerere and Kaunda have been presidents of their countries. Massacres which can only be described as genocide have occurred. No one can doubt that they are abhorrent to both men. But they cannot prevent them nor remove their causes by constant condemnations. These have to be reserved for those occasions when either the security of their own countries or the survival of the machinery of African unity is endangered. Nyerere has described the OAU as 'a crucible within which the chemical elements of African nationalism mix with each other'. He considers it a victory that the organisation has held together during the troubled years since its inception in 1963. Most of the foreign policies of both presidents are devoted to maintaining it as a coherent organisation.

Yet, despite their accord, Kaunda and Nyerere approach their international responsibilities from slightly different angles. During a visit to the United States before independence Kaunda addressed students at Fordham University. He explained his global view of the human predicament in these words:

> We believe both the East and the West are failing mankind. We see far too much emphasis placed on material development, which in fact is very quickly leading to the eclipse of man as the centre of all human activity. Can they recover from this, or is there going to come out of Africa a new ideology to help our fellow men in these two camps? I should also point out that if we ourselves in Africa are not careful, we might also find ourselves slaves to the machine.

Compare this with a speech made by Nyerere at a banquet in honour of Chou en Lai in 1968:

> . . . my country is free. It is because of that freedom that I am able to come here on behalf of my countrymen to cement the friendship which exists between our two peoples. Yet at the same time my country feels that it is not free, because Africa is not free. My countrymen know that they are insulted because the blackness of our brothers is being insulted in Africa. And my country, with the other independent nations of Africa, is determined that this situation will be changed. Africa will be free. Africans will be respected in Africa. For Africa will liberate Africa. The struggle before us may be a long one; the machinations of neo-colonialism may sometimes cause us to stumble in our progress to liberation. But the Organisation of African Unity will succeed in both its objectives. It will lead Africa to freedom and human dignity, and it will lead Africa to unity . . . I look forward to the day when I cannot come to China as President of the United Republic of Tanzania, because to the outside world there is no Tanzania – only Africa.

Both men would approve of the other's sentiments. But whereas Kaunda has always been concerned over the moral condition of mankind itself, Nyerere deals with the practical issues facing contemporary Africans. Kaunda seeks harmony in national and international society. He believes that man should be guided by values which bring together God, the community, the material world and the self. Nyerere considers that injustices provoke conflict, that battles have to be fought, whether physical, mental or diplomatic, before they can be remedied. The two work in harness, complementing each other, but displaying distinct differences of temperament.

The friendship, mutual understanding and constant co-operation of these two men profoundly influences the current development of society in Africa, ideas in the Third World and, perhaps, the future of human society. Both are genuine philosophers in that they have a real sense of history and a perspective of the long-term future of the human race. Despite their varying emphases, both are offering human beings a different kind of social life from that which has been assumed for centuries to reflect the essentials of 'human nature'. Both assert that human beings are only avaricious, aggressive and competitive in certain social contexts; that in others they can be generous, loving and co-operative. They both aim to build the institutions in their nations which will encourage the latter human characteristics and inhibit the former.

Nyerere stated this proposition with lucid clarity in his Introduction to *Freedom and Unity*. He first established his premise that 'Man's existence in society involves an inevitable and inescapable conflict − a conflict of his own desires. For every individual really wants two things : freedom to pursue his own interests and his own inclinations. At the same time he wants the freedoms which can be obtained only through life in society . . .' He then suggested that three main principles guided life in the African family which he argued was the kind of society which has given most satisfaction to its members:

. . . an attitude of mutual respect and obligation which bound the members together − an attitude which might be described as love, provided it is understood that this word does not imply romance, or even necessarily close personal affection. The property which is important to the family, and thus to the individual members of it, is held in common. And every member of the family accepts the obligation to work. These three principles weld the family into a unit which is so obviously important to the individual members that each individual thinks of himself, and of others, in the framework of their membership of the unit. A man or woman knows that he or she is a unique person with private desires. But he also knows that his actions must, for his own good, be restricted to those which are consistent with the good of his social unit − his family. [He then asserts that] The principles which worked in this one case are equally valid for larger societies because, however large it is, men are always the purpose and justification of society.

Finally, Nyerere met the criticism of those who attack these principles. 'The principles are challenged first by those who maintain that the purpose of society is not man but a glorification of some abstract notion, such as "the nation", "the flag", or even God.' He argued that the nation is a social group which cannot have a purpose separate from the good of its members; that to glorify a piece of cloth is absurd; that worship of God is for the benefit of man. In short, that the 'purpose of society is in all cases man . . .':

> The other major challenge to the validity of the principles of love, sharing, and work as a basis of society is made on the grounds that they are too idealistic, particularly for large groups where the members cannot know each other. This criticism is nonsensical. Social principles are, by definition, ideals at which to strive and by which to exercise self-criticism. The question to ask is not whether they are capable of achievement, which is absurd, but whether a society of free men can do without them. Like democracy, they are easier to approximate to in smaller societies than in large ones. But like democracy, they remain equally valid for both small and large societies – for both traditional and modern Africa.

This, then, is the essence of the proposition offered by Nyerere in his socialism and Kaunda in his Humanism. It may be that Kaunda places a higher expectation on man's innate spirituality and Nyerere on the importance of institutions which encourage mutual aid. Essentially, however, both men are offering an alternative to the aggressive, competitive, materialistic world which has grown out of industrial society, whether capitalist or communist. Both are trying to build such alternative societies in their own countries. Both find it good in their own lives to believe in a God and a future, in man's progress which gives him the abilities to improve his own life and his society. Each places his main reliance on adherence to principles, from which can be built institutions which will curb anti-social tendencies and foster harmonious human relationships. Each is anxious to establish such institutions before he retires from public life so that his ideals will be firmly rooted, his nation continues to pursue him after his personal time. Neither is sanctimonious, dogmatic nor fanatical; but rather good-humoured, relaxed, humble, balanced, accompanying his philosophy lessons with playing golf, reading, translating, joking, watching football, playing with children. Their proposals for new social values, for a different form of society, for changed relationships between human beings, are being listened to by even more Africans, especially by the young.

In a world in which competitive materialism has provoked continual war, frequent famine, growing mental sickness and widening social injustice, the ideas of these two Africans are due to be heard by a larger audience.

Index

(continued from front flap)

plex and significant task: combining a rural renaissance with urban prosperity, on an egalitarian basis.

Two African Statesmen traces Nyerere and Kaunda's developing attitudes from childhood; the impact of tribal codes, trade unions, and colonial politics on their contrasting countries; and their respective roles in world affairs, particularly the degree of their support for the non-aligned bloc and the concept of the Third World.

John Hatch, author of ten other books about Africa, including *Africa Emergent,* has been visiting or living in Africa for more than two decades. He has been Commonwealth correspondent of the *New Statesman* and a broadcaster for the BBC; he is editor of *Third World* magazine, and founder and director of the African Studies Program in Houston, Texas.